Self-Defense

by Damian Ross

T0049389

for **dummies**®

A Wiley Brand

Self-Defense For Dummies®

Published by: **John Wiley & Sons, Inc.,** 111 River Street, Hoboken, NJ 07030-5774, www.wiley.com

For general information on our other products and services, please contact our Customer Care Department within the U.S. at 877-762-2974, outside the U.S. at 317-572-3993, or fax 317-572-4002. For technical support, please visit https://hub.wiley.com/community/support/dummies.

Wiley publishes in a variety of print and electronic formats and by print-on-demand. Some material included with standard print versions of this book may not be included in e-books or in print-on-demand. If this book refers to media such as a CD or DVD that is not included in the version you purchased, you may download this material at http://booksupport.wiley.com. For more information about Wiley products, visit www.wiley.com.

Library of Congress Control Number: 2023946341

ISBN 978-1-394-19708-8 (pbk); ISBN 978-1-394-19709-5 (ebk); ISBN 978-1-394-19710-1 (ebk)

SKY10058351_102523

Contents at a Glance

Table of Contents

Introduction

I f you follow the news, or maybe just look out your window, you can tell that the world is an increasingly dangerous place. Nations are becoming more divided along political, social, and economic lines; incidents of senseless violence are skyrocketing; alcohol and drug abuse is on the rise; political and social protests are growing more violent; and human trafficking has become commonplace. At the same time, calls to defund the police are growing stronger, and more and more prosecutors are unwilling or limited in their ability to bring violent criminals to justice.

The message is clear: Although threats to your life and safety, your loved ones, and your property are on the rise, you're increasingly on your own when it comes to protecting them. Unfortunately, you probably lack the training and even the time to develop the skills required to defend yourself. You need a practical, effective, and affordable solution. Welcome to *Self-Defense For Dummies*.

About This Book

The conceptual framework for this book started in the basement of a church where I received training under the tutelage of a beast of a man named Carl Cestari. Carl stood about 5'10" and was a barrel-chested 215 pounds with thick forearms and hands that looked like they could smash rocks.

Carl taught *combatives* (a wide variety of close quarters combat systems with military roots). What Carl showed me was nothing short of a revelation. It was so simple, it just made sense. It was like nothing I had ever seen before or since — not in all my years of collegiate wrestling, my many years of martial arts training, or any of the self-defense classes or seminars I had attended over the years.

Through Carl, Yohisada Yonezuka, and other legends, I discovered the truth about self-defense — that it's not a sport or a style; it's an instinct that every living creature on the planet has . . . including you. What you're about to discover wasn't conjured up in a *dojo* (martial arts school) or developed solely by one person. It's a system of tactics and techniques gathered over a century of modern warfare and close combat created and tested by men and women whose lives depended on it.

When I was first introduced to this system, we called it "Defendu" in reference to the title of a book written by close combat pioneer William Fairbairn. In the 1900s, Fairbairn assembled a team and devised a method of close combat that was later taught to the commandos and allied forces of World War II, as well as the Office of Strategic Services (OSS), which later became the Central Intelligence Agency (CIA). These methods eliminated the sport and ceremony of the martial arts until only the most effective techniques and tactics remained. Fairbairn's Defendu found success at all levels of warfare, from the battlefield to the back alley. Later, these methods were abandoned because they were considered too brutal, but they were kept in circulation by people who faced real violence on a regular basis.

I was lucky to stumble into it, and now you are, too.

Think of this book as your "self-defense code breaker." Here, you discover that self-defense isn't complicated. You find out how to apply a handful of tactics and techniques to any possible situation instead of trying to learn hundreds of different, specialized, counter-moves for each individual attack. And you discover how to identify your attacker's weaknesses and exploit them.

How far you go with your self-defense training is up to you. You can read this book, use the awareness tactics, get some pepper spray, and call it a day. Or you can dig in, develop and fine-tune your close-combat skills, and be ready for any and all situations. It's your call.

Look, I won't tell you what you should fight for; that's not my place. It's a personal decision. Some people will give up their wallet, others will fight over a dime. All I show you in this book is what will give you the highest chance of success in the shortest amount of time when the general laws allow you to defend and protect.

Whatever you do, don't wait until it's too late. Start now to equip yourself with the knowledge and skills you need to protect yourself and your loved ones.

Within this book, you may note that some web addresses break across two lines of text. If you're reading this book in print and want to visit one of these web pages, simply key in the web address exactly as it's noted in the text, pretending as though the line break doesn't exist. If you're reading this as an e-book, you've got it easy — just click the web address to be taken directly to the web page.

Foolish Assumptions

All assumptions are foolish, and I'm always reluctant to make them, but to keep this book focused on the right audience and ensure that it fulfills my purpose in writing it, I had to assume the following:

>> You want to be able to defend yourself from people who pose a threat to your life and safety, your loved ones, or your property.

>> You don't have a lot of time or a deep desire to work out in a gym or train in a dojo for hours on end to master a system of complex counter-maneuvers. You just want a simple set of self-defense tactics and techniques that work.

>> You're a responsible, caring individual who normally wouldn't hurt a fly, but you realize that sometimes good people have no other option than to perform some brutal acts to defend themselves . . . or you're at least open to the idea.

>> You have no training in the martial arts, such as judo, aikido, karate, kung fu, wrestling, boxing, or mixed martial arts. Or you have lots of training in one or more martial arts but have an open mind to self-defense systems that may be easier and more effective.

Other than those four foolish assumptions, I can honestly say that I can't assume much more about you. I don't know your gender, size, or fitness level. You may be a gym rat or a couch potato, rich or poor, white collar or blue collar, doesn't matter. Whoever you are, you need to be able to protect yourself, your loved ones, and your property, regardless of how small you are, how weak you are, or how old you are. And in this book, I show you how.

Icons Used in This Book

Throughout this book, icons in the margins highlight certain types of valuable information that call out for some special attention. Here are the icons you'll encounter and a brief description of each.

REMEMBER

I want you to remember everything you read in this book, but if you can't quite do that, then remember the important points flagged with this icon.

TIP

Tips are tidbits of information and insight that I've gathered from my many years of self-defense study, training, practice, and experience that I've distilled to save you time and effort.

WARNING

"Whoa!" Before you take another step, read these warnings. I provide this cautionary content to help you avoid the common pitfalls that are otherwise likely to trip you up and may get you seriously injured . . . or worse.

Beyond the Book

In addition to the material in the print or e-book you're reading right now, this product also comes with some access-anywhere goodies on the web. Check out the free Cheat Sheet for some tips for avoiding and preventing physical attacks, how to end a fight before it starts, the four pillars of self-defense, and more. To get this Cheat Sheet, simply go to www.dummies.com and type **Self-Defense For Dummies Cheat Sheet** in the Search box.

Where to Go from Here

Make self-defense training a habit. Start with the awareness drills, get yourself some pepper spray, and carry it with you at all times. If you do only those three things, you'll be better off than most people, who wander around clueless.

But if you're serious about this, you need to develop those hard skills (combat skills). Get something to hit and someone to practice with from time to time. Even if it's for only a few minutes a week. I find it very therapeutic. There's nothing like taking your day out on a training dummy; it really gets rid of the toxicity.

To take your self-defense training and skills to the next level, visit my website at www.myselfdefensetraining.com/self-defense-for-dummies-free-videos, where you can access free training videos of what I cover in the book. Through that same site, you'll find a variety of courses you can take with the support of my team of certified instructors. You can also order self-defense products including bulletproof jackets and backpacks that fit seamlessly into your everyday life.

Finally, share your knowledge with someone you care about. Invite a friend or family member to one of your training sessions. The more people who have this knowledge, the safer and more respectful and disciplined the world will be.

1

Getting Your Head in the Game

Explore the difference between soft skills that engage your mind and hard skills that require you to get physical with an attacker.

Discover a self-defense system that's not only more effective but actually easier to master than something like mixed martial arts (MMA), Brazilian Jiu-Jitsu, judo, or karate.

Tell the difference between self-defense, combat sports, and police and military defense tactics, and understand why their differences matter.

Master the four pillars of self defense — position, distance, momentum, and balance — and find out how to leverage them to your advantage.

Find the most effective and efficient means of self-defense, from firearms and knives to hand-to-hand combat maneuvers.

Develop a self-defense mindset so you're prepared mentally and emotionally to do whatever's necessary to defend yourself and your loved ones.

Recognize and appreciate what you're up against — the various types of criminals and their means and methods — so you're better prepared to avoid, escape, and resist attackers.

Chapter **1**

Laying the Groundwork for Self-Defense

Self-defense involves both mind and body. I can present and demonstrate self-defense techniques, but to avoid attacks, train effectively and efficiently, and apply what you learn to real-life situations, I encourage you to approach the topic with a higher level of understanding — a bird's-eye view. This overall understanding serves as the framework for grasping more detailed and nuanced concepts, tactics, and techniques.

In this chapter, you begin to formulate your general understanding of self-defense by developing a clear idea of what you're up against, getting up to speed on the two main components of self-defense, taking a reasonable approach to training, and finding out how to incorporate self-defense into your life. And, if you happen to be a victim of violence, I encourage you to start working through that traumatic event as you make yourself less vulnerable to future attacks.

Getting to Know the Real Enemy

Knowing who your attacker is — what they want, what they're capable of doing to get it, how they operate, where they strike, and more — improves your ability to avoid and respond to attacks. Here are some details about attackers to enable you to develop the insight you need:

>> **People who commit violent crimes are not like you.** They're willing to do things you would never dream of doing to a fellow human being. Don't make the mistake of projecting your thoughts and reasoning onto them. They're making choices based on broken values, and they'll use your reasoning and good sense against you.

>> **They may be intelligent and skilled fighters.** Don't underestimate an attacker. Just because someone doesn't train in a gym, doesn't make them "inferior" or "weak" — in fact, it can make them even *more* dangerous. They don't play by the rules that govern martial arts competitions.

>> **They're probably armed.** About one-third of all attacks are committed by unarmed attackers. The other two-thirds involve an *impact weapon* (a club of some sort), a firearm, or an *edged weapon* (such as a knife). And just because they don't threaten you with a weapon initially, doesn't mean they don't have one. They may think you're going to be a pushover, but after they discover you're not, out comes the weapon.

>> **They may not be alone.** You should assume they have friends nearby, ready to pounce on you if you put up any resistance.

>> **They probably have a plan and a track record of getting what they want through force or coercion.** They've probably done it before. They know what to say and how to say it. They know how to isolate you and distract you.

WARNING

Don't believe anything an attacker tells you. Anyone who uses or threatens violence to get what they want isn't likely to tell the truth.

>> **They're probably not looking for a fight.** Attackers choose victims they determine to be easy marks — people who look like they can't or won't put up a fight. By making yourself appear less vulnerable, you decrease your odds of being targeted. Resisting an attack increases your odds of ending it in your favor.

WARNING

Although you can make some basic assumptions about an attacker, you never know who you're going to face. They could be an ex-con, a street fighter, an athlete, or a soldier. They could be emotionally disturbed or jacked up on PCP or meth. Assume the worst and seek to end the conflict as quickly as possible by whatever means possible.

REMEMBER

Assailants don't "come out of nowhere." They need to find an opportunity to strike, which requires time and observation. Be aware of your surroundings, pay attention to that little voice in your head, and manage your personal space. Taking these precautions enables you to sense when you're being set up or stalked, so you can take evasive action and be prepared in the event that the assailant closes in on you.

Recognizing the Two Components of Self-Defense

Self-defense can be broken down into the following two components:

>> **Soft skills:** Soft skills involve developing a heightened awareness, avoiding places of ambush, maintaining your personal space, knowing how to spot a setup, deciding when to stand your ground or escape, and being able to unleash your inner beast when you're threatened. You can develop these skills very quickly and with little effort.

>> **Hard skills:** Hard skills involve techniques for fighting off an attacker, with and without the use of weapons. These skills require some practice. You need consistent repetition to program them into your muscle memory — to build new neuropathways in the brain that make them instinctive. The more you practice, the more powerful and confident you'll become, and the better your chances of responding effectively at the moment of truth.

Soft skills: Getting your head in the game

Soft skills can be broken down into two groups: those that enable you to avoid danger, and those that empower you to defeat it. In this section, I offer guidance on how to develop your rational and intuitive mind (to avoid trouble) and your animal nature (to deal with unavoidable threats).

Avoiding attacks

The best way to avoid an attack is to make yourself a hard target, as opposed to an easy target. An easy target is a person who's in the wrong place at the wrong time, distracted (not paying attention), confused or afraid, and smaller/weaker than the attacker. In contrast, a hard target avoids high-risk places and situations (such as poorly lit streets), stands tall, walks confidently, and makes eye contact (a quick glance is all it takes). A hard target also listens to that little voice inside their head warning them of trouble and engages in whatever evasive maneuvers are necessary to move out of harm's way in a hurry. In Chapter 5, I provide additional information and guidance on how to make yourself a hard target.

Being ferocious

You're a nice person. The thought of hurting another human being probably sickens you. That's good. You're normal. I feel the same way. However, sometimes good people need to do bad things. When you're facing someone who wants to assault, rape, torture, or murder you, you have to be willing to do whatever is required by whatever means necessary to survive.

The British Special Air Service's motto is "Who Dares Wins." In an attack, whoever dares to attack first, whoever dares to do whatever it takes, whoever launches the most brutal and effective attack first and doesn't stop 'til it's over wins.

REMEMBER

Deliver the most brutal strike you can, fast and first, before your assailant has a chance to do it to you. Then don't stop. Continue driving forward into your assailant giving them everything you've got until you can escape safely or until the assailant can no longer harm you.

Don't play "tit for tat" (someone pushes you, and you push them back), and don't wait for someone threatening you to throw the first punch. As soon as you sense that an attack is imminent, as soon as the attacker even twitches toward you, smash 'em in the face and keep smashing them until they no longer pose a threat. If you can't escape, you *must* attack!

Don't take any chances. If you let an attacker make the first move, you stand to lose your last chance to defend yourself. If they stab you, shoot you, club you, or hit you just right, it's game over. Even if they just shove you, you could fall and hit your head on the concrete, and — you guessed it — game over. Don't play that game.

REMEMBER

Your willingness to protect yourself and your loved ones at all costs doesn't make you a violent person. In fact, the opposite is true; when you're trained, you're confident and you have a respect for violence. You understand that any altercation can result in serious loss, so you're less likely to get angry and get involved in altercations. However, when necessary, you'll be able to flip the switch from Peaceful Citizen to Brutal Combatant. Think of yourself like the family dog — playful and cuddly most of the time, but a ferocious beast as soon as somebody threatens their family.

To train your mind to flip the switch, take the following steps:

1. Get comfortable. Sit in a comfortable chair or lie down on your couch or bed — wherever you're most comfortable.

2. Think of someone you love — a family member, friend, pet, whoever. Imagine, for a few minutes, a great time you had together doing something you totally enjoyed. Then let that memory fade away.

3. Think of something you did that you're proud of, a major accomplishment in your life — something at school or work, an athletic achievement, a performance. Think about that for a few minutes. Enjoy it. Then let that memory fade away.

4. Imagine your worst nightmare — a big, mean, armed attacker moving toward whoever you imagined in Step 2. The attacker intends to subject them to an unthinkable cruelty. Feel the panic, the frustration, the rage.

5. *Attack!* Imagine what you'd do to the assailant, whatever it takes to stop them. Attack and keep attacking — kick, hack, bite, gouge, stomp every part of that assailant's anatomy. Picture yourself *winning* and *defeating* the enemy! Enjoy that accomplishment.

TRAINING PARTNER REQUIRED?

If you're training in a combat sport, such as judo or tae kwon do, you need training partners for sparring, but when you're training for self-defense, you don't need a partner as often. In fact, you can develop some bad habits training with a partner — for example, pulling your punches, stopping and saying "sorry" when you hurt them, and letting up when they start begging for their life.

In self-defense, you need a training partner only about 10 percent of the time, just to get a feel for some of the positions. For the primary and most critical self-defense training, train on a dummy, which you can attack with 100 percent force and zero regard for its safety. Going all out on a dummy is the only way to develop the correct technique, power, and attitude. It's the only way to program ruthlessness and relentlessness into your muscle memory.

6. Go and train, unleashing all that emotion on your training dummy. (When you're training with a partner, you need to hold back to prevent harming them, but with a training dummy, you can go all out.)

Hard skills: Fighting back

Like soft skills, hard skills can be divided into two groups — fighting *without* weapons and fighting *with* weapons, such as pepper spray, a gun, a knife, a club, or some other implement that can cause bodily harm.

Fighting empty-handed

Your body is equipped with some very effective, natural weapons, which you can deploy easily to disrupt an attack and injure your assailant. Any dense bone and a few other parts of your body can cause some damage. Let's start at the top and move down:

>> **Skull:** The forehead, *crown* (just above the temples), the top, and the upper part of the back of the skull are great for headbutting an assailant or grinding into their face.

>> **Chin:** Drive your chin into an eye socket, the throat, or the side of the neck when *grappling* (wrestling).

>> **Mouth:** Bite anything soft that comes close to your mouth. However, grab hold of whatever you're going to bite before chomping down to protect your teeth as your assailant tries to pull away. You can also use your mouth to tell the assailant "No!" and "Stop!" Sometimes, that's all it takes to stop an attack (see Chapter 6).

>> **Shoulder:** Drive your shoulder into your attacker.

>> **Elbows:** Hold up an elbow and tuck your face behind it to defend yourself as you close in on your attacker. Throw elbows to the head, face, neck, throat, stomach, *solar plexus* (just below the sternum) . . . really any part of the attacker's body.

>> **Forearms and hands:** Strike your assailant with the edge of your hand, heel of your hand, or forearm (see Chapter 9 for details).

>> **Fingers and thumbs:** Gouge, rip, and tear the eyes, ears, testicles, nose, mouth, and fingers, and use your hands to choke your assailant.

>> **Hips and butt:** Drive a hip or your buttocks into an assailant to throw them off balance or to create space if they have you in a bear hug, so you have some space to strike back.

>> **Knees:** Drive your knees up into your assailant's groin or any body part for that matter. You can also use your knee as an anvil, for example, grabbing the assailant's head or hair and smashing their face into your knee.

>> **Feet:** Kick the living daylights out of your assailant and stomp the tops of their feet to crush their arches. If you're wearing boots, especially steel-toe boots, kicking can be especially effective.

Turn to Part 3 for more about fighting without weapons.

Improving your odds with a weapon

A weapon is any object you can use to distract, injure, and stop your attacker. It could be designed specifically for combat, such as pepper spray, a club, a knife, or a firearm. Or it could be an improvised weapon, such as a rock, a baseball bat, a chair, or a fistful of dirt. Anything that increases your reach, impact, or odds is a weapon, which is why weapons are also referred to as *force multipliers* or *force equalizers* (they even the odds in what might otherwise be an unfair fight).

WARNING

Don't just stand there. . . . Many martial artists train to face their attacker unarmed like in some bad karate movie. If someone comes at you with a knife (or any weapon), *move!* Run and dodge behind and around furniture, walls, doorways, cars, trees, utility poles, anything that will trip up and slow down your attacker. Grab a chair and play lion tamer to keep them at a distance. Don't ignore your environment — use it to your advantage.

See Chapter 7 for details about choosing and using weapons and Part 4 for guidance on how to neutralize weapon attacks.

Making Self-Defense Training Less Overwhelming

People often avoid or put off self-defense training (or any self-improvement challenge) because it seems so overwhelming at first glance. I get it. You don't have the time, the equipment, the space, or the energy to take on something new, especially something that requires training. Don't let any misconceptions you may have about self-defense discourage you from getting started. I'm not going to promise that it's easy, but it is probably much easier than you think, especially if you accept the following advice:

>> **Incorporate self-defense into your everyday life.** You can practice anytime, anywhere — you don't need to join a gym. To some degree, you're already practicing self-defense. Now that you're reading this book, you're simply discovering ways to do it better.

>> **Take a gradual approach.** Look, you're not training for a prize fight or the Olympics. The skills you develop in one chapter or even one section of this book improve your ability to defend yourself and others. You don't need to know everything right now to be effective.

>> **Advance from one level to the next.** Self-defense has three levels:

1. Awareness and avoidance
2. Escape and evasion
3. Control and domination

You can develop awareness and avoidance skills and start using them immediately to significantly reduce your risk of attack. When you're ready, you can move up to the next level. In contrast, martial arts require that you train for weeks or months to develop some low level of proficiency.

>> **Follow my system.** My self-defense system doesn't have a lot of complex moves, countermoves, holds, and so on. It's built on the repetition and slight variations of fundamental tactics and techniques. As such, it's much easier to master and to program into your muscle memory than something like judo or jujitsu.

REMEMBER

The more you can do and the sooner you can do it, the better off you'll be. Like the old saying goes, "Don't wait until you're thirsty to start digging the well."

In the following sections, I detail what it really takes to develop self-defense skills. How often and how long you should practice to get proficient in self-defense is often exaggerated. Because these skills are simple and natural, they require a lot less time to master than martial arts and combat sports do.

Everybody lies

Part of what drives people away from getting started with self-defense is the people who exaggerate their training or abilities. When you hear people telling you that they train full contact every day, they either don't know what full contact is or they're lying. Stop reading posts and comments on social media from self-defense experts and afficionados. You should know by now that nearly everyone on social media bends the truth — it's just not possible for everyone to always be "doing great" and feeling so "blessed."

People love to glorify the past and exaggerate their accomplishments, especially when it comes to martial arts training. You'll read things like, "I trained eight hours a day, seven days a week for ten years, and we always went *full contact!*"

That's nonsense. I played Division 1 sports in college (wrestling and football); I've trained with Olympians in wrestling and judo; I've even seen professional and amateur fighters prepare for contests — and I'm telling you that you can sustain intense training on the elite level only for a few weeks before your body and your mind start to break down.

Besides, they're not you.

Less is more

Slow and steady wins the race. Self-defense is a marathon, not a sprint. When you start practicing the hard skills, the tendency is to jump in and get after it, and while I love the enthusiasm, I'm going to urge you to start slowly, especially if you've never "hit" anything before.

TIP

Start slow and soft and slowly build your power and intensity. Let pain be your guide. A little sore is okay; bruised and bloody, not so much. You don't want to injure yourself so you're unable to defend yourself. That kind of defeats the purpose.

Over time, your hands will toughen through training. You're going to be striking primarily with the edge and the heel of your hand, which are naturally pretty tough. Your other primary weapons (forearms, elbows, knees, and boots) are extremely tough.

Start with five- to ten-minute sessions. Don't even change your clothes, in fact, it's better to train in what you normally wear; your attacker won't wait for you to change into your yoga pants.

A practical approach

Self-defense isn't a sport; it's an education and a life skill. The best way to develop skills is to incorporate them gradually into your daily routine. That may include improving your physical fitness, practicing striking or using weapons (see Part 3), heightening your awareness of your surroundings (see Chapter 5), practicing tactical driving (see Chapter 5), and taking the position of advantage (see Chapter 8) whenever you're interacting with someone in person.

Here are a few more suggestions for taking a practical approach to developing self-defense skills:

>> **Don't try to learn everything in a day.** Focus on one skill and work on it until you feel comfortable and confident. In fact, studies show that shorter, more frequent sessions improve retention.

REMEMBER

The number of repetitions doesn't matter so long as you practice until the skill is instinctive and convulsive (like a reflex). *Don't do it just until you get it right; do it until you don't get it wrong.*

>> **Maintain your physical fitness.** The better shape you're in and the more punishment you can dish out and take, the less likely you are to be targeted for attack (because you look like you're prepared to put up a fight) and the faster you'll recover from any injury.

>> **Practice even if you're sick or injured.** If you can leave the house, you'd better be able to defend your life regardless of any injury or illness you have.

>> **Keep training regardless of your age.** You may age and lose muscle mass, agility, and endurance, but you continue to be exposed to attackers at their peak of strength and agility, and the older you are, the more likely you'll be targeted.

Imagine your attacker is a ripped, tattooed, mixed martial arts (MMA) fighter. Imagine fighting the guy in your prime and then fighting that same guy when you're older, slower, and weaker. No doubt, you'll take a different approach when you're older; for example, you may be more inclined to use a firearm or a crowbar to improve your odds.

Incorporating Self-Defense Skills into Your Everyday Life

Unlike a sport, which requires training for a specific contest or competition, self-defense demands that you adapt your current physical and mental ability to a constant threat. (Your physical ability may diminish over time, but your attacker will always be the same — same age, same size, same strength.) As long as you're alive and breathing, you're under threat of a possible attack. The threat level varies according to the self-defense condition:

>> **Condition green:** You're in your home, relaxed; the doors are locked and the security system (if installed) is armed (on).

>> **Condition yellow:** You're out in the world, going about your day, paying attention, and managing how you interact with your environment.

>> **Condition red:** You're being attacked or threatened.

As you go about your day, pay attention to changes in condition from green to yellow to red and from red to yellow to green. Adjust your level of awareness and vigilance accordingly. Imagine different scenarios at the different threat levels and how you might respond to them. Train for the different threat levels and scenarios.

As you incorporate self-defense into your daily routine, you'll find that you're constantly practicing self-defense. You don't have to spend an hour in the gym every other day. You're practicing as you're going about your business. You're paying attention to areas of ambush. You're getting comfortable carrying one or more weapons.

By combining this everyday training with more formal training sessions to develop specific hard skills, you're transforming yourself into a formidable foe for anyone who makes the mistake of attacking you. In terms of training for hard skills, do as much as you can when you can. Five minutes is better than zero minutes.

Recovering After an Attack

Any potentially dangerous or deadly situation will impact different people in a variety of ways. I've seen people who were able to recover from the most brutal attacks relatively quickly and others who've agonized after a close call. There's no timetable or specific process of recovery, but you will recover.

The two biggest questions people have after an assault are "Why me?" and "How did this happen?" To answer the first question, you were probably singled out because you were in the wrong place at the wrong time, you had something they wanted, and you looked like an easy mark. To answer the second question, it happened because this big, beautiful world has some twisted and desperate people in it. There's a reason it's called *senseless* violence. As hard as you try, you may never make sense of it. Just realize that it wasn't your fault and there are things you can control moving forward.

Every victim of violence goes through a recovery process. It usually begins with any physical recovery that's necessary and continues with a typically longer process of psychological recovery. Much of the psychological damage is the result of a lost sense of control — control over your own will and even over your body. You've been violated in some way.

In my experience working with victims of violence, I've found that the sooner someone starts preparing to prevent this from happening again, the faster they recover. Through self-defense training, victims start to rebuild the control they lost during the attack. They develop a plan for dealing with something they previously didn't have a plan for.

If you're a victim of a violent attack, the good news is that you can do something to minimize the chances of it ever happening again. Self-defense is about percentages. There are no absolutes, but there are ways to increase your chances and minimize your risk.

Chapter 2

Wrapping Your Brain around Self-Defense Concepts

E very discipline has a set of fundamental concepts that collectively form its foundation and framework. These concepts provide the rationale (the *why*) behind the various practices and techniques characteristic of the discipline. For example, the concept of the fight-or-flight response explains why complicated martial arts techniques are often useless in self-defense situations. In fight-or-flight mode, when your sympathetic nervous system (SNS) is engaged, your rational thought processes and fine motor skills are impaired, making it difficult, if not impossible, to execute complex martial arts moves.

Understanding the concepts that underpin effective self-defense tactics and techniques makes you more receptive to those tactics and techniques. It's like becoming more receptive to adopting a healthy diet and exercising regularly when you have a better understanding of the impact of those factors on your health and fitness.

In this chapter, I introduce you to several key concepts that form the foundation and framework of self-defense.

Distinguishing Self-Defense from Martial Arts

Self-defense is most often confused with cultural fighting arts such as kung fu and aikido and combat sports such as mixed martial arts (MMA). Although you can use some techniques from those martial arts to defend yourself (after all, a punch is a punch), at the end of the day, martial arts are tactically inefficient and practiced for a purpose other than self-defense.

Modern martial arts are a celebration of sport and culture with a loose connection to their roots in warfare (real or fictional). They're designed to promote national pride, competition, and self-improvement through discipline, and they include rules to minimize serious injury and death. Fighting in martial arts is against a single opponent of equal size and ability in a secure area at a specific time and date. The techniques (though they can inflict severe pain) are not fully intended or executed to cause severe and debilitating injury or death.

In contrast, self-defense is survival by any means necessary — gun, knife, baseball bat, biting, gouging, kneeing, stomping, tearing of flesh. . . . Self-defense happens at the time of your attacker's choosing, against an unknown number of assailants who are usually larger, stronger, and most likely armed.

Martial arts competitions are athletic events. If you're injured or you don't make weight, you don't have to fight. With self-defense, you must fight regardless of how old you are or whether you're sick, injured, or out of shape. In fact, you're most likely to be targeted when you appear vulnerable.

Martial arts schools do teach self-defense, but only nominally. Defenses are scripted, and counters are choreographed, making these maneuvers not only ineffective but detrimental to your safety. They build false confidence, which can make you even more vulnerable.

In the following sections, I give you a closer look at specific martial arts and explain in greater detail what makes self-defense so different.

REMEMBER

I'm not belittling combat sports or cultural fighting. They all require time, discipline, and sacrifice. They're a pursuit of excellence and perfection, which should be applauded. I'm just pointing out the differences between martial arts and self-defense, so you understand why I don't recommend martial arts styles or techniques for self-defense.

Exploring cultural fighting arts and combat sports

Cultural fighting arts and combat sports comprise a wide variety of systems and styles. In the following sections, I introduce you to some of the most common of these martial arts.

Japan's big three

Japan was the first country to systematically export martial arts to the West for the purpose of promoting Japanese culture. Judo emissaries were sent around the globe to put on demonstrations and teach the art. Although Judo was the primary export, Japan is home to three major martial arts:

>> **Karate** offers a hard edge and an attitude that focuses on killing the enemy with brutal and violent strikes.

>> **Aikido** is the opposite of karate, stressing harmony, movement, and leverage, with the goal of using your opponent's momentum against them.

>> **Judo** relies on *grappling* (wrestling), throws, and submissions to defeat the opponent in a way that's symbolic of a victory on the battlefield. In some ways, judo is the middle ground between karate and aikido.

You would think that Japan would've settled on one, single martial art as the best one, but martial arts are an expression of combat and heritage, not actual combat. Karate, aikido, and judo provide unique experiences for the practitioner while still connecting to Japan's heritage; they just do it in three different ways.

PRESERVING JAPAN'S WARRIOR HERITAGE

Karate, aikido, and judo all evolved after World War II. Japan was demilitarized by the United States, and all forms of Bushido were forbidden. (*Bushido* is the code of honor and morals developed by the Japanese samurai that was the driving force behind Imperial Japan.)

A few years into the reconstruction of Japan, the practice of martial arts was allowed — first judo, then karate and aikido. These three completely different approaches all symbolically connect the student to Japan's warrior heritage.

Other cultural fighting arts

Other cultural fighting arts include *kenjutsu* (sword arts), Chinese kung fu, wushu, and other heavily stylized arts. These fighting styles are deeply rooted in a country's culture and are practiced to celebrate the nation's history and traditions.

Combat sports

Combat sports focus on sparring competition. These sports include judo, wrestling, boxing, Brazilian Jiu-Jitsu (BJJ), tae kwon do, and MMA. Each of these sports is defined by rules of competition that dictate and inform the style. In other words, the rules shape the style.

Variations in styles

Within each category of cultural fighting arts and combat sports are further divisions of style. For example, BJJ is a derivative of judo. Judo was brought to Brazil as part of Japan's efforts to spread its culture. The famed Gracie family of Brazil developed their own style by focusing on the *ground* elements of judo, while judo focused more on *standing* techniques.

Tae kwon do and Shotokan karate are other prime examples. The founder of tae kwon do, Choi Hong-hi, was a black belt in Japanese Shotokan karate but wanted to create a martial art that was distinctly Korean, so in 1954 he founded tae kwon do. To distinguish it from karate, he stressed the use of the feet with higher, acrobatic kicks instead of the straight punches and lower kicks of Shotokan. Even the untrained eye won't mistake Shotokan karate for tae kwon do.

RULES SHAPE STYLE

Any restriction on a contest shapes the fighter's techniques and tactics. For centuries people have been trying to determine the best martial arts style, but the outcome always comes down to two factors: the fighter and the rules. If the fighter is tough and the rules are in their favor, that fighter wins; style has little to do with it.

One of the most obvious illustrations of rules shaping a style happened when MMA evolved into what we know it to be today. If you watch the very first Ultimate Fighting Championship (UFC), you can clearly tell which style each fighter used.

Today, you see very little difference in fighting styles. A fighter may have a foundation in a particular discipline, but when they get into the octagon, they're fighting the same style as their opponent. One may be a better grappler or a better striker, but the overall approach is generally the same for both fighters.

Understanding what makes self-defense so different

Self-defense is vastly different from both cultural fighting arts and combat sports. Table 2-1 summarizes the key differences.

TABLE 2-1 **Self-Defense versus Martial Arts**

Self-Defense	Martial Arts
The goal is to stop the attack as quickly as possible, either by escaping or by damaging your attacker enough to neutralize them.	The goal is to defeat your opponent and hug each other at the end of the fight.
There are no rules.	You're protected by mutually agreed-upon rules.
Your attacker may be armed or have accomplices ready to pounce on you.	You don't have to worry about your opponent pulling out a concealed weapon or someone from their corner entering the ring.

(continued)

TABLE 2-1 *(continued)*

Self-Defense	Martial Arts
Your fight-or-flight response is engaged, which enhances some of your fighting abilities while diminishing other (see the later section "Fight-or-flight mode affects your ability to fight").	The fight-or-flight response rarely occurs, and when it does, it usually means you're out of control and you'll lose the fight or be disqualified.
Your attacker will be larger and stronger than you.	Your opponent will be about the same weight and skill level as you.
Your attacker will be intent on seriously injuring you (or worse).	Your opponent will stop when you're injured or in trouble.
You must be able to fight at the time and place of your attacker's choosing, on any terrain, regardless of whether you're injured, weak, or distracted.	You compete at a set time and place on a smooth (often padded) surface free of debris with a coach in your corner and your friends and family cheering you on.

Comparing Self-Defense to Police and Military Defensive Tactics

Many civilians seeking self-defense training turn to law enforcement or the military. Unfortunately, self-defense recommendations from these sources can be misleading because the parameters they have in place for use of force are vastly different from those of a street fight. Note the following differences:

>> Both the police and the military are trained to respond to calls and seek to perform missions with superior numbers, weapons, and intelligence.

>> When police engage in hand-to-hand combat, they're usually not alone. The situation typically involves multiple officers taking down a single subject, and they can call in backup if the situation calls for it.

In the military, the difference is even more exaggerated. They defeat the enemy with overwhelming numbers, weapons, intelligence, and firepower.

Only when an officer or a soldier is alone with a violent criminal or a vicious enemy combatant are they in a situation similar to what you can expect on the street. And when that happens, they do what I recommend — launch a brutal attack to survive.

>> Many law enforcement and military academies develop programs approved by government and civilian oversight committees who look to limit their exposure to lawsuits and liability. The result is a sanitized (nice) version they can point to when they need to defend officers in use-of-force lawsuits.

>> The training in most police academies and military camps ends after several weeks. Without continued training, most officers lose whatever they learned in the academy in a matter of weeks. If a police officer or a soldier is serious about their close-combat skills, they usually join a civilian martial arts school to get some consistent training.

>> Many police officers and soldiers don't need much close-combat training. If you're a special forces soldier, even if you didn't make it through selection, chances are, you're tough, and anyone who puts their hands on you is going to regret it because your will to survive is light-years beyond that of the average person.

The context in which you may find yourself dealing with violence is completely different from that of a law enforcement or military operation. An attack can occur anywhere at any time; you're alone and you may be outnumbered; you may be unarmed facing an armed attacker; you probably know nothing about the enemy; and you have no backup. For these reasons, you need a completely different approach to self-defense.

Gaining Insight from the Predator-Prey Paradigm

You can gain a great deal of insight into self-defense by studying the predator-prey relationship in nature. Here are a few key lessons to be learned by examining how animals that would otherwise be vulnerable to predators defend themselves:

>> **Find strength in numbers.** Animals often travel in groups (herds, flocks, schools) for protection, so you're safer in

public places with lots of people or when you're with one or more friends or companions.

>> **Assume your attacker has friends nearby.** Intelligent predators, such as orcas and wolves hunt in groups to improve their efficiency and success, so don't assume that the person threatening you is the only one you'll have to deal with.

>> **Having a weapon improves your odds of survival.** Many animals — think porcupines, armadillos, and venomous animals of various species — would be extremely vulnerable if not for their weapons or body armor.

>> **Your appearance can be enough to discourage an attack.** That distinctive white stripe down the back of a skunk is enough to deter most predators. Carry yourself on the street in a way that tells would-be attackers you're no easy mark.

>> **Speed counts.** If you can outrun an attacker, you can defend yourself without suffering even a scratch. You don't even need to be the fastest potential victim in the crowd — you just need to be a little faster than the slowest one. When a lion attacks a herd of antelope, they all bolt, and the lion picks off the one that's left behind.

>> **You can outsmart your attacker.** Some prey defend themselves by being smarter than their predators. Case in point, the clown fish, which hides amid the poisonous tentacles of sea anemone to keep predators at bay.

REMEMBER

Self-defense isn't about defeating your enemy; it's about breaking the predator-prey paradigm between you and your attacker. You don't need a black belt in judo, karate, or tae kwon do; you just need to be smart and vigilant and know how to fully exploit whatever natural abilities and weapons you have at your disposal.

Using the Four Pillars of Self-Defense to Your Advantage

The four pillars of self-defense are position, distance, momentum, and balance. These four factors are crucial for moving and attacking effectively. Understanding and using these factors to your advantage can significantly improve your effectiveness while diminishing your attacker's ability to move and strike effectively.

In the following section, I cover these factors in pairs because distance and position are closely related as are momentum and balance.

Position and distance

Every self-defense situation can be broken down to position and distance. *Distance* is how far the threat is from you, and *position* is where you and your assailant are in relation to one another. That's it. The type of attack doesn't matter — a punch, a body grab, a stab, or even a firearm. Focus on where and how far away your attacker is from you.

Positions

You and your assailant can only be in one of the three following positions:

>> You're both standing.

>> You're both on the ground.

>> One of you is standing while the other is on the ground.

In Chapter 8, I explain how to assume the position of advantage when you're both standing. In Chapter 12, I explain what to do if one or both of you are on the ground.

Distances

Distances can vary quite a bit, but you can narrow the variations down to the following three:

>> **Far range:** Far enough away that they need to shift their weight to touch or strike you

>> **Close range:** Close enough that they don't have to shift their weight to touch or strike you

>> **Extreme close range:** Close enough to grapple with you

Positions at different distances

By combining positions with distances, you can develop a better understanding of the various situations you may find yourself and your assailant in during an attack.

If you're both standing, the threat can be in front of you, behind you, or to the left or right of you, far, close, or extremely close.

If one of you is standing and the other is on the ground, you can be in any one of the following three positions:

>> **Far range:** The person standing is outside the reach of the legs of the person on the ground.

>> **Close range:** The person standing is inside the reach of the legs of the person on the ground — close enough to kick them.

>> **Extreme close range:** The person standing is close enough to the person on the ground to stomp on them.

If you're both on the ground, distance is no longer a factor. You can be in one of the following three positions (see Chapter 12 for details):

>> **Mount:** The person on top is straddling the waist or chest of the person on the bottom.

>> **Guard:** The person on the bottom has both their legs wrapped around the waist or legs of the person on the top.

>> **Half-guard:** The person on the bottom only has one leg wrapped around the waist or leg of the person on the top.

That's it. You and your attacker can be in no other conceivable position/distance combination. The type of attack doesn't matter. Whether your attacker is armed doesn't matter. The tactics and techniques I teach focus on improving your position relative to your attacker to gain the position from which you can mount an effective and decisive counterattack.

Momentum and balance

Momentum and balance are the two factors you need to control during an assault. Everything you do to defend yourself is intended to stop your attacker's momentum and build yours while disrupting your attacker's balance and maintaining yours:

>> **Momentum:** Momentum is force moving in a certain direction. You can use momentum to your advantage in three ways:

- Increase the momentum of your attack into your assailant to deliver more powerful and devastating blows.

- Make your assailant miss, so their momentum throws off their balance and they waste energy.

- Strike your assailant as they move toward you to multiply the force of your strike.

REMEMBER

To win the battle for momentum, strike first and continue to strike. If you pause, even for a moment, you give your attacker an opportunity to shift the momentum in their favor.

>> **Balance:** Balance is firm footing, which enables you to deliver powerful, accurate strikes and, if you're using a firearm, shoot straight. Your goal is to maintain your balance while keeping your attacker off-balance, which takes both the force and accuracy out of anything they try to do to you. If you can get your attacker to trip and fall and crack their skull open on the sidewalk, all the better.

Grasping Key Tenets of Self-Defense

You can leverage an understanding of various physical laws and traits of human biology and physiology to gain an advantage in self-defense. In this section, I introduce you to four key tenets of self-defense.

Force = Mass × Acceleration

The heavier an object is and the faster it moves, the more force it has behind it, so the faster you strike your attacker and the heavier whatever you're swinging happens to be, the more pain and injury it's likely to cause. Because your body mass is constant (well, maybe not after the weekend), you have only two options for increasing the force of your attack:

>> **Increase your acceleration.** Drive forward into your attacker and keep driving.

>> **Use a force multiplier.** Any weapon is a tool that multiplies your force, the most obvious of which is a club. When you swing a club, it multiplies both the mass and acceleration of

the strike. Other weapons act as force multipliers in other ways — for example, a firearm multiplies the force required to pull the trigger, and a knife concentrates the force of an attack on a tiny point or narrow edge, which can puncture or slice the skin and puncture vital organs.

Inflicting pain and injury on your attacker is the only way to stop a physical attack in progress. Pain comes before injury; it tells the body to stop whatever the heck it's doing before it gets seriously injured.

WARNING

Don't accept the common misconception that hurting your attacker will only make them angrier and more violent. The overwhelming majority of attacks stop after the assailant encounters resistance. They're more likely to feel emboldened by any *lack* of resistance.

Fight-or-flight mode affects your ability to fight

When you sense a significant threat, your SNS shifts into high gear to prepare your body to fight or flee. In fight-or-flight mode, your body experiences several physical changes that enhance some physical and mental capabilities while impairing others. Understanding these changes provides insight into why some self-defense tactics and techniques can be so effective while others can be completely useless or even difficult or impossible to do:

>> Adrenaline and other stress hormones pour into your bloodstream, increasing your heart rate and respiration rate. Small airways in the lungs expand to take in more oxygen with each breath. Increased oxygen in the brain sharpens your senses and makes you more alert. At the same time, glucose and fats are released, boosting energy.

WARNING

If your heart rate and respiration rate increase excessively, you'll black out and then pass out. So, when you experience SNS activation, try to control your breathing. I'm not telling you to stuff your emotions, because many of the physiological changes are to your advantage. Just be conscious of your breathing and try to breathe more deeply and regularly. In other words, don't hyperventilate.

» Blood flow is redirected away from your extremities to your large muscle groups and vital organs, increasing your muscle strength and enhancing your *gross motor skills,* such as running away, charging forward, throwing, lifting, and kicking.

At the same time, your fine and complex motor skills are impaired. *Fine motor skills* are movements that use the smaller muscles of the hands, such as the ability to use a pencil or scissors, fasten buttons, and tie shoelaces. *Complex motor skills* are movements that require more intricately coordinated body movements, like waving or flapping your hand or arm, rotating and closing your hand, and wiggling your fingers. Complex motor skills incorporate greater neuromotor fitness components and require learning and practice.

» Vasoconstriction of minor blood vessels in your extremities reduces any bleeding in places like your fingers and hands.

» Your pupils dilate, narrowing your focus to the immediate threat in front of you, giving you tunnel vision. At the same time, you may experience auditory exclusion — not registering anything you may be hearing.

» Digestive processes slow or shut down. When fear is severe, you may even evacuate your bowels and bladder (yes, poop and pee your pants).

» Your brain's cerebellum takes a back seat, suspending your ability to think rationally or speak coherently and articulately. Your hypothalamus takes over, essentially placing your body on autopilot.

The logical conclusion you can draw from this list of SNS activation changes is that complicated self-defense techniques that are recommended in the martial arts don't work on the street for two reasons:

» Your body and mind are incapable of doing them effectively (or at all) in fight-or-flight mode.

» They don't take full advantage of your enhanced gross motor skills, such as your increased ability to knee, kick, stomp, and deliver devastating open-hand strikes.

For these reasons, the best self-defense techniques are these:

>> A handful of simple, large movements that you execute effectively in any situation

>> Tactics and techniques that involve either moving toward or escaping from the threat

TIP

When you sense a threat, being mindful of your heart rate can help your body maintain the optimal heart rate for self-defense: 115 to 145 beats per minute (BPM). At this rate, you're at your peak performance in terms of visual and cognitive reaction times and the balance between gross and complex motor skills. To understand the relationship between heart rate and self-defense performance, check out the effect of different heart rates on your body (see Table 2-2).

TABLE 2-2 The Effect of Different Heart Rates on Your Body

Heart Rate (in Beats per Minute)	Condition	Description
60–90	White	Normal resting heart rate.
91–120	Yellow	Fine motor skills start to deteriorate.
121–140	Red	Complex motor skills start to deteriorate.
141–175	Gray	Cognitive processing deteriorates. You experience *vasoconstriction* (reduced bleeding from wounds), loss of peripheral vision, loss of depth perception, loss of near vision, and *auditory exclusion* (a form of temporary hearing loss caused by stress).
176 or higher	Black	You experience an irrational fight-or-flight response. You may freeze (with the inability to move), black out, void your bladder and bowels, and exhibit submissive behavior. Your gross motor skills may also peak.

TACHYPSYCHIA

Tachypsychia is what happens to your mind under extreme conditions of stress and can be developed by engaging in regular self-defense training. In short, it's your mind's ability to slow down or speed up under fight-or-flight conditions. Tachypsychia is a neurological condition that enables you to process and respond to traumatic situations.

Sometimes called the *stop-clock condition,* tachypsychia increases your brain's anticipatory ability in self-defense situations.

Keep it simple

The reason why complex self-defense counter-maneuvers taught by the vast majority of martial arts fail in the real world is because you can't recall them, and your body won't let you perform them when you're in fight-or-flight mode. The more effective approach to self-defense is one that employs a much smaller set of simple tactics and techniques. Keep it simple.

REMEMBER

Don't try to fight Mother Nature. You can't circumvent your body's natural response to danger. The only thing you can do when your SNS is activated is to channel your newly found power through simple, large motor movements.

Action is faster than reaction

A core reality largely ignored by self-defense experts is that action is faster than reaction. When applied to self-defense, this means you're better off attacking first and forcing your attacker to react than waiting until your attacker acts first, forcing *you* to react. By acting first and continuing an unrelenting attack, you keep your attacker on the defense. By keeping them off-balance and with momentum in your favor, you have the upper hand.

WARNING

Act, don't wait to react. In one study, researchers measured the reaction times of police officers in a use-of-force situation. The average reaction time was 21 milliseconds. That may not seem like a long time, but that's all an attacker needs to knock you out, stab you, or shoot you.

And keep in mind that that study was conducted on trained police officers trying their best to react as quickly as possible. In the real world, you're going to be distracted, lost, looking for your car or your keys, and your reaction time will be a bit longer.

And if you're thinking a little martial arts training is all you need to improve your reaction time, think again. Traditional martial arts self-defense training can actually *increase* your reaction time as you proceed through all the steps necessary to calculate your counter-maneuver:

1. Allow your attacker to approach.
2. Wait for your attacker to make the first move.
3. Determine the type of attack — punch, kick, stab, or grab.
4. Recall the specific counter-maneuver.
5. Execute the counter-maneuver before the attacker hits you first. (Good luck with that, by the way.)

Imagine you're leaving work. You're thinking about your day and what you're doing that night. Maybe you're in a good mood, or maybe you're upset over something that happened at work. All of a sudden, you're approached by some guy looking for his lost dog.

The next thing you know, this guy is right in your face demanding your cash. Do you really think when he attacks you that you're going to have the time to "block" whatever he has in store for you? What if he grabs your collar? Are you going to remember the specific defense move?

No.

And that's just the *first* attack. Because it's not going to be just one punch, one kick, or one grab. It's going to be a barrage of punches and kicks. And that grab is going to be followed up by something much more devastating. Your attacker has a plan, and it doesn't stop with the initial assault.

WARNING

You'll never be able to react with a specific defense counter-maneuver. Nonspecific tactics and techniques based on position and distance don't require you to first identify the type of attack and calculate your response before taking action. They enable you to act immediately, forcing your attacker to react to you.

Recognizing the Three Levels of Self-Defense

Self-defense has three levels. Ranked in order from least to most difficult, they are

>> Awareness and avoidance

>> Escape and evasion

>> Control and domination

Awareness and avoidance

Awareness and avoidance involve spotting or sensing danger, looking like someone who's willing and able to resist an attack, and making savvy decisions about the places you frequent, the situations you place yourself in, and the people you hang out with. Being vigilant, avoiding places of ambush, managing your personal space, making wise decisions, carrying yourself with confidence, and identifying potential setups are all very easy skills to develop. (See Chapter 5 for details.)

REMEMBER

If you're not aware of your surroundings, no self-defense style or system on the planet will work for you.

Escape and evasion

Running away solves a lot of issues. Even if you face an attacker with a firearm, most after-action reports show that when you simply run away, even getting shot at is unlikely.

Techniques that focus on your ability to remain mobile and escape are easy to learn and execute. In most cases, as soon as you resist, your attacker will stop because they weren't planning on your fighting back — they were planning on your voluntary compliance and submission. Your resistance breaks the predator-prey paradigm.

Control and domination

This is, by far, the hardest level of self-defense. Outside the use of a weapon, imposing your will over another human being requires skill, power, and fitness, all of which require more time in training.

However, training exclusively for control and domination, as martial arts practitioners often do, can build false confidence. In a *dojo* (a Japanese martial arts school), you can observe this practice daily as small women and children take out bigger, stronger opponents or get them in holds that force them to tap out. The larger attacker charges the smaller defender, who then executes the technique (almost effortlessly), leaving the attacker lying helpless on the ground. These demonstrations make for good theater, but they work only because the attacker is letting the defender win. In the real world, your attacker is going to be hell-bent on getting what they want from you, regardless of your training. They're not impressed by your kung fu fighting.

REMEMBER

Martial arts are mostly focused on control and domination. The goal is to knock out the opponent, throw them to the ground, or get them in some complicated hold that makes them submit. Those are the hardest things to do in a street fight. The good news is that you'll rarely, if ever, need to do them.

Ranking Self-Defense Tactics on the Use-of-Force Hierarchy

All the options you have for defending yourself can be ranked based on effectiveness and efficiency (the amount of strength, effort, expertise, and physical contact with the attacker they require). I would much rather use a predator drone than grapple.

As you choose the means for defending yourself, consult the following use-of-force hierarchy, which ranks your options from most to least effective and efficient:

>> **Projectile weapons:** Any weapon that can injure an attacker from a distance — predator drone, gun, bow and arrow, or slingshot (or just throwing a rock). I don't include knives in that list because throwing a knife is a waste of a good weapon.

WARNING

Consult your local law enforcement agencies or other reliable sources of information for rules and regulations that apply to owning, carrying, and using any weapon in your area. See Chapter 7 for more about choosing and using weapons and Part 4 for guidance on how to neutralize weapon attacks.

>> **Nonlethal weapons:** Any weapon that slows, distracts, or temporarily disables your attacker without causing physical injury, such as personal alarms and pepper spray. (Everyone on the planet should carry pepper spray in public, where legally permitted.) At the bare minimum, you can use nonlethal weapons to pause the attack long enough for you to escape.

>> **Impact weapons:** Any weapon that causes blunt-force trauma and improves your ability to knock out your assailant (for example, a blackjack, a lead pipe, an axe handle, a hammer, brass knuckles, sap gloves, or fist packs).

>> **Edged weapons:** Anything with a sharp edge or a point, from daggers and hatchets to ice picks. Even though these are more lethal than impact weapons, using them requires more physical contact with your attacker, and even if you succeed in causing severe bleeding, your attacker may be able to continue fighting until they lose enough blood to pass out.

WARNING

Never throw a knife unless you need a free hand to draw a gun.

>> **Striking (hand-to-hand combat):** Striking your assailant with empty hands (edge of hand, heel of hand, or hammer fists, as explained in Chapter 9) is low on the list, but it's the best option if you don't have a weapon and can't pick up something to use as a weapon. Empty-hand strikes require the least amount of physical contact and have the most impact on your target, and they're easier to master than grappling techniques.

>> **Gouging, biting, ripping:** Gouging the eyes, biting your attacker, and ripping the flesh (for example, the nose, the mouth, or an ear) are the most primal means of inflicting pain and injury, and they're highly effective.

Imagine a date-rape scenario, during which your attacker continues to impose their will on you after you've told them "No!" Biting what's in front of your mouth and gouging an eye can create enough pause and space to get their weight off you and escape. It might even sober them up.

>> **Grappling:** Wrestling, judo, jujitsu, aikido, and other martial arts that involve close contact and rely on grabbing, holding, tripping, and throwing an opponent are at the bottom of the list for good reasons: They require the most skill, power,

strength, and leverage; they increase your exposure to risk; and they're unnecessary.

Don't get me wrong — I love grappling. I wrestled in college, have a black belt in judo, and have ranks in Brazilian Jiu-Jitsu. If you have the time and inclination, I recommend adding a grappling martial art to your skill set — it builds confidence, gets you in great shape, creates toughness, and makes you more comfortable in close quarter situations. But it's much easier to knock someone out with a strike than it is with a strangle. It's easier to bite someone than it is to choke them. Grappling limits your mobility and makes you vulnerable to multiple attackers and weapons.

REMEMBER

Never choose the ground; the ground is unforgiving. In the gym, the mat is there for safety. On the street, you have concrete, rocks, debris, and other items that can do more damage than your attacker.

TIP

Which techniques work the best? That's your call, and you can make that call only in the heat of battle. The best technique is the one that gives you the greatest tactical advantage at the time and has the greatest chance of stopping the assault. Generally speaking, however, you should always be trying to improve your position on the use-of-force hierarchy. If you're on the ground grappling, gouge, bite, and rip your attacker to create room to strike or time to grab a weapon and escalate your counterattack.

Chapter **3**

Developing a Self-Defense Mindset

S elf-defense is physical, no doubt about it, but it also has emotional and psychological elements that you need to factor in. For example, confidence is a biggie. If you have a victim mentality and feel that the entire world is against you, you're going to walk around feeling dejected; you'll appear weak and vulnerable, making yourself a more likely target. And if you are attacked and assume you don't have a chance, you're probably going to lose.

On the other hand, if you're confident in your ability to destroy anyone who messes with you, you'll walk tall and strong and be a less attractive target. And, if anyone does mess with you, you'll enter the fray confident that you'll come out on top. As that old saying goes, "Whether you think you can or think you can't, you're probably right."

In this chapter, I encourage you to develop a healthy and resilient mindset and explain how to get in the right frame of mind for defending yourself and destroying anyone who makes the mistake of threatening you or a loved one. I also address any legal concerns you may have about the use of force in self-defense, so you have a better idea of what's legal and what's not, and those concerns won't distract you when you're threatened.

Coming to Terms with Your Emotions

I don't know about you, but the thought of fighting for my life scares me. I don't want to do it. I would rather go about my business and never, ever have to hurt or get hurt by another human being. The risk of injury and humiliation is something I would rather avoid. However, there is one thing I hate more: the thought of not being able to protect and defend myself and those I love. The potential humiliation of not being able to stand up for myself and my loved ones outweighs my fear of being defeated or humiliated on the street.

Growing up, I was a bigger, stronger kid and was never one to back down from a bully. Not only was I a bigger, stronger kid, but I started wrestling in second grade, and if you wrestle and you fight a kid who hasn't wrestled, it's no contest. Even with those advantages and regardless of the many schoolyard scraps that ended in my favor, I was always afraid to fight. Fighting, even when I won, wasn't easy.

As I got older, those schoolyard scraps got a little more serious and a lot more dangerous. I guess that's why I got into martial arts. Believe it or not, the kid who was all-state in both football and wrestling was scared. And to this day, I'm still scared. But being scared is still not as bad as the frustration and humiliation I would face if I didn't stand up for myself or my loved ones.

I share my story to make the point that regardless of a person's physical fitness and self-defense skills, having to fight can be scary, and being afraid is okay. In fact, fear and other emotions (anger comes to mind), can work in your favor. In this section, I explain how to leverage fear and other emotions without allowing them to become debilitating.

Harnessing the power of your emotions

Fear is like a tornado siren, giving you an early warning signal that something's not right and you need to get ready for action. It activates your sympathetic nervous system (SNS) to trigger your fight-or-flight response, preparing your mind and body for battle or escape. (See Chapter 2 for more about the biological and physiological changes resulting from SNS activation.)

Many self-defense experts advise remaining calm in a life-threatening situation. I don't recommend trying to remain calm for two good reasons: (1) You can't, and (2) You shouldn't. You can be more mindful of your breathing to keep your heartbeat and respiration from going off the charts, but trying to remain calm when your life is threatened will probably only ramp up your anxiety. Besides, your built-in fight-or-flight response is there to protect you — don't resist it, *harness* it.

One of the great aspects of fear (and frustration for that matter) is that it can quickly turn to anger, and when that blood gets pumping and you're jacked up on adrenaline, you're capable of performing superhuman feats. When you're threatened or attacked, get angry — get very, *very* angry — and then unleash all that pent-up violent emotion on your attacker.

All right, now you can calm down.

Keeping panic at bay

Panic is fear with no outlet. It's how you feel when you're frustrated or afraid and believe you have no escape or effective response. When panic is extreme, your heart rate soars over 175 beats per minute (BPM), you hyperventilate, and you may even black out or pass out. Instead of fighting or fleeing, you freeze or engage in an endless loop of useless, ineffective thoughts and behaviors.

REMEMBER

The only way to avoid panic is to prepare. You're already in the process of preparing by reading this book. Developing new self-defense skills and engaging in self-defense training make you even more prepared and confident. The result is that when you're attacked, your fear has an outlet. You have an effective response at the ready for whenever you need it.

Managing anxiety

Anxiety is a product of uncertainty — fear of the unknown and, in the context of self-defense, not knowing what to do when you're approached or attacked. Anxiety is also the result of not feeling in control. When you're the victim of a violent crime, your power and control are taken from you, resulting in instability, which ripples through every aspect of your life.

Again, the best way to prevent anxiety, and alleviate any recurring bouts of anxiety after an attack, is to prepare for the exact issue that causes it — in the context of self-defense, that means preparing yourself to respond effectively to a threat.

I can't tell you the number of people who've started self-defense training after they've been assaulted. But all the victims of violence I've had the pleasure of training have found they were able to regain some semblance of control and reclaim their lives through self-defense training and preparation.

Clearing a major mental hurdle

The biggest emotional/mental hurdle you face when you're being threatened is giving yourself permission to violently attack another human being *before* that person has a chance to attack you. Responsible, caring human beings aren't programmed to do that. In fact, we're all programmed *not* to do it. We're programmed — and this is insane — to let someone physically harm us before we permit ourselves to harm them. And at that point, our response is, tragically, too late.

Whenever there's a fight, people ask, "Who started it? Who threw the first punch?" as if those two actions are the same. When someone threatens you, *they* started it. You didn't ask for it. Now it's your turn to throw the first "punch." Strike first and ferociously. They started it. You end it.

In martial arts competition, you don't have to decide when to take action. The ref says, "Go!" In the real world, you don't have that luxury. In self-defense, you take your cues from your attacker and the situation. When you sense that an attack is imminent, you look for an opening and strike immediately.

TIP

Taking the first step is the most important part of surviving a physical assault because the person who strikes first usually wins. Every good street fighter knows this; now you do, too.

You can take comfort in the fact that fear and nervousness are normal and that they disappear as soon as you take action. If you've ever competed in combat sports such as wrestling, boxing, judo, jujitsu, or mixed martial arts (MMA), that nervousness you feel right before the start of the match is at its peak — but right after first contact, it melts away and you're in the moment. The same holds true for self-defense. When your SNS is activated, your heart rate goes through the roof and adrenaline courses in your veins, but after you take the first step, it dissipates and you're in the moment.

Never let your attacker throw the first punch. Would you let Mike Tyson throw the first punch? You never know who you're facing out there, and that first punch leads to two, three, and four . . . and you on the floor.

Lessening the Emotional Trauma of an Attack

Being the victim of violence can be very traumatic. In addition to any physical injury you suffered, you lose your sense of power, control, and self-determination to some degree. You may feel violated and humiliated. You may even blame yourself. If you're a victim of violence, I encourage you to visit Chapter 1 for guidance on how to recover and reclaim your life, along with Chapter 16, in which I offer an additional ten tips for survivors of violence. Here, I discuss how to prevent or lessen the emotional and psychological trauma of an attack by acting proactively — planning and preparing for an attack.

The key is to resist. Don't give up your power and control. Make your attacker work for it.

According to at least one study (and I've witnessed proof of this time and time again through my work with victims), the people who fought back, successfully or not, recovered faster than the victims who did not. Another study showed that most victims who submitted to their attackers regretted doing so. One study participant said, "I remembered hearing somewhere once that the best way to survive a violent sexual assault was to give in, so I did. The guilt of doing so haunted me for years."

What you decide to fight over and whether you decide to fight back is your decision. Don't let me or anybody else tell you what's worth fighting for.

What I do recommend is that you start training for self-defense and make it an integral part of your life, as I explain in Chapter 1. Engaging in self-defense training gives you the option of fighting back, whether you choose to or not, while inoculating you against the emotional trauma of an attack. It makes you stronger and more capable physically and mentally and gives you more control over the ultimate outcome. It makes you more resilient.

REMEMBER

Some people are more resilient than others, some are naturally better equipped, physically and mentally, to fight back. When you're attacked, there's no right or wrong response — the only right way to respond is the way *you* choose to. Training and preparation give you more choices and increase your odds of survival.

Getting Up to Speed on Your Legal Right to Defend Yourself

What most people know about the law and self-defense is based on urban legend, the movies, and the media. Even the notion that you can use deadly force (a firearm) only when your attacker is armed is *totally false*. Laws differ from state to state and country to country. However, in every country on the planet, you have the right to defend yourself, others, and even your property.

In this section, I clear up any misunderstandings you may have about your right to defend yourself and others and present the facts about your legal rights.

Dispelling common legal self-defense myths

The first order of business is to purge any common misconceptions you may have about your legal right to defend yourself. Here, I bust six common myths that drive me nuts.

Myth #1: You must wait for your attacker to throw the first punch

False. If someone looks capable, has the means, and has demonstrated an intent to do you bodily harm, you have the legal right to use force to physically defend yourself. Any act of aggression or aggressive display that causes you to believe a physical attack is imminent can justify your use of force.

Myth #2: If your attacker is unarmed, you must fight them unarmed

False. You can defend yourself by any means necessary. You can use mechanical force (clubs and batons) and even deadly force (a firearm). Edged weapons, such as knives, are a category between mechanical and deadly force. The more meaningful the threat, the more force you can use. If you're faced with a strong, determined, and capable attacker, you can use deadly force to protect yourself. You wouldn't expect a little 90-year-old lady to go mano a mano with a young, violent criminal; the law doesn't either.

Myth #3: The law prohibits you from defending other people

False. You have the right — and the moral obligation — to help others who are in harm's way. The law supports this notion. However, the law does not *compel* you to act. If you choose to stand there and do nothing (or capture it on video), you won't be held accountable. The law allows you to intervene, but it doesn't punish you for not intervening. That gives you more reason to assume that when you're attacked you're on your own.

Myth #4: You need to wait for an attack to defend yourself

False. This myth is similar to the first one but provides you with a little more leeway to launch a preemptive strike against what you have reason to believe is a threat to your safety. For example, suppose someone's stalking you; the mere sight of your stalker is enough justification for you to act. Another example: You get into an argument with someone on social media, and that person threatens you. The next day, you see that person walking toward you on the street with an angry look on their face. If you believe they're about to attack you, you have the legal right to strike first.

The same holds true if you have a war of words with somebody who has threatened to harm you, your family, or even your property and then you see them coming up your driveway; you would be justified in using force to protect yourself.

Myth #5: You'll get arrested if you carry a concealed weapon like a knife

False. Unless a weapon (like pepper spray or blackjacks) is strictly prohibited in your state, you can lawfully carry weapons to defend yourself. However, laws vary regarding firearms; for example, some jurisdictions allow concealed carry, whereas others permit only *open carry* (carrying a gun in a way that others can see it).

WARNING

Check with local law enforcement or other reliable sources to find out what your legal rights are concerning which weapons you can own and carry, how you can carry them, and in what situations you're permitted to use them. Laws can be tricky; for example, in New Jersey, according to my source, you can defend yourself with a knife, but you can't carry a knife for self-defense. So, for example, you can carry a knife to open boxes at work, and then use it to stab someone who's physically threatening you, but if a police officer stops you and you say that you're carrying a knife for self-defense, you could be in legal trouble.

Myth #6: Trained fighters must register their hands as lethal weapons

False. A very common myth perpetuated by the media is that anyone who's highly trained in any sort of fighting art must register their hands (or feet or whatever) as lethal weapons. That's nonsense.

I have three black belts — two from the United States and one from Japan — and I've *never* been required to register *anywhere.* This is just another case of martial artists allowing the "folklore" to perpetuate, because — let's face it — being considered a lethal weapon is *awesome!* But it's still BS.

However, it is true that lawyers may try to use your training against you to prove that you used excessive force or were capable of gentler techniques because of your training. The best way to protect yourself legally is to stop your counterattack as soon as you feel the threat is over.

Consulting the deadly-force diamond

One way to determine whether the use of deadly force in a self-defense situation is justified is to consult the deadly-force diamond, which stipulates the following four criteria:

>> **Weapon:** The subject is capable of causing you physical harm — weapon or no weapon. To meet this criterion, the attacker must be armed, trained, or considerably larger or stronger than you.

>> **Opportunity:** The subject is in a position to impose their will on you.

>> **Subject's actions:** The subject is threatening you or moving toward you.

>> **Duty to retreat:** You're unable to disengage from the confrontation safely. In other words, you have no other option but to fight back. This doesn't mean you have to turn your back on someone who's in your face threatening you — when they're that close, you're usually unable to retreat safely.

REMEMBER

The only place you don't have a duty to retreat is in the living area of your own home (see "Defending your 'castle'" later in this chapter) or in states that have stand-your-ground laws. Your duty to retreat also doesn't apply to protecting others. If you see someone in danger, you're legally justified to use force to protect them. I know this is viewed as "taking the law into your own hands," but that notion doesn't apply when someone poses a credible threat to you or others. Case in point, in August 2012, when an assailant was shooting it out with police at a trailer park in Early, Texas, a Good Samaritan grabbed his pistol and shot the assailant. Police hailed him as a hero.

A person poses a *credible threat*, when all three of the following apply:

>> They're capable of causing physical harm.

>> They're displaying aggression.

>> You have reason to believe they intend to harm you.

These use-of-force criteria are similar to those used to justify use-of-force for law enforcement agencies except that police officers have no duty to retreat.

Checking three key criteria

Regardless of whether you use deadly force, your legal right to defend yourself must meet all three of the following criteria:

>> **Opportunity:** Conditions are such that the person who's threatening you can harm you physically. For example, if someone's yelling at you from across the street and waving their fist at you, they're not in a physical position to harm you. However, if they're up in your face yelling at you or across the street pointing a gun at you, they are in a position to harm you.

>> **Intent:** The person threatening you expresses, by word or action, their intent to harm you. The threat could be verbal, but it doesn't have to be. If you tell the threat to stay away, and that person moves toward you, that's a sign of intent.

REMEMBER

An attack is usually the culmination of a series of events that lead up to it. You may have been approached, exchanged words, or engaged in an argument. After you establish your position of advantage (see Chapter 8) and tell the attacker to back off and that you don't want to fight, any move that person makes toward you is a demonstration of intent.

>> **Ability:** The threat is capable of harming you physically. Getting yelled at by an elderly man in a wheelchair is much different from getting into an argument and being threatened by Dwayne "The Rock" Johnson (not that he would ever do that). The old man may *say* he wants to kill you, but he probably doesn't have the capacity to do so. The Rock, on the other hand, is well equipped to do so.

Defending your "castle"

The *castle doctrine* enforced in many jurisdictions eliminates the duty to retreat from a legally occupied space — your home or even your vehicle. It also lowers the criteria for use of deadly force that you would need to meet in the street.

Some jurisdictions have variations on the castle doctrine and what constitutes your castle. For example, in New Jersey, you can legally use force to defend yourself only when you're already home when the intruder unlawfully and forcibly breaks into your home and only after they have crossed the threshold (a few feet inside your entrance). If you come home from work, and the intruder is already inside, you're prohibited from using force because you have a path to escape. In Florida, on the other hand, if the intruder is inside when you arrive home, you're allowed, under law, to use force to defend yourself, your loved ones, or your home.

REMEMBER

Even if an intruder unlawfully and forcibly enters your home, you can use force to defend yourself, others, or your property only if the person poses a credible threat. The more deadly your response, the more evidence you need in court to demonstrate the intent and ability of the intruder.

Gauging your level of force

Judges, juries, and people in general frown upon excessive use of force, whether used by a civilian, the police, or even the military. When deciding to use force, try to use the least force required to prevent or stop the attack. In the following list, I rank level of force from least to greatest:

>> **Constructive force:** A command with clear cause and effect; for example, you tell someone, "Get off my lawn if you know what's good for you" or "Leave her alone or I'll shoot." You can use constructive force with or without a weapon; even pointing a firearm at someone can be considered constructive force, but in some jurisdictions, that's considered brandishing a weapon and is illegal.

>> **Physical contact:** Comprises actions that reinforce your commands without causing physical injury or shock to the body; for example, sternly, but gently, taking someone by the arm to move them or guiding their head into a police cruiser.

>> **Control techniques:** Methods of controlling or restraining the subject by holding or pinning them down against their will.

>> **Physical force:** Methods of striking the subject without the aid of a weapon. You can deliver the strike with any part of your body, so long as a weapon isn't used. Physical force is also referred to as *active resistance tactics.*

>> **Mechanical force:** Involves the use of weapons intended to cause pain and injury but not death, such as *impact weapons* (for example, clubs, batons, or lead pipes), pepper spray, tasers, and other items that increase your effectiveness yet enable you to maintain control over their lethality.

> **» Deadly force:** Involves the use of weapons that are lethal by intent and provide the user with no means to control their lethality. Firearms and edged weapons fall into this category.

If someone looks as though they're going to hurt you, your property, or others, you can use force to stop the situation, and you can use the amount of force needed to stop the threat. As soon as the threat is stopped, you stop.

REMEMBER

Even when you abide by the law, chances are good that you'll need to defend your use of force in court, where the definitions of terms such as *reasonable use of force* and *credible threat* will decide your fate.

In some ways, you're damned if you do use force and damned if you don't, and only you can make that decision for yourself based on the circumstances and your interpretation of them. Personally, I'd rather be judged by 12 than carried by 6, as the saying goes. In other words, I'd rather be judged by a 12-person jury of my peers than carried in a coffin by 6 pallbearers. Anytime someone tries to forcefully impose their will on you, you're at risk of being seriously injured or killed.

Knowing when to stop your counterattack

Throughout this book, I recommend that you respond to a threat by striking first and using the most effective means at your disposal. However, that doesn't mean you should continue your attack past the point of incapacitating your attacker. You must stop at that point. Knocking out someone is okay, but continuing to attack their unconscious body may be considered an excessive use of force and expose you to criminal charges. Shooting someone until they fall down is okay but putting two more rounds in them "execution style" is not.

Making use-of-force decisions as an officer of the law

Whenever a police use-of-force incident hits the news, it stirs a lot of debate, mostly uninformed, over whether the officers used excessive force. The increased use of body cams has gone a long way to clear up these types of misunderstandings, but unless you're in that situation, you can never truly understand what the officers were experiencing, feeling, and thinking at the time . . . unless they tell you and they're honest about it.

Officially, the rules of engagement that deal with use of force in law enforcement are based on the following four types of threats:

>> **Passive compliant:** No threat. The subject complies with directives from the officers. Use of force is not warranted.

>> **Passive resistor:** No threat. The subject complies with directives from the officers but verbally protests. Use of force is not warranted.

>> **Active resistor:** Moderate threat. The subject is not compliant or is aggressive. Use of force is warranted. For example, an environmentalist chains themselves to a tree to prevent loggers from cutting it down. Although the protestor isn't posing an immediate threat to anyone, they're actively resisting an order to move out of the way and let the loggers do their jobs. The use of force must be appropriate for the level of resistance; if the subject isn't combative, physical contact would be sufficient.

>> **Active aggressor:** Dangerous threat. This subject is capable of causing physical harm and has expressed an intention, by their words or actions, to cause harm to others and property. Use of force is justified. Note that in this case, the subject doesn't have to be actively attacking an officer. The subject could've uttered a threatening statement, could've made an aggressive move toward the officer, could be holding a weapon, or could have a history of violence or criminal behavior.

Deciding whether to use force

Deciding to use force as police officer or as a citizen requires making grave decisions under extreme stress. This is why I recommend methods that take a lot of the guesswork out of it.

Assuming you're the type of person who would prefer not to fight, I show you how to keep people out of your personal space in a way that reveals their true intentions before that "first punch" is ever thrown (see Chapter 8). This approach gives you the greatest chance of success while ensuring that your decision to use force is justified.

» Distinguishing an attack from a street fight and a fight in the street

» Recognizing various attacker types

» Exploring the motivations of violent criminals

» Analyzing different types of attacks

» Discovering the three things every criminal fears

Chapter **4**
Knowing What You're Up Against

Self-defense training is an exercise in preparing to be attacked, and part of that requires knowing what to expect. The more you know about the enemy and their motivations, fears, and methods of attack, the better prepared you are to avoid, prevent, and respond when you're threatened or attacked.

Of course, in the real world, you have no way of knowing specifically who your attacker is or what they're thinking, and it really doesn't matter much. You're going to treat every attack and attacker the same because they all pose a threat to life and safety. Whether you're dealing with a career criminal, a serial killer, or a bully, you'll respond at the first sign of a threat. Whether the perpetrator plans to steal from you, rape you, kidnap you, or kill you, you'll take action to incapacitate them or escape.

However, having some knowledge and insight about the type of people who commit violent crimes, what motivates them, what commonly foils their attacks, and so on empowers you to turn the tables on these deviants. For example, just knowing that resisting an attacker decreases their odds of success may be enough to convince you to resist rather than comply with a criminal's request.

In this chapter, I pull back the curtain to reveal what attackers are really like and shed light on the common types of attacks so you'll have a better understanding of what you're up against and a clearer idea of what works and what doesn't to avoid, prevent, and stop an attack.

Assuming the Worst

You never know who you're going to face on the street, so you must assume the worst. Assume that your attacker will be larger and stronger than you, is intent on harming you, is armed and dangerous, and has friends nearby ready to step in for backup. Assuming anything less puts you at an extreme tactical disadvantage.

Another factor working against you is that the attacker chooses the time and place to attack (typically, a time and place where you're most vulnerable) and probably isn't going to give you a heads-up that the attack is imminent — they're going to try to blindside you, or at least get you to drop your guard.

With all these factors stacked against you, what chance do you have? The biggest factor working in your favor is the element of surprise. Your attacker isn't expecting you to resist. If they had thought you'd resist, they wouldn't have targeted you. Launching a violent counterattack before the would-be attacker has a chance to strike is your best chance to survive.

REMEMBER

Never trust your attacker. They're smart and cunning, and they'll use your good will and sense of morality and decency against you. They'll reason with you, threaten you, and negotiate to convince or coerce compliance. Look, if they use or threaten to use force, or if they restrain you or restrict you from leaving, they intend to harm you. Their smooth talk or threats, spoken or unspoken, are only their first and most gentle means of gaining your compliance. You can count on much worse to follow, regardless of whether you comply.

If you notice yourself even considering going along with an attacker's request, remind yourself that you're not dealing with a rational, decent human being who's anything like you or the people with whom you normally associate. You would never use force or restrain someone against their will to get what you want from them. The mere fact that they approached you to coerce you to do something against your will tells you something about their moral compass. You can't trust them. They're not playing by the same rules you are.

Violent criminals are like rabid dogs in the sense that they're broken. Something is wrong with how they interact with other humans that is beyond your comprehension. The family pet would never bite you, just like your true friends and loved ones would never attack you. So, treat anyone who approaches you and tries to make you do anything against your will as a threat to your life and safety.

WARNING

When you're being threatened or attacked is no time for politics. After you incapacitate your attacker or escape to safety, you can volunteer at the local jail to help rehabilitate criminals. I'm all for that. But out in the street, it's a battlefield. It's kill or be killed. That's it — you or them. Sorry to be so blunt, but this is what you're up against.

Busting a Common Myth about Attackers

Many people mistakenly believe that violent criminals are looking for trouble and want to "pick a fight." Further, they think that a self-defense situation is like a prize fight or martial arts competition in which both attacker and defender fight until someone wins (gets knocked out or worse). Nothing could be further from the truth.

Your attacker doesn't want a fight. You have something they want, and they plan to get it in a way that requires the least amount of effort. Think of it as their job; they want an easy job, so they pick a target they think is vulnerable — someone they believe can't or won't put up a fight. So, if you resist and make their job harder or increase their chances of getting caught and jailed, they're likely to let you be and move on to an easier mark.

UNTRAINED ATTACKERS ARE *MORE* DANGEROUS

A common myth is that an attacker who has formal training in the martial arts is more dangerous than someone who lacks such training. If that's what you think, I have a question for you: Would you rather deal with someone who has been training a few times a week in a martial art with rules, etiquette, and community, or someone who's been surviving off the streets, using violence to get what they want from a really young age?

I'd much rather face someone who has dedicated their life to following the rules than the one who has survived outside them.

Don't ever underestimate your attacker, and don't assume that because you have a black belt, this person is going to roll over. Trust me, they don't care, and they're not impressed. They'd rather be fighting someone who fights fair and follows the rules, too.

Most self-defense situations end when the attacker feels it's too much effort. If you watch many street fights, you start to notice a pattern — the fight starts and, within minutes, sometimes less, the combatants stop fighting and go their separate ways. The reason is that one or both combatants have suddenly realized that the risk and effort outweigh any potential reward — it's no longer in their best interest to continue fighting. Even street fights that begin for the most inane reasons end this way. Each participant goes in expecting to kick ass, but when they realize that's not going to be so easy or when they get hurt or tired and realize that they had unreasonable expectations, they stop. It's just not worth it.

The lesson in all this is that any resistance you put up is likely to foil an attack. Compliance emboldens attackers.

Comparing an Attack, a Street Fight, and a Fight in the Street

Informal physical confrontations, outside the ring or the dojo, are not all created equal. Some are attacks, and others are street fights or fights in the street. All three are different, carry varying levels of risk, and call for unique responses. Here are the differences among the three:

- **Attack:** An attack involves an assailant trying to take something they want — sex, money, your car or jewelry, or something else — by force or coercion.

- **Street fight:** A street fight is a brutal physical altercation during which the assailant intends to cause serious physical harm or worse. They'll use whatever means necessary to dismantle you and eliminate you from the planet.

- **Fight in the street:** A fight in the street is a glorified sparring session that just happens to take place outside. It's like a schoolyard scuffle. The combatants have no intention of harming each other, and they stop when someone taps out or stops fighting. These sparring matches are often mislabeled "street fights." Don't participate. You can still get seriously hurt, and for what?

REMEMBER

When you're training for self-defense, you're training for attacks and street fights — life-threatening situations. The tactics and techniques presented in this book are not intended for sparring. They're not something you try on your friend who does Brazilian Jiu-Jitsu . . . unless, of course, you're willing to gouge, bite, rip, and stab them.

Profiling Your Attacker

In law enforcement, *profiling* involves analyzing data about criminals to help identify the most likely suspects in a criminal investigation. The practice has gotten a lot of bad press, and rightfully so, for its use in racial profiling — focusing investigations on members of specific racial or ethnic groups based on the cultural biases of the investigators or society at large.

When I encourage you to profile your attacker, I'm talking about profiling by personality type, motivation, and modus operandi (MO) — their preferred methods — like FBI profilers do. The practice of profiling attackers enables you to develop a better understanding of who they are, why they commit the crimes they do, and how they operate, so you can be better prepared to avoid them, prevent attacks, and stop an attack that's unavoidable.

You can expect to encounter various types of attackers as you go about your daily business. Some have spent their lives surviving on their wits and using violence and intimidation to get what they want and what they need to live. Others have deep insecurities, which they choose to address by forcing their will on others. Some have deep-seated mental or emotional issues that make them enjoy harming their fellow humans. And some are under the influence of alcohol or other mind-altering substances.

In the following sections, I divide attackers into four groups:

>> Criminals

>> Bullies

>> Sociopaths

>> Deeply disturbed or highly intoxicated people

REMEMBER

These personality types can overlap; for example, you could be dealing with a criminal who's a sociopath high on methamphetamine and chooses to mug people to feed their drug habit.

Criminals

Criminals use violence, trickery, or coercion to get what they want instead of using legal, socially acceptable ways to meet their needs. For example, they steal money instead of working for it. They rape instead of engaging in traditional courting behavior or using Tinder for consensual casual sex. They jack cars instead of using rideshare services.

Although criminals pose a threat to your property, your safety, and even your life, a pure criminal is probably the easiest attacker to deal with, because they're usually not willing to work very hard for what they want. If they meet with resistance, they typically stop in a hurry and move on to an easier mark.

Bullies

Bullies are all about feeding their egos. For whatever reason, they have low self-esteem. By imposing their will on others, by gaining power over others, they feel better about any inadequacies they perceive in themselves.

Like criminals, bullies want something from you — your power and self-determination — and they're usually not willing to work very hard for it. They target victims they believe they can easily bully into compliance. Standing up to a bully is the best way to get them to back down and to discourage them from bullying others.

Sociopaths

From rapists to serial killers, sociopaths want to harm you on a profound level. They're cunning, manipulative, and sadistic. They have no regard for human life. They lack empathy and remorse. They lie about anything to anyone. They feel superior to others.

If you're dealing with a sociopath, you're in a life-threatening situation. This person will do anything by any means to get what they want. *Remember:* They still fear the three things every criminal fears (detailed later in this section). The dangerous difference between sociopaths and criminals and bullies is that the sociopath's goal is to cause you extreme harm or death.

WARNING

Don't be fooled by appearances or smooth talk. You can't tell that someone's a sociopath just by looking at them or talking with them. They may seem very attractive, friendly, and even helpful. They could spike your drink and drive you to a remote location to prevent you from resisting. Be careful out there, especially when you're dealing with people outside your usual social circles. Don't be alone with someone you barely know. Do your research and trust your gut.

Deeply disturbed or highly intoxicated people

Emotionally disturbed people (EDP) and people who are under the influence of alcohol or other mind-altering substances (methamphetamine, PCP, ketamine, and so on) may suffer from impaired judgment and engage in erratic behaviors, including physically harming themselves and others. They are often unpredictable and may be impervious to pain, and that's a dangerous combination. Imagine having to deal with an ex-pro boxer on meth. I assure you, it's not a good time.

Many law enforcement agencies invest considerable time and resources training to de-escalate situations involving deeply disturbed or highly intoxicated individuals. As I point out in Chapter 2, the police have the added advantage of being able to respond with overwhelming force and call in for backup, if necessary, for their own protection. You don't have that luxury.

WARNING

When dealing with someone who's deeply disturbed (mentally or emotionally) or highly intoxicated, or anyone who's acting irrationally, you can't afford to give them a chance to attack you. Take the position of advantage and assume the interview stance (see Chapter 8), let the person know you don't want to fight, and then, if they make the slightest move in your direction, destroy them before they have a chance to destroy you.

Analyzing Common Motivations for Violence

Understanding why some people resort to violence can improve your chances of avoiding, preventing, and responding effectively to an attack. Based on my experience and observations, I see most violent crime being driven by desire or desperation and a much smaller percentage (miniscule in comparison) driven by violence for the sake of violence.

Desire or desperation

By some estimates, including my own, desire or desperation is the motivation for 99 percent of all attacks. The attacker wants or needs something you can provide (money, sex, whatever) badly enough that they're willing to use force or coercion to get it.

The good news for you is that these attackers engage in continuous cost-benefit analysis. Leading up to and during an attack, they're doing the math and wondering, "Is this worth it?" You do the same thing throughout the day. For example, you're sitting at your desk and you drink your last sip of coffee. You want another cup, but do you want it badly enough that you're willing to get up and walk over to the coffee maker? Every decision involves a cost-benefit analysis, and nearly every attacker performs that analysis.

Your best defense against criminals who perform cost-benefit analysis is to make it more costly to commit the crime and/or reduce the perceived benefit. For example, if you're accompanied by two armed bodyguards, you're less likely to be targeted for attack. Likewise, if you're walking around like you don't have a penny in your pocket or a pot to piss in, you're probably not going to get mugged either. Turn to Chapter 5 for more practical ways to tilt the cost-benefit calculation in your favor.

Violence for the sake of violence

For a very small percentage of criminals, violence is intrinsically rewarding: They get off on it. In fact, committing violent acts is so rewarding to them that they're willing to risk their freedom, life, and limb to satisfy their urges. Their cost-benefit analysis is severely slanted toward the benefit side of the equation.

However, they still engage in cost-benefit analysis, so anything you can do to increase the cost to them of attacking you while reducing the benefit can improve your chances of surviving an attack and perhaps even facilitate your attacker's arrest and conviction.

WARNING

People who think they have nothing to lose or are willing to lose everything to satisfy their desires or needs are the most desperate and dangerous criminals. They will stop at nothing, which means you must stop at nothing to stop them.

Recognizing Four Common Attack Types

Attacks fall into the following four primary categories:

>> **Attacks of opportunity:** You don't know the perpetrator.

>> **Attacks of familiarity:** You do know the perpetrator.

>> **Attacks of ego:** The perpetrator is a bully.

>> **Sociopath attacks:** The perpetrator has no moral compass.

Attacks in every one of these categories involve violence or coercion, they all pose a threat to your life and well-being, and they all follow the predator-prey paradigm, as I explain in Chapter 2 — the assailant is looking for the most vulnerable targets with the highest perceived value.

Attacks of opportunity

Attacks of opportunity are crimes people commit when circumstances arise that make committing the crime seem like a good idea. For example, you park your Tesla on a poorly lit street in front of a payday loan storefront, step out of the vehicle, and start counting a thick wad of bills. A bystander, standing in the shadow of a building, can't believe what they're seeing. They sneak up behind you, smash you on the head with a crowbar, take your money, and drive off in your Tesla.

Attacks of opportunity account for most street crime — it's the mugger looking to target you in a parking garage, on a subway platform, or at a mass transit terminal, or the rapist looking to approach you in your apartment or dorm or while you're out jogging. Whenever you go out, become more keenly aware of your surroundings and avoid places of ambush (see Chapter 2 for details).

Attacks of familiarity

Attacks of familiarity are those perpetrated by someone you know — for example, incidents of domestic violence and most sexual assaults. Your attacker has increased access and opportunity as a result of the relationship you've established.

Unfortunately, attacks of familiarity can be the most difficult to avoid, prevent, and even survive, especially in an intimate relationship, which requires that you let your guard down to establish intimacy.

Avoidance and prevention are crucial to reduce your exposure to risk in these situations. Do your research and get to know someone for a while before letting them get close. Introduce them to your friends and family members to get their take on whether the person seems trustworthy. Trust your instincts if you notice any flashes of violent or erratic behavior. Get out of toxic relationships.

Attacks of ego

Attacks of ego are those committed by bullies, who need to oppress others to make them feel better about themselves. Fortunately, bullies are usually easy to identify. They need to be in control and the center of attention. They're usually loud and abrasive.

The best course of action is to keep your distance and be prepared to respond to violence with violence squared if the threat approaches you. Nonverbal cues, like simply taking the position of advantage, will demonstrate confidence and send a signal that you're not an easy mark.

Sociopath attacks

Because sociopaths have no moral compass or sense of empathy, and because they can disguise themselves as sweet, caring individuals, you need to remain in a state of heightened awareness whenever you're around anyone you don't already know well and trust. Like most criminals, a sociopath will use any means at their disposal to get you alone so they can commit their unthinkable crimes.

This is why managing your personal space and privacy and interacting effectively with your environment are critical. If you're struggling with groceries, a potential threat may offer to help you carry them into your apartment. Once there, you're in a potential world of pain. If you don't really know them, *don't let them in!*

WARNING

Don't ever go alone with someone you've just met or known for only a brief period. If anyone tries to restrain you or prevent you from moving or leaving, launch a violent counterattack. The only reason they want you restrained is so they can do something much worse to you. Fight for your life.

Leveraging Every Attacker's Three Biggest Fears

When you're being attacked, you're not the only one who's afraid — your attacker is afraid, too. You can use these fears to your advantage. Every attacker fears the following:

>> **Pain and injury:** No one wants to get hurt. Unless the person is under the influence of drugs or alcohol, or emotionally disturbed, pain or even the threat of it can be a huge hindrance. Injury is an even higher price to pay. A broken bone, a severed tongue, a detached ear, a gouged-out eye . . . all those call for a trip to the hospital, and that means answering a lot of uncomfortable questions.

>> **Being identified:** A criminal's need to conceal their identity works in your favor, especially in a world permeated with surveillance and smartphone cameras. Even making casual eye contact with a would-be attacker when they're sizing you

up could be enough to discourage them from attacking you. Staying in close proximity to others, avoiding poorly lit streets, frequenting establishments with security cameras, and taking other precautions can reduce your risk.

>> **Getting caught:** Being captured means spending time in prison, losing quality time with loved ones, and having to cover the high costs of legal expenses. Most violent criminals aren't released immediately, and multiple offenders will do a longer stretch. Anything you can do to increase the probability of your attacker being identified increases the chance of their being captured and brought to justice.

Recognizing the Importance of Trusting Your Instincts

Attacks don't happen at the spur of the moment. Your attacker sizes you up and conducts their cost-benefit analysis to determine whether you have something they want badly enough to take the risk of being physically hurt, identified, or captured. It doesn't get more complicated than that.

Every criminal sizes up their prospective victim first, observing their target over a period of time to see if they can get away with it. They watch to see if their target is lost or distracted. They analyze their target's body language. They wait until their target is alone and nobody's watching.

The greater your perceived value, the more time they'll spend sizing you up, and the more risk they'll take. If you're wearing a Rolex, you're going to get more attention than if you're wearing a Timex.

When you're being sized up is when your awareness and natural instincts kick in, so pay attention to them. Your subconscious is always at work, always gathering and processing sensory input, even input that you may not be consciously aware of. And when you get that tingly sensation, when the hairs on your body start to stand up, pay attention to those early warning signals. Your subconscious is telling you that you're in danger.

Changing your direction of travel, going back inside a restaurant, or waving off your Uber driver doesn't require a great deal of effort, and it just might save your life. The risk of being assaulted far outweighs having to casually offend or inconvenience someone. If you're walking down the street, you see a group of people hanging around, and the situation doesn't feel quite right, simply cross the street. Pretend to look at your phone and react as though you forgot to do something, and then abruptly change direction. Acting on instinct isn't racist, agist, or any other "–ist" — it's pragmatic. Don't let reason put you in peril.

WARNING

Don't disregard your instinct as paranoia. Don't let reason override your gut feeling. As human beings, we're animals, and we share animals' gift of fear. Fear, even to the point of paranoia, is there to protect us; it's part of our built-in early warning system.

REMEMBER

The biggest killer out in the street isn't a person; it's *denial* — believing that nothing bad will happen, that the stranger approaching you would never do such a thing, that it can't happen in your neighborhood.

2

Starting with Basic Self-Defense Tactics

Find out how to make yourself a hard target as opposed to an easy target.

Discover ways to safely navigate public spaces and gatherings, including streets, parking lots, bars and nightclubs, restaurants, events, and protests.

Improve your safety when you're out driving, commuting using mass transit systems, using ride-sharing services, and traveling to unfamiliar destinations.

Train yourself to be loud, angry, and violent when your life or safety is threatened — which may be all you need to do to drive a would-be attacker away.

Gear up for self-defense with body armor and weapons — everything from pepper spray and personal arms to clubs, knives, and firearms — and know how to use them.

Chapter **5**

Deterring Attacks and Attackers

For most people, self-defense is about stopping an attack, but the most effective self-defense tactics are those that prevent an attack from occurring in the first place. These tactics involve avoiding situations that make you vulnerable, traveling with one or more other people, carrying yourself like someone an attacker wouldn't want to mess with, and trusting your instincts — all of which can be collectively referred to as *deterrents*.

Deterrence is all about preventing yourself from becoming an easy target. Violent criminals target the most vulnerable people in the most vulnerable situations. If you look as though you're capable of defending yourself and you're in a safe location with a lot of people around, most criminals are going to skip you and look for an easier mark. It's like that story about the two guys in the woods. A bear confronts them, and the first guys yells, "Run!" The second guy says, "Nobody can outrun a bear." And the first guy replies, "I don't have to outrun the bear. I only have to outrun *you*."

In this chapter, I present some general suggestions for making yourself a hard target and then I go into greater detail on what that approach looks like in a variety of situations — when you're out in public, in or near your car, traveling, commuting, and so on.

Becoming a Hard Target

When someone singles you out to attack you, they're not looking for a fight, and they certainly don't want to lose. They're going to choose a soft target — the most vulnerable person who has what they want and is someplace where they're unlikely to be caught or identified.

To discourage someone from identifying you as a soft target, you need to make yourself a hard target. In this section, I present specific ways to do just that.

Exuding strength and confidence

Being a hard target starts with your appearance, posture, and body language:

>> **Be neat, well groomed, and organized.** Criminals avoid targets that look like they have their act together (see Figure 5-1). Having your act together demonstrates control and confidence. If you're sloppy or disorganized or you seem lost or confused, you're more likely to be targeted.

>> **Hold your head up, back straight, shoulders back, chest out.** Move like you own the place to make yourself appear as big and strong as possible. Good posture projects confidence and sends a clear message, albeit subconsciously, that you *will* fight back. Contrary to what you might think, good posture doesn't antagonize a potential threat; it just lets them know that if they attack, they're likely to fail.

>> **Walk like you know where you're going.** Walk at a comfortable pace with a comfortable stride. Don't walk too fast or too slow. Don't take strides that are too long or too short. Anything out of the ordinary signals that you're lost, slow, or afraid.

FIGURE 5-1: Looking like you have your act together makes you a hard target.

WARNING

- **»** **Make casual eye contact.** A one-second glance at the faces passing by you is all it takes to let everyone know that you see them and acknowledge their presence. Don't stare — that makes people uncomfortable. Just give a casual glance.

  Don't follow the standard advice to look down and walk fast in an area where you feel threatened. That makes you look like a lemming, which is exactly what a potential attacker is looking for. Your attacker can spot that behavior a hundred yards away, giving them enough time to size you up and set up an ambush.

- **»** **Don't talk or text on your cellphone.** When you're talking or texting, you're distracted and your hands aren't free for self-defense, which makes you more susceptible and vulnerable to attack.

>> **Drink in moderation in public.** I'm not a teetotaler by any stretch of the imagination, but alcohol and other substances and even some prescription medications can impair your judgment, balance, and reflexes. Moderate your intake in public — be social, not sloppy.

If you act like prey, you'll be treated as prey; if you act like a predator, you'll be regarded as such.

Finding safety in numbers

Criminals don't want to be noticed or outnumbered, so you're generally safer in public places with lots of people around. The one exception is when you're a stranger in a crowd of people who are friends or associates of a would-be attacker, in which case, you're outnumbered and whatever the attacker does to you is easier to conceal.

Being alone, without a close friend or companion, always makes you more vulnerable to attack, but having a companion isn't always possible. When you're alone, be more vigilant than you normally are and put more effort into some of the other precautions I recommend throughout this chapter.

Avoiding risky places and situations

When you were a kid, your parents probably told you to stay out of trouble. That's good advice in the context of self-defense as well. Staying away from risky places and dangerous situations can significantly reduce your risk of being attacked. Here are some places and situations to avoid (see the later section "Navigating Public Spaces" for details):

>> **Anywhere after midnight:** That old saying, "Nothing good happens after midnight" holds a lot of truth.

>> **Poorly lit areas:** Darkness helps conceal criminals and the crimes they commit.

>> **Sketchy neighborhoods:** If everywhere you look you see rundown buildings, liquor stores, strip joints, massage parlors, cannabis dispensaries, and payday loan firms, you're probably on the wrong side of town.

>> **Arguments or fights:** Don't try to play peacemaker. Call 911 and keep walking.

WOMEN'S INTUITION IS REAL

I believe wholeheartedly in the existence of women's intuition and in the common theory that women are more sensitive to threats of violence because they're typically smaller and weaker and have a greater need to spot potential threats. The theory suggests that around the time women hit puberty they develop an increased awareness because they're much more likely to be attacked. Men, on the other hand, are less likely to be attacked (and most likely the aggressor) so they can enjoy a higher level of ignorance.

My wife is a much better judge of character than I am, and she has better insight into business dealings and opportunities. I have no interest in arguing gender politics — I'm just helping you survive. And if your radar goes off before mine, I'm listening to you.

Trusting your gut

Always listen to that little voice inside your head. Your subconscious mind is constantly observing and evaluating your surroundings. It senses danger even before your rational mind has a chance to think about it. In fact, your rational mind is likely to question and challenge that little voice inside your head and convince you to stay in a dangerous situation.

WARNING

Don't let your rational mind talk your intuitive mind out of taking immediate action. Trust your gut. Listen to what that little voice inside your head is telling you and act accordingly. I've heard many victims say, "I thought that guy looked familiar, and I had a weird feeling, but then I told myself, don't be ridiculous. . . ."

That little voice is usually right. And even if it's wrong, who cares?

Sizing up a room

Part of becoming a hard target is being able to size up a room — the entrances and exits, the furnishings, the people, and the overall vibe.

Entrances and exits

Identify all the ways out of the room or building. Most people try to leave the same way they came in, but if that exit is blocked, having an alternate exit can save your life. From the Aurora, Colorado, movie theater murders to the Station Night Club fire in Warwick, Rhode Island, more lives could've been spared had people used the emergency exits.

TIP

In a restaurant, you can always leave through the kitchen. The kitchen has its own exit, and only the kitchen staff will use it, so it'll probably be clear.

Obstacles

Notice the location of any stairs, railings, changes in elevation, or other obstructions that could impede your speedy exit. After you've identified all exits, you need to evaluate your options to know which is best and how you're going to navigate that route.

Weapons

Scan the room to identify anyone who's obviously carrying a weapon, such as a handgun or knife and to identify any objects in the room that you could use as a weapon. Turn to Chapter 7 to find out more about weapons.

The room's vibe

Take the room's pulse. Is this a high-energy or low-energy crowd? Are people looking at you as though you don't belong? Do you feel an impending sense of doom, like something is about to go down? If you feel uncomfortable for any reason, you may just want to turn around and leave.

Avoiding traps

Don't expect a criminal to approach you, point a gun at your face, and say "Stick 'em up!" They're a little smarter than that. They may ask you for directions or spare change. Serial killer Ted Bundy had a cast on his arm and asked for help loading boxes into his car.

REMEMBER

For anyone to impose their will on you, they need to get close to you, and they have only two ways to do that: They go to you, or they have you come to them.

One way they can get close to you is to ambush you. They hide in a doorway, behind a parked vehicle, or behind the corner of a wall and pounce on you as you walk past. To avoid being ambushed, simply give these places a wide berth (see Figure 5-2). If you're crossing an alley, walk toward the street side of the sidewalk. When passing a doorway, step several feet away from it. Anything that increases the distance between you and a potential threat improves your ability to identify and react.

FIGURE 5-2: Avoid areas of ambush by giving them a wide berth when you walk past.

Another way they can close the distance is to use a *dodge* (a ruse for disarming you, getting into your personal space, and gauging how much they can get from you). They may ask for help or spare change, but that's just the beginning.

WARNING

A good dodge occupies your eyes and hands, impairing your mental focus and ability to defend yourself (see Figure 5-3). If someone asks you for directions, what's the first thing you do? Probably point and look in the direction you're sending them, and that's all it takes for them to close in on you.

FIGURE 5-3: A dodge will occupy your hands and attention.

The only foolproof way to avoid being sucked in and set up is to say "No" and keep moving away.

If they say . . .	You say . . .
Can you give me directions?	No.
Do you have spare change?	No.
Have you seen my dog?	No.
Have you seen my child?	I'll call 911 for you.
Anything unintelligible.	Bless you.

You have no reason to interact with people you don't know. If you met them under different circumstances, sure, but not if this is a parking garage at 10 p.m. It's not a dinner party. Just call the police and have them deal with it.

WARNING

Now, if you tell them "No" and they continue to follow you as you walk away, you have a problem, because they obviously didn't want what they asked you for — they want *you*. Now you must act (see Part 3 for details).

Assume that your threat has friends or associates. Usually, an attacker has one or more partners hiding outside your field of vision. While the primary threat is distracting you, the secondary threat is going to come up behind you and take you out, which is why continuing to move is crucial.

Your attacker won't appear out of a puff of smoke; chances are, if you're paying attention, you'll catch them sizing you up, and that may be enough to deter them. At the bare minimum, you'll recognize them when they approach you, which now gives you an advantage.

Navigating Public Spaces

You're under constant surveillance, and it's not just Big Brother watching. Common, blue-collar criminals, more beast than human, are watching you, sizing you up, and trying to answer their all-consuming question every animal asks: "Do I fight it, mate with it, or eat it?"

You want them asking a different question: "Is it worth it?" And you want to make them answer that question with a resounding "Nope." In this section, I explain how to make yourself a hard target in various public places and situations.

Walking down the street

I know, you've been walking down the street since you could, well, walk. And you're going to keep doing that, but with a small tactical adjustment.

Avoid places of ambush — anywhere a body can hide to quickly close the distance on you, such as doorways, alleys, hallways, and behind and between parked vehicles. Give yourself a wide berth when passing these potential hiding places.

Moving through parking lots

Parking lots and garages are popular places of ambush because they're either deserted (no witnesses) or packed with cars (offering plenty of hiding places, as shown in Figure 5-4). People are usually distracted, trying to find their vehicle or their keys or focusing on what they're doing or what they're planning to do, and they may be too overburdened with packages to use their hands to defend themselves.

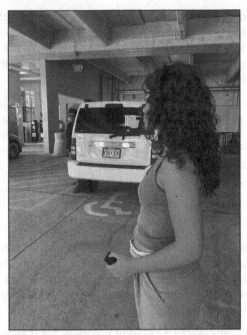

FIGURE 5-4: Parking lots provide many potential places of ambush.

After you reach your car, you're focused on loading it up and getting in. That's all it takes for you to be distracted and your hands too occupied to fight off an attacker.

TIP

Before leaving the building and going to your car, make sure you're holding your car keys in one hand and your pepper spray in the other (see Figure 5-5). Hang your bags on your arm or use a cart. This approach enables you to get into your car quickly and defend yourself immediately. Walk to your car just like you're walking down the street, head up, aware, and putting distance between you and potential places of ambush.

Staying aware in bars, restaurants, and nightclubs

Bars, restaurants, and nightclubs pose unique risks. People are often packed into close quarters; some/most are drinking, mingling, bumping into one another; some have personal agendas or percolating frustration and disappointment. Some may even be there specifically to commit a crime — to steal something or dose someone's drink.

FIGURE 5-5: After shopping, make sure you have your keys in one hand and pepper spray in the other.

Any small infraction (spilled drink, foot stepped on, looking at someone else's date) could be grounds for attack. If you have a negative interaction, you must now maintain awareness of that person and keep track of them the entire night . . . or just leave (usually the wiser option).

You never know who you're dealing with or how many friends someone has. As the night goes on and they increase their intake of mind- and mood-altering substances, they may escalate your "stepping on their new sneakers," see it as disrespectful, and decide to take their bad day out on you.

TIP

Here are a few tips for avoiding trouble at your favorite nighttime venues:

>> **When you enter a bar, restaurant, or nightclub, if you have a choice, sit with your back to the wall facing the main entrance.** It's a cliché, but it does give you a better view, and no one can approach you from behind.

>> **Always maintain control of anything you put in your body.** Drink something straight from a bottle that you can see the bartender open. If you must drink wine, stick with familiar brands so you're more likely to notice if something tastes odd. When ordering a mixed drink, watch the bartender prepare it.

>> *Never* **leave your drink unattended.** Popular comedians who starred in sitcoms in the '80s aren't the only ones to spike drinks; sometimes people do it just for kicks. Hey, it's a big, beautiful world with some really messed up people in it.

Two drugs are commonly used to spike drinks — a powerful sedative called Rohypnol (commonly called "roofie"), which is odorless and tasteless, and a general anesthetic called ketamine (commonly called "Special K"), which tastes bitter. You can buy a variety of test strips and gadgets to test for foreign substances in drinks.

>> **Try to avoid hanging out with people who increase your risk profile.** Maybe you know someone who's an angry or sloppy drunk, or someone who tends to get into fights or go home with just about anybody. Choose the people in your posse very carefully.

Paying attention in sketchy neighborhoods

One wrong turn, one road closure is all it takes, and you could wind up on the wrong side of town. If you look around and all you see are liquor stores, payday loan services, massage parlors, graffiti, trash, bars on the storefronts, and homeless encampments, chances are good that you made a wrong turn.

If you're driving, just practice the tactical driving techniques I detail later in this chapter. Keep at least a half-car length in front of you when your vehicle's not moving, and be prepared to pull away if you're approached. Keep the windows rolled up and stop for nothing (other than stoplights or stop signs, of course). If someone kicks your car or pelts it with rocks, drive away and call the police. If you do get into a little fender bender, call the police and stay in your car.

If something, anything, is blocking the road completely — for example, a disabled vehicle or burning tires (yep, that happens) — escape immediately. Don't stop and get out to see what's going on. Consider where you are before you act.

If you're on foot and you think you're being followed or you're approaching a person or group of people and your radar goes off, simply change direction.

REMEMBER

Listening to your radar isn't about being racist — ethnicity has nothing to do with it. It's the location and the situation that's making your radar go off. Don't fall into the trap of exposing yourself to a risk because you're afraid of appearing to be racist. If you saw that same group of people chatting over produce at your local supermarket, I'm sure you wouldn't change direction. Of course, if you *would*, then yeah, you might be racist.

TIP

To mask your change in direction, quickly look at your phone or pretend you forgot something and go another way. Enter an open business and call the police if you need help. Even if you tell the cops you're lost or you think you saw something, their job is to respond.

Being extra vigilant in a crowd

Whenever you're in a crowd — for example, at a festival, concert, sporting event, or political rally — you're at an increased risk of being attacked, especially if security is light. To protect yourself and others, do the following:

» **Be extra vigilant.** Scan the crowd every so often for anyone who's not "going with the flow." Be suspicious if you see anyone who's a little stiff. They'll be scanning the crowd, too, working up the nerve and looking for an opportunity to attack.

» **Look for anything out of the ordinary.** Maybe someone is wearing a jacket or coat when everyone else is in T-shirts and short pants. The person in the jacket may be concealing a weapon.

Years ago, when I was a young lad working security in a nightclub, the crowd was dancing and interacting. There was a sea of motion as you would expect, except for several individuals who were standing like statues, stone still. Turns out, they were members of a local biker gang looking to get some payback on a rival gang member.

>> **Keep an eye out for any unattended backpacks or bags.** They could be concealing an explosive device.

>> **Pay attention to any areas where a vehicle can drive off the road and into the crowd with little resistance.**

REMEMBER

I'm not encouraging you to be paranoid or start a stampede every time your Spidey senses tingle. I'm just encouraging you to look for signs of trouble and, when a real threat appears, to warn others and report your suspicions to a security officer or the police.

Keeping your head in protests and civil unrest

I'm all for people exercising their first amendment rights to free speech and peaceful assembly, but if you choose to attend a political rally or protest, realize that you're putting your safety at risk. Several factors contribute to the heightened risk, including the following:

>> Any crowds are attractive to shooters or bombers who want to cause mass casualties, especially if they have strong beliefs contrary to those held by members of the crowd.

>> Peaceful protests can turn into chaotic riots in a matter of seconds.

>> Nearly every peaceful protest attracts one or more provocateurs who will try to whip emotions into a frenzy. Every time I see a protest turn into a riot, I'm suspicious about how it started and who instigated it.

>> Law enforcement officers can be provoked to violence. Some may even look for opportunities to impose their will on protesters.

REMEMBER

If you really want to attend a rally or protest, one of the best ways to protect yourself is to stay on the fringe of the crowd — avoid the front line. If the situation turns into a powder keg, you have a much easier escape route. And if someone is inciting violence, that's the last person you should listen to — and be sure to distance yourself from them.

WARNING

Don't antagonize the police. Protests can get intense, and officers may fear for their own safety. Fear can make people — even police officers — respond in unpredictable and even irrational ways. The point of a protest is to express, in numbers and words, your beliefs. The First Amendment gives you the right to speak your mind and assemble peacefully; it doesn't give you the right to verbally or physically attack another human being — especially someone who's putting their life on the line to protect the rights and safety of others.

Tactical Driving

You don't need to be a Secret Service agent to operate a motor vehicle in a way that enables you to avoid and escape potential threats. Carjacking, mugging, and road rage are the three biggest threats, and you can avoid most of them by following these simple rules:

» **Keep your vehicle in good repair.** Every time you break down, you're at an increased risk of being attacked.

» **Keep your vehicle fueled.** If you get down to a quarter-tank (or 25 percent charge in an electric vehicle), fuel up. Running out of fuel or power is just as bad as breaking down.

   I'm the worst at keeping my car fueled; I like to see how far past the "E" I can go, but I do that only when I'm in familiar surroundings. When I'm traveling and I hit a quarter-tank, I fill up. When you're in a strange area, you don't know when you'll have the next opportunity for fuel.

» **Keep your doors locked and windows up.**

» **Don't tailgate.** Leave at least one car length for every 10 miles per hour (mph) you're driving. If you're driving 60 mph, that's six car lengths.

» **Always leave at least a half-car length between you and the car in front of you at stop signs and stoplights.** You should be able to see the rear tires of the vehicle in front of you. This distance enables you to pull out and around the car in front of you if you're approached by a potential carjacker (or an irate driver who thinks you cut them off).

» **When stopped, check your mirrors every moment or two for anyone approaching your vehicle until you're moving again.**

» **Pay attention to your surroundings.** If you notice suspicious behavior, act accordingly. If you think you're being followed, call the police and drive to the nearest police station.

Road rage happens because humans perceive the speed of driving as unnatural and life threatening and interpret any accident or near accident subconsciously as a life-threatening attack. Regardless of whether you're angry at another driver or they're angry at you, try to deescalate the situation. Don't engage. Stay safe and mobile in your vehicle. Back off. Give the other driver time and space to cool down.

In the following sections, I offer additional safe-driving tips.

Gearing up for safe driving

I recommend that you carry the following items in your car to handle mishaps and threats to your safety:

>> Cellphone

>> Pepper spray

>> Firearm (if so inclined) or other weapon (crowbar, tire iron, baseball bat)

>> Knife, which can be used for self-defense and other purposes

>> Jumper cables

>> Extraction tool (glass breaker and seat-belt cutter) in case you're ever trapped in your vehicle when it's on fire or in water

>> First-aid kit

>> Bolt cutters (to cut a chain or lock to gain access to a road that's closed and preventing your escape in the event of a fire or other emergency)

In addition to packing those items in a convenient location in your vehicle, take the following precautions:

>> **Keep essential items in your pockets, including your wallet, keys, and cellphone.** In the case of a carjacking, you don't want the bad guy driving away with your whole life. This is tough for me because I hate having anything in my pockets, but the alternative is worse. At least keep the keys to make jacking your car a little more difficult.

>> **Check with your auto insurance provider to see whether they offer roadside assistance.** If they do, add it to your

policy (if it's not already included), post the phone number in a convenient location in your vehicle, and add it to your cellphone's contact list.

>> **Look into the latest available technologies for automatically alerting first responders in the event of an emergency.** New technologies are constantly in development for both vehicles and smartphones. In some cars, you simply press an SOS button in your vehicle to call in the troops.

Avoiding common dodges

Criminals use two common dodges to get you to stop and exit your vehicle so they can steal from you, kidnap you, or harm you in some other way — the fender bender and the Good Samaritan.

The fender bender

With the fender bender, the criminal either taps your bumper or pulls in front of you and suddenly slams on their brakes. You both pull over, and you're really riled up because you know you're right and you're not looking forward to the hassle of filling out an accident report, notifying your insurance company, paying a deductible, and taking your car to the shop to have it repaired. You immediately get out of your vehicle. Now you're exactly where they wanted you.

The best way to handle this incident depends on the situation:

>> **If you're on a crowded highway, stay in your car and call the police.** Don't even roll down the window. If they leave the scene, get their license plate number and wait for the cops.

>> **If you're on a deserted road or in a sketchy part of town, call the police and have them direct you to the nearest police station or squad car.** *Don't stop.* If you can get a photo of the license plate or the vehicle, great. Chances are, the plates are stolen, but a photo of the plates or the vehicle may help the police track it down.

Don't worry about leaving the scene or about leaving your vehicle in the exact position of the accident. If your car is drivable, pull it over to the side of the road — don't stay in a lane. I know people think they need to preserve the "scene of the accident," but it's not necessary. The cops can tell who hit whom by examining the damage to the vehicles.

The Good Samaritan

The Good Samaritan dodge involves the criminal offering to help you when you're broken down or out of gas. They grab you, knock you out, or offer to drive you home or to the nearest town, gas station, or mechanic. Then they drive you somewhere else to rob you, rape you, or harm you in some other way.

Criminals may also pretend they need help or a ride to prey on well-intentioned passersby. You'll see someone broken down or in trouble on the side of the road (usually a woman), and while you're helping her, her boyfriend comes up and puts your lights out. To avoid this, just call 911. No cell service? Then make a note of the mile marker or street sign and the direction you were traveling, and tell the cops when you have service.

WARNING

Never drive anybody anywhere. Give them your car if you must, but if they want you to take them someplace, it's because they can't do to you what they want to do at your present location.

Commuting on Mass Transit

Buses, trains, bus stops, and train stations/platforms are home to a variety of crimes and criminals — pickpockets, muggers, gropers, and even violent criminals. And not only do you need to be careful not to get robbed, mugged, shot, or stabbed, but you also have to watch out for somebody sneaking up behind you to shove you onto the train tracks or in front of oncoming traffic.

To protect yourself in these situations, I suggest you take the following precautions:

>> **Arm yourself.** Turn to Chapter 7 for more on weapons.

>> **Maintain a heightened level of awareness.** If your eyes are glued to your phone, you won't be able to see a pending threat.

>> **Sit or stand close to a door, if possible.** That way, you have an easier escape route if someone starts acting up.

>> **Identify all the exits.** Again, this way, you have multiple escape routes.

>> **Maintain your space as much as possible.** When passengers are packed in like sardines, that can be tough. In the event of an active shooter, drop your level and use the other passengers as a shield as you close the distance on the shooter and attack.

WARNING

At a train station, never stand on the edge of a crowded platform. Stand with your back against the wall of the platform until the train arrives or at least three rows back from the edge to keep from getting shoved onto the tracks or into the train. You may not get on the first car or even get a seat, but that's not worth risking your life over.

Using Rideshare Services Safely

Rideshare services such as Uber and Lyft provide affordable transportation that's generally safe, but you still need to be careful. Maintain heightened vigilance and take the following precautions:

>> **Ride with a friend or companion when possible.** You're less likely to be attacked or abducted when you're not alone.

>> **When your rideshare arrives, verify that the driver and the car's make, model, and license plate number match the info provided by the rideshare app.**

>> **If you're riding alone, call someone and keep your phone on until you get to your destination.**

>> **Keep pepper spray in hand.** If carrying pepper spray is legal in your area, carry it. If not, carry a small can of aerosol bug spray instead. Anything that distracts and irritates an attacker will work.

>> **Pay attention to the route and make sure you're in route to your destination.** If anything feels off, call the police. Give them your location (nearby intersection, landmarks) and your direction of travel.

>> **If you're going to or from your home, specify an address a few doors down and pretend that's where you live until the car drives off.** Even a driver with a top rating can be a psychopath.

Staying Safe When You Travel

Travel poses additional self-defense challenges. You may need to deal with restrictions on your *everyday carry* (EDC; weapons and other self-defense tools you always have with you); you may be visiting unfamiliar locations; and you'll be dealing with travel situations, such as going through airport security and staying in a hotel room.

In this section, I provide guidance on how to overcome some of the most common and challenging self-defense obstacles you'll face on your next trip.

Researching your destination

When you travel, you lose your home-field advantage. You're out of your element, and the local criminals can tell. When choosing a travel destination and before you depart, research the destination by taking the following steps:

>> **If you're traveling to a foreign destination, check your home country's travel advisory alerts for that destination.** If you live in the United States, visit https://travel.state.gov/destination to search for travel advisories and alerts related to your destination country. You can also sign up to receive travel advisories and safety alerts via text or email.

>> **If you're traveling domestically, check your destination's local news to identify areas where the most shootings and other crimes occur.** That way, you'll be better informed about which areas to avoid. A good place to start is https://news.google.com, where you can specify a location to focus on its local news.

Packing for your trip

When traveling anywhere by any means, you need to know the rules and restrictions governing the items in your EDC. Check the laws in place at your travel destinations and any locations you may be passing through. Check for any additional restrictions in place at airports and the specific airlines you'll be flying with and other modes of travel (trains, boats). Find out what you can carry with you and what you can carry in your checked luggage — for example, firearm, ammo, knife, club, body armor. When traveling by plane in the United States, I check a bag so I have my full complement of EDC when I arrive at my destination.

In the United States, you can carry the following items through airport security and on the plane with you:

>> **Tactical pen:** A *tactical pen* (an inexpensive metal pen) will typically pass through the X-ray machine without getting flagged, but even if security staff take it, it's no big financial loss.

>> **Flashlight:** A tactical flashlight or just a plain, everyday flashlight is perfectly safe to carry on a plane.

>> **Personal alarm:** A personal alarm is an electronic device that produces a loud, unpleasant sound when activated.

>> **Bulletproof backpack or jacket (see Figure 5-6):** Body armor is not prohibited and can come in very handy when you're waiting in line at a security checkpoint — the area at an airport that's most vulnerable to an active shooter.

FIGURE 5-6: A bulletproof backpack can go through airport security.

See Chapter 7 for more about these and other self-defense tools.

REMEMBER

When traveling by plane, you're most vulnerable standing in line, waiting to go through airport security. Anyone can come in and spray the entire line with gunfire. At my local airport, we have armed law enforcement, but they're not everywhere (they're mostly directing traffic). Transportation Security Administration (TSA) agents are unarmed, and security doesn't start until after you pass through the security checkpoint.

TIP

To pass through airport security faster and with less hassle, enroll in a service that uses your biometrics, such as your eyes and face, instead of documents, such as a driver's license and passport, to identify you. These services include CLEAR (www.clearme.com) and Global Entry (www.cbp.gov/travel/trusted-traveler-programs/global-entry).

Securing your hotel room

Hotel room security needs to address two situations — what happens when you're in your room and what happens when you're not in it.

When you're in your room, bolt the dead bolt and the locking latch on your side of the door. If your room has a door to an adjacent room, make sure that door is locked, too. As an added precaution, if you have a personal alarm with a door attachment on it (they're really cheap), slip that into the crack of the door (see Figure 5-7) — just be sure to remove it before *you* open the door. A variety of portable door locks, door jams, and alarms are available to keep out uninvited guests.

When you're out of your room, take all your valuables with you — money, jewelry, firearm (if allowed), and so on. Don't trust the hotel safe; it's there to protect your valuables from the people who have access to your room — and those are the same people who have the master code that unlocks any safe in the hotel. Keep your jewelry to a minimum — only the items you'll wear all the time when you leave the room.

FIGURE 5-7: Personal alarm with door attachment.

If you do travel with a firearm, always bring a travel safe. There are a variety of them on the market and only you know the combination. Plus, you can store your other valuables in it as well.

REMEMBER

Hotel staff have full access to your stuff 24/7. And all those people have friends and family. Chances are, if you have something worth taking, somebody in that network will find out about it . . . and take it.

Asking the locals for advice

The best source for information about neighborhoods that are safe and those that aren't are the locals. Be friendly with all the staff. Ask the people at the front desk for recommendations about restaurants, recreation, and areas to go shopping. They're likely to recommend more touristy locations, which is fine because "touristy" generally means safe.

For less touristy recommendations, ask the valet or other hotel staff. If they recommend something different, return to the front desk and ask them about that neighborhood and what it's like at the time of day you plan to go there.

Neighborhoods change over the course of the day and may be totally different on weekends compared to weekdays. A corporate street becomes desolate after 6 p.m. A sleepy neighborhood may be invaded by partygoers after 10 p.m. All you need is one meeting to run late, and that once-bustling neighborhood is now a ghost town.

To stay safe, follow these precautions:

>> Before leaving a meeting, restaurant, business, or building, ask the people you're with for advice about how to safely get where you're going next.

>> If someone you trust offers you a ride, accept the offer.

>> Never walk alone. If you're only a few blocks from your hotel and you feel like walking because the neighborhood that morning was filled with coffee shops and fruit stands, remember that it may be a completely different place now.

If you don't know, don't go.

Chapter **6**

Getting Loud, Angry, and Violent

Whenever you're in a scary situation — when you feel your life is threatened — you'll feel the effects of fear, which, when channeled in the right direction, can be a powerful ally. Fear is your early warning system that fuels your fight-or-flight response. Fear gets your body weaponized; jacked up on adrenaline, you can perform some amazing physical feats.

In this chapter, I encourage you to harness the power of your emotions to supercharge your self-defense response and send a clear and unambiguous message to your attacker that you're not going to be a victim — that they need to stop or they'll suffer the consequences.

WARNING

The fight-or-flight response is actually the fight-flight-or-freeze response. When threatened, some people in some situations, are unable to move or even speak — they're "deer in the headlights." That's the worst thing that can happen — and what this book will help you avoid. With the proper knowledge and training, you can program yourself to act decisively and ferociously to stop an attack.

Using Your Voice as a Weapon and an Alarm

You can use your voice as both a weapon and an alarm. Like coyotes that howl to draw the pack together and warn off potential predators, humans have the same instinct to become more vocal when they need help or are confronted by a potential threat. What you say and how you say it function as your initial act of resistance.

In this section, I tell you what to say and how to say it and provide insight into the importance and effectiveness of using your voice as a weapon and an alarm.

Knowing what to say and how to say it

When you feel threatened, raise your voice and say, "Stop!" or "No!" State the command authoritatively. This isn't a question, a suggestion, or even an option. Yelling "Help!" can also be effective, especially if other people are nearby. If an assailant believes that others may intervene to help you, they'll be less likely to attack.

REMEMBER

What you say to an attacker is less important than your volume and tone. Whether you say "No!," "Stop!," "Help!," or even "Fire!," as some self-defense trainers advise, doesn't matter as much as saying it in a loud and commanding voice. Your defiance is what really counts; the words you use are secondary. Just make them simple and loud.

Think about it: When a family member yells your name from another room, you can usually tell just from the volume and tone of their voice whether the situation is urgent.

TIP

Whatever you choose to say, keep it simple. When your sympathetic nervous system (SNS) activates, it diverts function from your *cerebrum* (the part of your brain that controls speech and rational thought) to your *cerebellum* (which controls gross motor skills, balance, and equilibrium). When you're in a high-stress situation, you may be less able to think rationally or speak articulately, so you want to preprogram yourself to think and say something simple such as "No! Stop!" — something that doesn't require you to put much thought into it.

SHOULD I YELL "FIRE!" OR "HELP!"?

Many self-defense experts strongly recommend yelling "Fire!" instead of "Help!" during an assault because they believe that people are more likely to respond to a fire than to an attacker who could potentially harm them. After all, people generally want to avoid being attacked, or they may suspect that a cry for help is actually a ruse to lure them into a dangerous situation.

I understand the rationale behind the argument, but the data doesn't support the claim. No study shows that yelling "Fire!" works better than yelling "Help!"

However, one study looking into violence against women revealed that outside intervention occurred in only 6 percent of all cases. In other words, no matter what you yell, you have a 94 percent chance of having to deal with the attacker yourself.

Knowing when to employ verbal resistance

Most people think of self-defense as the *physical* act of resisting, but self-defense involves a series of escalating actions (see Chapter 2). It starts with awareness and how you present yourself to the world, followed by escape and evasion, then verbal resistance, and finally the use of physical force. Verbal resistance is the start of your active resistance.

REMEMBER

According to several studies on violence against women, the benefits of resistance — whether verbal or physical — outweigh any potential drawbacks:

>> **More than 50 percent of women who resisted an attack verbally stopped and ended the attempted assault or rape.** Simply yelling "Stop!" worked half the time.

>> **Resisting did not increase the victim's risk of serious injury beyond the sexual assault itself.** In other words, the victims were not punished by their attackers for resisting. Some people advise not to resist because you'll make it worse. According to the studies, that's just not true.

>> **Women who resisted the initial assault were less likely to be raped than women who did not.**

>> **Women who resisted suffered less psychological trauma than those who didn't resist.** In my experience, the psychological trauma is primarily the result of feeling violated and powerless to stop it. When you resist, you take that power back.

In fact, self-defense training can be very therapeutic for victims of violence — something I hadn't expected when I started teaching self-defense. Training gives survivors an answer to something they thought they didn't have a response to. I never imagined that teaching someone how to crush the testicles could be therapeutic.

REMEMBER

Intensive resistance is effective because it's not part of the attacker's plan. They're counting on your eventual (and quick) submission. In the street, when you verbally resist, you're increasing the likelihood of them being caught or identified. In the case of sexual assault, such as date rape, you expose your attacker to those same risks with the addition of the sobering realization that they're committing the unforgivable act.

@#$%!: Let your words fly

I get a kick out of instructors who are training people to survive the absolute worst event in their lives and correct them when they utter a four-letter word. *Seriously?!* You expect a person to kick someone in the nuts and gouge out their eye but not say *motherf**ker?!?!*

Let your inner badass out. Get mean, get beyond angry, get intensely aggressive, let those NC-17 words fly!

Embracing Your Inner Beast

Self-defense is a nasty business that requires good people to do the unthinkable. Breaking bones, crushing throats, smashing testicles, boxing ears, gouging out eyes, or snapping someone's neck is not normal, civilized behavior. It isn't how good people treat one another. No normal person should ever fantasize about causing such harm to an innocent individual. In fact, most people would have a really hard time envisioning themselves delivering such brutal punishments.

Not wanting to beat another human being senseless is a *good* sign. It's what separates you and me and most people from the socio-paths of the world. However, to survive, and more than that, *to win*, you must be willing to do what most people won't. You must be more ruthless and brutal than your attacker. Embracing, and then unleashing, your inner beast gives you the greatest chance of success, perhaps the only chance.

REMEMBER

I would love to tell you that the Vulcan nerve pinch (from *Star Trek*) works — that all you need to do is pinch a nerve on the side of an attacker's neck to make them crumble to the ground and wake up an hour later, unharmed and abandoning a life of crime. But that's fiction. Effective self-defense requires more than a simple, harmless technique, and it doesn't work with a Vulcan mindset. You need to leave your rational, caring self behind and embrace your inner, brutal beast. In this section, I explain how.

Develop the protector mindset

People generally have trouble imagining themselves brutally attacking someone in self-defense. Yet, these same folks have no trouble imagining themselves dismantling someone who attacked or even threatened a loved one.

TIP

Develop the protector mindset. Don't think about protecting yourself. Think of someone you love, someone you care deeply about — a family member or close friend, your dog, your goldfish. Now, imagine someone going out of their way to cause harm to that loved one. Imagine them kicking down your door and trying to kill the being you love most in this world. All of a sudden, doing the nasty bits needed to stop the attacker is a little easier, right? It's easier to think about protecting others than it is to think about protecting yourself. Practice this mental exercise to program a sense of ruthlessness into your being.

Train to be brutal and relentless

TIP

Self-defense is most effective when the mind and body are in sync. Both your mind and your body need to be geared toward being ferocious and relentless, so train that way. Spend some time training with a self-standing training dummy. Having a training partner is great, but you need to train on something you can strike with *full power* — you need a training dummy. Now, hit with hate, with no regard for your target. Imagine your worst nightmare bearing down on your loved ones. Let that image sear itself into your brain cells as you unload on your training dummy.

REMEMBER

When you make the tough decision to use violence to defend yourself, you need to approach it with extreme prejudice, a blood lust, and a desire to do or die. Then, when the threat is over, you stop.

Get your head right

A mistake people often make is that they project their value system onto their attacker. They assume that their attacker is operating within the same rational, moral system and mindset. That's like assuming a rabid dog will act like a friendly family pet. Would you pet a rabid dog? Of course not, so don't approach an attacker as you would a peaceful, law-abiding individual. You can't reason with someone who's unreasonable, someone who's made a conscious decision to threaten you or a loved one.

TAKE A LESSON FROM A SERIAL KILLER

Dennis Rader, the serial killer who called himself BTK (short for "bind, torture, kill"), reasoned with his victims to make them more submissive. He installed security systems in homes and businesses, so he knew exactly what to say to convince someone to let him in their home.

Once inside, he would produce a firearm and proceed to rob the home. Then he would convince the victims to let him tie them up. He'd say something like, "Look, I know you're going to call the cops as soon as I leave, so I'm going to have to tie you all up. As soon as you're tied up, I'm going to leave and that will give me a head start."

Sounds reasonable, right?

Ten people fell for that line and met a gruesome end. As soon as they were bound, the real horror began, as Rader proceeded to torture and then kill them over the course of several hours.

Never believe your assailant, and *never* project *your* thoughts and reasoning onto someone who's doing something *you* would never do.

Chapter **7**

Adding Weapons to Your Self-Defense Arsenal

The ability to use only your body to defend yourself is essential — you may not always have access to a weapon, or you may lose your weapon during an attack. However, having a weapon of any kind and knowing how to use it safely and effectively gives you an advantage.

In this chapter, I provide the guidance you need to choose the right weapons for you and use them safely and effectively to defend yourself. In the process, I bring you up to speed on the most common weapons used in self-defense — from nonlethal weapons, such as pepper spray and stun guns, to lethal weapons, including blackjacks, knives, and handguns.

THE RULE OF THE LESSER WEAPON

In Hollywood, the lesser weapon almost always wins. Empty hand defeats sword, sword defeats gun, gun defeats tank. Without fail, the unarmed hero defeats the platoon of highly trained commandos armed with automatic rifles.

The rule, of course, is preposterous, but Hollywood has been successful, to some degree, in programming audiences to think that weapons are an ineffective means of self-defense.

The opposite is true — the person with the better weapon usually wins. That's why you're well advised to "never bring a knife to a gunfight."

REMEMBER

Don't fall into the trap of thinking that weapons make you a bad or violent person or that they give you an unfair advantage (a form of cheating). Weapons are tools that improve your ability to defend yourself against someone who's bigger, stronger, meaner, and perhaps more skilled than you are. Think of a weapon as an *equalizer* — a tool that increases your odds in what might otherwise be an unfair fight.

Choosing a Weapon

The variety of weapons you have at your disposal can be overwhelming. One way to narrow your choices is to consider only those weapons that meet the following three key criteria:

>> **It works.** Many weapons out there (for example, most stun guns) simply don't work. Do your research and test a weapon before you carry it to make sure it works and is durable. Never go into battle with an untested weapon.

>> **You'll carry it.** Some weapons are too big or bulky to carry. If you don't have it with you, it's useless.

>> **It's legal.** Research local laws regarding which self-defense weapons you're allowed to carry and any restrictions limiting their use. If you travel, research your destination and your means of travel; for example, you're prohibited from taking pepper spray on a plane.

ATTACKED WITH YOUR OWN WEAPON?

One thing that infuriates me is when I hear a self-defense guru advising someone who's relatively small and weak not to carry a weapon because an attacker could take it way and use it against them.

Nonsense!

If the weapon works, if you know how to use it, and if you don't hesitate to use it, that weapon gives you an advantage. If you merely hold it in front of you with no intention of deploying it, then yes, someone can take it from you and use it against you.

TIP

Gear up with multiple layers of self-defense for a variety of situations (a tactic known as *stacking*). You may have pepper spray for the immediate assault, a neck knife for *grappling* (wrestling), a bulletproof backpack for an active-shooter situation, and finally your empty hand techniques if all else fails.

REMEMBER

Never take an untested weapon into battle. Test and train with every weapon you carry. If it's pepper spray, make sure it works. If it's an impact weapon, hit a training dummy or a heavy bag. If it's an edged weapon, practice as I describe in "Using an edged weapon," later in this chapter. Finally, if you carry a firearm, not only do you need to know how to operate it safely and responsibly, but you must be able to draw, aim, and fire under stress; above all, you need weapon retention skills (see "Weapon retention," later in this chapter).

Wading in Gradually with Nonlethal Weapons

Nonlethal weapons (including pepper spray, flashlights, personal alarms, and stun guns) are the most popular self-defense weapons. They're approachable, affordable, and mostly legal in every state. In this section, I explain what you need to know about each weapon in this category.

Pepper spray

Pepper spray is a no-brainer. If your state allows you to carry it, get it. I carry it every day. It's quick and simple, and it enables you to end the conflict with the least amount of physical contact and liability. When you're in the market for pepper spray, here's what I recommend:

>> **Fogger:** With a fogger, all you do is point toward your target, squeeze the trigger, and draw an S shape in the air. Your attacker must walk through that cloud to get to you. Stream and foam require greater accuracy.

>> **Protective flap over the trigger:** You slide your finger or thumb between the flap and the trigger and press down. Avoid designs that require you to flip a switch or slide a button before you can spray. I'm also not a fan of pepper spray guns.

>> **¾ ounce with a clip:** You want something that's small and light and fits easily in a pocket.

Whenever you buy a new can of pepper spray, test it outside and upwind, using one quick burst to make sure it's working. Replace it about every eight months.

REMEMBER

Carry your pepper spray in a pocket or other easy-to-reach location and have it in your hand with your finger or thumb on the button whenever you're going through an area where you could be attacked or ambushed. If it's deep in your pocket or buried in the bottom of your bag, you won't have the time to retrieve it when you're approached.

WARNING

Don't depend on pepper spray to completely disable your attacker. Thirty percent of the time, it has little effect, but if it does nothing more than make your attacker blink, move their face, or simply pause their attack, that may be all you need to escape or launch an effective counterattack.

Tactical flashlight

Tactical flashlights are small, light, and durable, and they project an intensely bright beam. They also have a textured bezel with ridges that prove useful for self-defense.

When you're entering a potentially dangerous area, hold the flashlight firmly in the palm of your lead hand with the bezel toward the pinky side and your thumb on the power button. In low light conditions, shine the flashlight directly in your assailant's eyes to temporarily blind them. This could be all you need start your counterattack or get away. If the encounter gets physical, deliver hammer fists (see Chapter 10), driving the bezel into your target.

Personal alarms

A personal alarm is a plastic fob or small box that has a siren and a strobe light. You can attach it to a backpack, a bag, or your pocket and activate it by pulling a pin. When you're approached by a threat, activate the alarm and toss it a few feet away from you and your attacker. This distracts the attacker and forces them to make a choice — deal with you, deal with the alarm, or skedaddle. While they're making that decision, you can get the heck out of there.

WARNING

Be sure to throw your personal alarm only a few feet away. If you hold it, your attacker may come to you to disable it.

Stun guns

The effectiveness of civilian stun guns is a bit exaggerated. I haven't tested one yet that delivered more of a jolt than I'd get from putting my finger in a socket (I know, I have issues.) The typical stun gun sold to civilians requires you to press it against your attacker, meaning you'd have to be in a grappling situation to use it, and that's exactly what you want to avoid.

The Tasers used in law enforcement deploy projectile prongs that attach to a target from a greater distance (up to 35 feet) and deliver a more powerful jolt. These, too, have drawbacks: They require some degree of accuracy and give you only one or two shots to hit your target just right.

Stepping Up to Impact Weapons

Impact weapons are anything that can be used to bludgeon your target. To be effective, the weapon must have some weight behind it. It should be heavier and harder than your hand, but light enough to maneuver. In this section, I introduce you to popular impact weapons and how to use them.

Blackjacks

A *blackjack* is a small club typically made out of a spring with a weight on the end of it all wrapped in leather. The kinetic energy of your swing is transferred through the flexible handle and focused on the weight at the point of impact. It's so incredibly effective that I call it the "instant black belt."

When you sense that you may need to use your blackjack, hold it in your rear hand concealed behind your thigh. You'll use it to deliver your knockout shot. Launch your counterattack with your lead hand to clear the path for your weapon, and then swing the blackjack in a tight arc (see Figure 7-1) — no need for a big windup. Keep striking and taking ground as you drive forward. The more you injure your attacker, the more you can wind up to swing.

FIGURE 7-1: Swing the blackjack with your rear hand to deliver a knockout blow.

TIP

You can conceal a blackjack in a pocket but to be really sneaky, insert it into one of the fingers of a glove. Then it looks like you're hitting them with just a pair of gloves.

Collapsible batons

Collapsible batons are clubs that retract into themselves like old-fashioned radio antennas. They can be deployed with the flick of a wrist. Although they're popular, I don't like them for two reasons: (1) The act of "snapping it out" shows your attacker that you're armed, and (2) They're too lightweight. Remember, Force = Mass × Acceleration. No mass means no force. Call me old-fashioned, but I prefer the night stick, axe handle, or lead pipe.

Clubs and axe handles

Anything that's roughly the length of your forearm, has a little weight to it, and that you can wrap your hand around makes for a good impact weapon. This could be anything from a lead pipe to an umbrella. I'm sure if you look around you, you could probably find something that would do the trick. The only drawback is that it may be inconvenient to carry and difficult to conceal.

Most people's first instinct is to swing a club, which is effective, but in close combat, when you're starting at close range in your interview stance (see Chapter 8), the large motion of winding up and swinging telegraphs your intention, which is something you want to avoid, especially with a weapon.

In the following sections, I share two starting positions and a handful of strikes you can deliver from each position before getting into swinging motions.

The crossbar position

In your interview stance, hold your club in two hands horizontally, waist high, each hand several inches in from the end, lead hand gripping from below, rear hand gripping from above. From the crossbar position, you can deliver the following strikes:

>> **Crossbar smash up:** From the interview stance, drop-step while driving the club horizontally up the target's centerline into their throat and chin (see Figure 7-2).

>> **Crossbar smash down:** Follow up the crossbar smash up by bringing your club directly down onto your target's head or face.

>> **J-hook forward:** From your interview stance, step with your rear foot so your rear shoulder is facing the threat. As you step, cut the butt of the club across the attacker's midsection and then up as if you're drawing a small letter J in the air. You can use this move as an opening technique or a method of changing direction to face an oncoming threat.

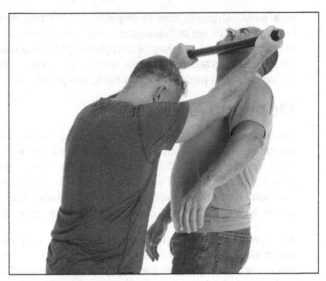

FIGURE 7-2: The crossbar smash up.

>> **Butt-stroke forward:** From your interview stance, drop-step while driving the butt of your club into anywhere on your target's centerline from the head group all the way down to their groin.

>> **Butt-stroke backward:** When your attacker is close behind you, step out while extending both arms out, away from your target. Drop your bodyweight while driving the butt of the club into your target's centerline anywhere from the head group to the groin.

>> **Butt-stroke left or right:** When the threat is approaching from the side, swing your arms out away from the target and then step in that direction and lower your body while driving the butt of your club into your target's centerline.

The figure-four position

To assume the figure-four position, hold the club with your dominant hand about 4 inches from the butt, tuck the other end under your opposite shoulder, and reach your free hand underneath the club to grab the wrist of your dominant hand (see Figure 7-3). Your dominant (lead) hand holds the club firmly to keep it from slipping while your rear hand provides the driving force.

FIGURE 7-3: The figure-four position.

Two basic strikes from the figure-four position can create openings and surprise and disrupt the threat, allowing you to move into more powerful strikes:

>> **Butt-stroke forward:** From your interview stance, drop-step while driving the butt of the club into your target's centerline. Continue your forward drive, kneeing and stomping while you pepper their centerline from top to bottom.

>> **Butt-stroke up:** From your interview stance, drop-step while driving the butt of the club straight up into the target's chin. Follow up with forward butt-strokes and stomping and driving footwork.

REMEMBER

You're not "stick fighting" you're "fighting with a stick." Don't neglect your empty-hand techniques. Combining a crossbar smash up or butt stroke forward with a knee to the groin, a kick to the shin, or a stomp to the foot can be very effective.

Swinging your club

After you've created some space and your attacker is on the defensive, you can swing the club to maximize impact.

When you swing, simply grip the club like a baseball bat. Squeeze and don't let go. Step with your lead foot and drive off your back foot, dragging your hip through the point of contact. Follow all the way through. Practice swinging horizontally (left to right and right to left), diagonally (down left to right and down right to left), and vertically (from over your head or shoulder down).

Fortified fists

Ever since the dawn of humans, people knew that breaking a hand in a fight was a problem, and they devised ways to fortify the fist. The Japanese used horse stirrups. Roman gladiators used the *caestus* (a glove made of metal and leather). Today, all sorts of products are available for fortifying the fists, including the following:

>> **Sap gloves:** Gloves with lead shot sewn into the outer knuckles, which not only protects and reinforces the knuckles but also adds some weight to your punch.

>> **Knuckle dusters (brass knuckles):** A knuckle duster is a device made of hard material (such as brass, lead, aluminum, or carbon fiber) that covers the knuckles, transfers the striking force to the palm of the hand, and gives your punch a little more weight. Some have spikes or other bits of nastiness on them.

Knuckle dusters are illegal to carry almost everywhere, so if you're going to carry them, be prepared to have an explanation as to why you have them, other than the obvious. This is why they're commonly sold as "paperweights" or "bottle openers."

>> **Fist pack:** A fist pack is anything that supports the fist from inside the palm and adds weight to the punch — a traditional yawara stick, a small flashlight, or even a roll of quarters. You can combine a fist pack with sap gloves for a knuckle-duster effect.

You can fortify both fists or only your rear hand (power hand). If you fortify only one hand, keep it hidden until you're ready to use it and then deliver it as you would a chin jab. For example, from your interview stance, drop-step and deliver a finger jab with your lead hand (see Chapter 9); then follow up with two rear hand strikes and continue your forward drive.

Exploring Edged Weapons

Edged weapons are instruments with a sharp edge or point. They can range from *katanas* (Japanese fighting swords) to ice picks. In this section, I focus on practical hand knives and other small, sharp instruments that you would use for self-defense. (A *hand knife* is any knife that can be held comfortably in one hand.) I also provide guidance on how to hold and use edged weapons.

REMEMBER

Keep it simple. Using a knife for self-defense is a topic some experts make overly complex. It's not that complicated. Using a knife for self-defense boils down to keeping it hidden, maintaining a firm grip, and sticking it into your target as many times as you can. Focus on the following essentials:

>> **Concealment:** Can you keep it hidden until it's sticking into them?

>> **Accessibility:** Can you access it quickly?

>> **Grip:** Can you hold onto it while using it?

>> **Effectiveness:** How many times can you stick it into your target?

Getting real

Before you commit to using a knife, wrap your brain around the following real-world considerations:

>> Driving a knife into a target requires a firm grip and a considerable amount of force. Fancy grips are more for show than combat.

>> People bleed when cut or stabbed, and blood makes everything slippery. You must be able to hold onto the knife not only when it's clean and dry but also when it's soaked in blood, sweat, and tears.

>> You're going to hit flesh and bone. Bone makes sticking the knife *in* difficult, while flesh seals around the blade making it difficult to pull *out.*

>> Unless you puncture an airway, a major blood organ, or a blood vessel, the person you stab isn't likely to fall over immediately and die. You need to keep fighting until their blood pressure drops and they pass out, which can take several minutes.

Breaking down the types of edged weapons

Most people think of knives when they think of edged weapons, but ice picks and tactical pens also fall into this category. In the following sections, I walk you through the types of edged weapons you may consider.

Knives

The variety of available knives can make your head spin, but the truth is all that really matters to you are how simple and fast you can deploy it with one hand, whether you can hold onto it as you use it, and whether it's long enough to penetrate to cause sufficient damage.

When you're in the market for a knife to use for self-defense, focus on the following two types:

>> **Fixed blade:** The knife consists of a single piece of metal that forms the blade and the *tang* (the strip of metal that extends through the handle).

>> **Automatic blade:** A folding knife that you can open with only one hand, such as a switchblade.

REMEMBER

Avoid knives that require two hands to open or fine motor skills to deploy, including manual folding knives, spring-assisted knives (nonautomatic), butterfly knives (balisong), or the straight razor, which is more for slicing than piercing. Here's a list of knives to consider:

>> **Fairbairn–Sykes knife (see Figure 7-4):** A fixed-blade knife with a slender blade that's long enough to penetrate a target and do sufficient damage, and a *quillon* (guard) to prevent your hand from slipping off the handle when you're stabbing a target. It's the quintessential fighting knife.

>> **Push (T-handle) dagger (see Figure 7-5):** A variation of the traditional dagger. You wrap your hand around the handle, fully enclosing it in the palm of your hand with the tang between your fingers and the blade projecting out from your fist. The handle enables you to push the blade into your target using the heel of your hand.

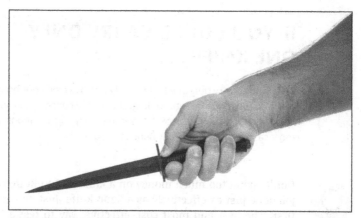

FIGURE 7-4: A Fairbairn–Sykes fighting knife.

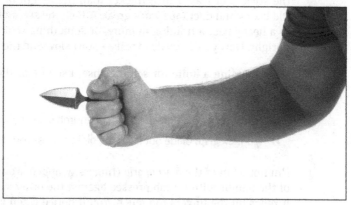

FIGURE 7-5: A push dagger is a very effective edged weapon.

>> **Finger hole knife:** A knife with a hole through it for inserting a finger to improve your grip.

>> **Neck knife:** A knife designed to be worn around your neck like a necklace, making it very easy to conceal and placing it in convenient reach.

>> **Boot knife:** A knife specially designed to be concealed in (you guessed it) the top of your boot. Carry two boot knives on the *outsides* of your legs. If one leg is trapped, you can still get the other knife.

TIP

Don't spend too much money on a knife. A $20 knife can get the job done just as effectively as a $200 knife. Just be sure to test it first. The best and most cost-effective way to test a knife is by stacking pieces of 10-x-10-inch panels of cardboard; make sure the stick is at least 1 inch thicker than the length of your knife. Old boxes and duct tape work great. Attach the stack of cardboard to a heavy bag, a training dummy, or something that will hold it upright. Now you're ready to test — start slow and then let 'er rip.

TIP

When holding a knife for self-defense, use one of the following two basic grips:

>> **Hammer grip:** Blade out from the thumb side of your hand

>> **Ice-pick grip:** Blade out from the pinky side of your hand

I'm not a fan of the *fencing grip* (fingers wrapped around one side of the handle with thumb pressed against the other side) because it relies on the fingers too much. You'll notice when you practice that it's very hard to maintain that grip.

Ice picks

Don't underestimate the lethal power of an ice pick. They're *extremely* tough and *cheap*. Unlike the tactical pen (see the next section), they go through clothing and penetrate deep enough to cause serious damage to the organs like the brain, kidneys, spleen, liver, and lungs. They have a rich history in organized crime because they're very effective when attacking the head group. Hey, I don't make this stuff up, I just report it.

Tactical pens

Tactical pens are made of metal and come to a narrow point for stabbing an attacker. I'm not a big fan of them because they're not very sharp. To penetrate the body, you need to strike a soft target like the neck or side of the head *very* hard. You're not going to penetrate clothing, and if the attacker is wearing a coat or sweatshirt, fuhgeddaboudit.

Using an edged weapon

You use an edged weapon in two situations:

>> **Proactive:** From your interview stance (see Chapter 8) when you have time to secure your weapon and have it concealed and ready to deploy

>> **Reactive:** When you're already engaged and you deploy your weapon in the heat of battle

In the following sections, I provide details on how to use an edged weapon in each of those scenarios.

REMEMBER

Regardless of when you deploy your edged weapon or the specific type you use, adhere to these two crucial rules:

>> **Never "brandish" your weapon.** Don't threaten with it or do or say anything that suggests you have a weapon. The only time your target should know you have an edged weapon is when it's sticking in them. If you brandish a weapon, you run the risk of escalating the situation and losing control of your weapon.

>> **Stab, don't slash.** When you stab, you hit organs and major blood vessels that get the bleed-out clock ticking. When you slash, the cuts are superficial, may not even penetrate light clothing, and don't stop the assault.

Proactive defense

To use an edged weapon in a proactive situation, take the position of advantage and assume the interview stance (see Chapter 8). Hold the weapon in your *rear* hand concealed in one of the following three positions:

>> Pressed against the back or side of your thigh — the best position if your weapon is long (see Figure 7-6).

FIGURE 7-6: Concealing the weapon behind your thigh.

>> Concealed behind your lead hand when your hands are crossed in the front, at your waist. This position works for a shorter weapon, depending on the size of your hand and the weapon.

>> Arms folded with the weapon under your lead arm. This can work for a longer weapon as well.

When you're ready to use your weapon, the main purpose of your initial strikes is to clear a straight path for the weapon to the target. After you deploy the weapon, keep a good grip on it and continue to attack until you feel the threat is no longer a danger to you and others.

Practice the following combination starting from the interview stance: Hold your edged weapon in your rear hand (concealed), drop-step, use your lead hand to deliver three short edge-of-hand strikes (see Chapter 9), and then stab your target's midsection and head group repeatedly. Try coming up with your own combinations, using your lead hand to strike and your rear hand to stab.

Reactive defense

Reactive defense is more about weapon concealment and accessibility than technique. I recommend concealing a weapon on both your upper and lower body. Consider the following options:

- >> Clipped to a front hip pocket, not inside the pocket
- >> Hung around the neck — just avoid anything with a locking mechanism
- >> Clipped to the belt or inside the waistband
- >> Inside each arm concealed behind a loose sleeve (always carry on both arms in case one is inaccessible)
- >> Outside of each boot (always carry on both legs)

Practice drawing the knife from its concealed position while grappling and using it to stab your target.

Use a rubber knife, a stick, or a very dull knife when practicing with a live partner, and even then, be careful.

WARNING

Improvised Weapons

Just because you don't have a weapon, doesn't mean you don't have a weapon. Look around — you can use almost anything as a weapon. If you can throw it, swing it, or hit or poke someone with it, it can at least distract an attacker.

Whenever you're in unfamiliar territory, scout for two things — a second exit (other than the way you came in) and any objects that can be used as weapons — for example, a hot beverage or even a cold one, loose change or a handful of dirt or gravel, something hard and heavy in a purse, spit, silverware, cups, glasses, bottles, pitchers, chairs, sticks, brooms, mops, canned goods, the list goes on. . . .

TIP

Firearms (Projectile Weapons)

Regardless of your politics, firearms work and are an incredibly effective means of self-defense. They enable you to stop a threat without having to come into physical contact with the target. They allow a much smaller, weaker person to stop a much larger, stronger person.

I could write an entire chapter or an entire book on firearms, but given the limited amount of space I have in this chapter, this section brings you up to speed on the basics.

For additional guidance, access educational resources provided by the National Rifle Association (NRA). The NRA has courses on gun ownership, training, conceal carry, range safety, and every other aspect of owning and operating a firearm. Your local gun range is a great place to start.

Following essential gun safety rules

In the spirit of safety first, follow these essential rules:

>> Always keep your firearm pointed in a safe direction.

>> Treat all firearms as if they were loaded.

>> Keep your trigger finger outside the guard and off the trigger until you're ready to fire.

>> Be certain of your target, your line of fire, and what lies beyond your target.

>> Always wear appropriate eye and ear protection when practice shooting and maintaining your firearm.

>> Always maintain control of your firearm.

>> Always make sure your firearm is secure when you can't control it.

Gun laws vary widely from one jurisdiction to another. Some allow *concealed carry* (carrying a concealed firearm), others allow *open carry* (carrying an unconcealed firearm), while in some buildings, such as schools and federal buildings, the public is prohibited from carrying firearms. Certain laws, such as the castle doctrine and stand-your-ground laws, also govern the *use* of firearms. Consult your state and local law enforcement agencies for detailed guidance.

Choosing a firearm

The variety of firearms available today is truly overwhelming, ranging from small pistols to shotguns to automatic rifles. For home use, a 12- or 20-gauge shotgun loaded with bird shot may be your best option. It requires less aiming and has less of a chance of a round going through the walls. I suggest keeping a round in the chamber and the safety *on*. (A 12-gauge packs a bigger punch, but if you're smaller, consider a 20-gauge.)

For self-defense when you're out and about, you'll want something smaller and lighter — a handgun. When you're in the market for a handgun, consider the following factors:

>> **Size and weight:** Smaller and lighter handguns are easier to conceal and carry. If you're planning to use the gun in your home, you can go with something larger and heavier.

>> **Semiautomatic or revolver:** Semiautomatics have detachable magazines that hold 6 to 20 rounds, they reload rapidly, and they have a thinner profile. Revolvers generally hold six bullets, are easier to fire, and are more reliable.

>> **Caliber:** Caliber is a measure of the diameter of a gun's barrel and the projectile it fires; for example, .22 caliber is 0.22 inch in diameter, and a 9mm is 9 millimeters in diameter. Larger-caliber guns are generally larger overall and more powerful. Smaller-caliber guns are smaller, less powerful, and have less recoil.

>> **Grip:** You want a handgun that's easy to grip and fire.

REMEMBER

What's most important is that the gun you choose is easy for you to carry, conceal (if permitted), and shoot accurately. Ask for recommendations from handgun enthusiasts you know or the person working behind the counter at your local gun store and, more important, try several handguns before buying one.

Carrying and concealing your handgun

If you purchased a handgun to carry with you for self-defense, your next decision is how to carry and conceal it, if permitted by law. Here are some options to consider:

>> **In the waistband (IWB) or outside the waistband (OWB):** IWB is a type of holster that keeps the weapon tucked inside your belt or the waist of your pants; it *prints* less (meaning people are less likely to see or notice the outline of your gun through your clothes) but it's less comfortable than an OWB holster.

>> **Appendix (front of your hip):** I think this is the best place to carry a handgun, where you have a better ability to maintain control of your weapon — it's in front of you, near your center of gravity, in the most defensible position on your body, and in the easiest place to conceal it because you can drape a shirt or jacket over it. The only drawback is that it's

uncomfortable, especially when sitting, if you have a full-size handgun or a bit of a belly.

>> **Hip (outside the hip):** The hip carry is comfortable and places the handgun in easy reach and where you can maintain control over it. However, it makes the gun more difficult to conceal and a little less easy to protect — it's in reach of someone standing next to you.

>> **Shoulder holster:** This rig straps around your shoulder and puts the weapon under your arm on the opposite side of the hand you'll use to draw the weapon. I like this option because it makes the handgun accessible, it doesn't print (the gun is under your arm), and it enables you to carry a full-size weapon comfortably. The only drawback is that you need to wear a jacket at all times to conceal it.

>> **Six o'clock carry:** This option involves tucking the weapon between your waist and pants at the middle of your lower back. It's comfortable when you're standing or walking, suitable for carrying a full-size gun, and less likely to print, but it makes the gun less accessible and more difficult to conceal and protect. Not a fan.

>> **Ankle:** I recommend the ankle carry only for backup and active-shooter situations when you can head for cover and then draw your weapon.

REMEMBER

If you're going to carry a firearm, you should also stack pepper spray, an edged weapon, and even body armor, such as a bulletproof backpack or jacket. Don't rely on any single weapon, and never rely only on a firearm. As the saying goes, if all you had was a hammer, then everything would look like a nail. If all you have is a lethal self-defense option, you're more likely to use it even in situations that could be resolved with a nonlethal option, such as pepper spray or even just saying "No!" in a commanding voice.

Training to use your gun

Before you even *think* about using a gun, train to use it properly and effectively. In this section, I cover the basics.

REMEMBER

Train for where you'll use your weapon. If you're going to conceal carry, practice drawing, aiming, and firing as well as protecting your weapon. If it's just for home use, practice accessing it from where you keep it secure, as well as *clearing your home* (searching every room carefully for hidden threats).

Focus your training on threats 20 feet away or closer. Most rooms and hallways aren't much longer than that, and most street crime occurs from a distance of just a few feet.

Training on and off range

Here are your training options:

>> **Dry fire:** Training with an empty gun. You can practice draws, site and target acquisition, trigger pulls, weapon retention, and clearing your house, all with an empty gun.

>> **Airsoft:** Airsoft is a brand of training guns that are the exact same dimensions and about the same weight as the real thing and use cheap, plastic pellets that you can shoot anywhere.

Wear eye protection when you practice.

WARNING

>> **Laser training:** Laser training products attach to your firearm and allow you to hit targets in real time. This option is great for training in your home to give you a *real* home-field advantage.

>> **Range:** Find a shooting range where the people are friendly and helpful and visit it once or twice a month just to get a feel for shooting the actual gun you may need to use someday to defend yourself.

>> **Force-on-force:** Force-on-force involves playing war games against another person. You can do this with an Airsoft training gun and eye protection.

TIP

To save on ammo, which can get expensive, and ensure a fuller training experience, I recommend breaking down your training time as follows:

>> **Dry fire, Airsoft, or laser training:** 85 percent

>> **Range:** 10 percent

>> **Force-on-force:** 5 percent

Drawing your weapon

As part of your training, practice drawing your weapon. Practice in two stages — first drawing your weapon, and then drawing and firing it.

When using your real weapon, check it multiple times to ensure that it's empty, and always point it in a safe direction — never at any living being.

To draw your weapon, take the following steps while continuing your forward drive (knees high, feet stomping, always claiming ground):

1. Using your nondrawing hand, clear your jacket or shirt and keep it out of the way, in the center of your chest, ready to receive the weapon (see Figure 7-7).

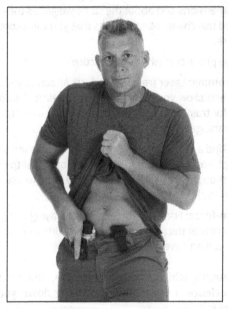

FIGURE 7-7: Clear your jacket or shirt with your nondrawing hand and hold it against the center of your chest.

2. Draw the weapon and raise it to firing position, bringing your other hand underneath for support (see Figure 7-8).

After you practice your draw and dry fire, go live with your Airsoft training gun at a target. Then practice firing and seeking cover as you take down the threat.

FIGURE 7-8: Raise your weapon to your clearing hand in the center of your chest.

Practice for both proactive and reactive situations:

>> **Proactive:** When you see the threat, determined that deadly force is needed, and have time to access your weapon before any shots are fired (for example, an armed robbery in progress).

>> **Reactive:** An active-shooter situation or when an assault escalates from a verbal confrontation to a physical confrontation. You have little time to react, and depending on your distance from the threat, you may have to seek cover first or fight to create enough space to draw your weapon.

Weapon retention

Weapon retention involves maintaining control over your firearm in a close-quarter combat situation. The good news is, you already have the skills to do this, the only difference is that once you've stopped your attacker's momentum, you're not escaping or continuing your attack. Instead, you're using that opportunity to draw your firearm. Train for the following two possible scenarios:

>> **Position of advantage:** Open with your favorite hand-to-hand combination, and then step back to create space and draw your weapon.

>> **Extreme close range:** The threat grabs your weapon. This is a code red situation. However, you have a slight advantage because the hand grabbing your weapon is not currently hurting you. Place your shooting hand on your weapon or grab the attacker's hand or wrist and hold it there. Don't attempt to move their hand, twist their wrist, or do any of the nonsense other people teach. You don't want to get into a wrestling match over your firearm.

While you're pinning their hand, use your other hand, elbow, head, knees, and whatever to go ballistic on them. Explode all over them with reckless abandon. *Do not stop!* Eventually, they'll need to let go to protect themselves. When they pause their attack, withdraw to a safe distance and draw your weapon. Practice this from all four directions within extreme close range of your dummy. Pin their hand and go nuts.

REMEMBER

You'll know when to transition from hand-to-hand to drawing your weapon because you've done it in practice. You'll know how long it takes for you to create space and draw. You may have to fight, try to withdraw, and then fight some more before you're at a distance that's safe enough for you to draw your firearm.

3

Developing
Hand-to-Hand
Combat Skills

Use the position of advantage and the interview stance to reveal a threat's true intention and strike first, if necessary, before they even have a chance to attack.

Identify the most vulnerable areas on your attacker's body so you can make every strike count.

Deliver devastating strikes with your hands in a way that minimizes the risk of injury — edge-of-hand strikes, heel-of-hand strikes, and hammer fists.

Get your entire body into the action with knees to the groin, headbutts, shoulder smashes, elbows, a simple choke hold, and more.

Find out how to free yourself when an attacker gets ahold of you and put your attacker on the defensive.

Avoid going to the ground at all costs, but know how to fight effectively and gradually improve your position if, despite your best efforts, that's where you end up.

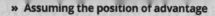

Chapter **8**

Knowing How and Where to Strike to Gain the Advantage

The outcome of an attack often depends on how you position yourself relevant to your attacker before the attack and where you choose to strike. In this chapter, you find out how to gain the position of advantage and target the most vulnerable areas of your attacker's anatomy.

REMEMBER

Your goal in self-defense is to *stop the attack* as quickly as possible. Assuming the right position and striking the most vulnerable areas on the human body give you the best chance of achieving that goal.

Taking the Position of Advantage

The position of advantage allows you to gain a tactical edge *before* the physical assault starts, providing you with the following benefits:

>> Forces your attacker to shift their weight to strike you, so you can more easily break their balance

>> Creates space to give you time to react

>> Reveals the threat's true intentions

>> Gives your attacker a false sense of confidence

>> Decreases the chance that your attacker will use a weapon because they assume they won't need one

>> Demonstrates to witnesses that you're not the aggressor (in case you need to defend yourself in court)

>> Enables you to focus your power on your attacker's weakest point of balance

>> Takes your centerline "offline" and puts you right on theirs

Step 1: Set your distance

Stand far enough away so that your attacker must shift their weight or take a step to reach you. Sufficient distance gives you time and space to respond more effectively.

HICK'S LAW: LESS IS FASTER

Hick's law simply states that the more choices you have, the slower your reaction time. Making a decision when you have three options is much faster than when you have five. This is critical in the world of self-defense, when split seconds count.

Less is more. Focus on what works and what you can do. You're going to discover a variety of techniques, but you need only a few that feel comfortable to you. Practice those techniques until you're confident with them in any situation. Being great at a few things is more effective than being good at a lot of things.

Allowing a threat into your personal space is a grave tactical error, leaving you insufficient time to react.

Step 2: Position yourself on the point of entry

The point of entry establishes the path you'll take to exploit your attacker's weakest point of balance when you launch your counterattack. To identify the point of entry, draw an imaginary line between your attacker's feet and a perpendicular line across the center of that line (see Figure 8-1). The point at which those lines cross is the point of entry.

FIGURE 8-1: The point of entry establishes your path of attack.

Set your distance and align your lead foot with the point of entry. Then bring your palms together to the center of your chest and point them to the outside shoulder of your target (opposite the shoulder of your lead foot), as shown in Figure 8-2.

Don't point your hands during an attack — only do it when practicing proper alignment.

ALWAYS WALK AWAY?

The notion to always walk away is a noble but impractical one. No sane person wants to fight. It's painful and puts you at risk of getting seriously injured, killed, or simply embarrassed. Most of us seek peaceful resolutions, but walking away isn't always an option. What if a loved one were in danger, or you saw someone getting attacked on the street (and you were compelled to do more than record video)? What if you're attacked with no way out? Every day, good people are put in untenable situations in which their only option is to fight back.

FIGURE 8-2: Line up on your target's centerline for the position of advantage.

REMEMBER

Your centerline runs from your groin to the top of your head. It's where most of your vital target areas are located — groin, bladder, *solar plexus* (just below the sternum), heart, throat, nose, and eyes. Always seek to protect your centerline and exploit your target's centerline.

If the target turns their shoulder toward you and faces sideways or puts one foot forward, disrupting their balance becomes much more difficult. Adjust your distance and position accordingly and as casually as possible to retain the position of advantage. *Never* get into a fighting stance and *always* avoid deliberate, unnatural movements like hopping or jumping into the position of advantage.

REMEMBER

The position of advantage puts you in a position to win the fight before the physical attack starts.

Assuming the Interview Stance

As you place yourself in the position of advantage, assume the *interview stance* (see Figure 8-3).

FIGURE 8-3: The interview stance.

The interview stance puts you in the best possible position to react while concealing your intentions to do so. As the name implies, you're interviewing the threat to determine if they're going to escalate the contact into a use-of-force situation.

REMEMBER

Surprise is your friend. Signaling that you're trained or even that you're prepared to go on the offensive may cause your attacker to use a weapon when they may have just tried to strong-arm you. Even better, your reaction (other than complete submission or panic) can catch your attacker off guard and make them reevaluate the risk/reward of the assault and decide to look for an easier mark.

The interview stance has three primary components: foot positions, arm and hand positions, and body tension. In the following sections, I describe each of these components in detail.

Positioning your feet

Start by setting your feet properly:

>> **Strong foot forward:** To determine which is your strong foot, stand with your feet together and take a casual step forward. Whichever foot you naturally move first is your strong foot.

>> **Weight on your front foot:** Apply about 80 percent of your weight on your front foot with your toes pointing directly at the point of entry. If you raise your front foot, you should feel like you're falling into your first step.

TIP

The benefit of putting most of your weight on your front leg is that it improves your chances of staying on your feet if your attacker lunges at you or even tries to tackle you. With your weight on your back leg or evenly distributed, you're more likely to end up on the ground — something to avoid as much as possible.

>> **Back foot spring-loaded:** Rest the other 20 percent of your weight on the ball of your back foot, like a sprinter in the starting blocks. If you need to counterattack, you want to be able to put as much weight and momentum into your first move without telegraphing or winding up.

REMEMBER

If you wind up, you waste valuable time and let your target know that you're attacking before you actually inflict any damage. When you go on the attack, you have first-strike advantage. When an attack starts, taking your attacker by surprise is more important than inflicting serious damage.

Positioning your arms and hands

Your arms and hands can be in three basic positions:

>> **Position 1:** Hands joined in front of your body at your waist, lead hand on top. Your lead arm/hand is on the same side as your strong foot.

>> **Position 2:** Arms folded (not crossed) at your chest, lead arm on top (see Figure 8-4).

FIGURE 8-4: Arms folded over chest.

>> **Position 3:** Hands up to chest level, palms facing out, like you're talking with your hands, with your lead hand in front. We used to call this "talking like you're Italian," and I guess I can still use that expression because I'm Italian.

REMEMBER

Always position your hands one level higher than your attacker's:

>> If your attacker's hands are by their side, put your hands in Position 1.

>> If your attacker's hands are at their waist, put your hands in Position 2.

>> If your attacker's hands are across their chest or higher, put your hands in Position 3.

Having your arms and hands positioned properly enables you to counterattack more easily while protecting your head and neck.

Tensing up

During an encounter, your body tenses up naturally thanks to activation of your sympathetic nervous system (SNS). Don't fight it, manage it. Some "experts" may advise you to relax, but that's impossible under SNS activation. You want to consciously slow down your breathing and breathe from your diaphragm. Other than that, let your body do what it was designed to do.

Whenever you interact with someone, take the position of advantage in your interview stance. The more you practice, the more natural it feels, and the less people notice. Start with friends and family, then coworkers, and finally complete strangers.

Avoid the fighting stance

Never assume the traditional fighting stance — fists clenched and raised like a boxer. Why? Because by doing so, you:

>> Lose the element of surprise.

>> Escalate the situation. Now your assailant perceives you as a threat and is more likely to attack.

>> Convince your attacker to use a weapon they may initially have deemed unnecessary.

>> Trigger your attacker's accomplice to attack.

>> Make it seem to witnesses like *you're* the aggressor, which may cause problems for you when defending your actions in court.

Putting Your Attacker Off-Balance

The position of advantage and the interview stance significantly improve your chances of putting your attacker off-balance — a key tactic for stopping an assault, rendering your attacker powerless, and giving you the upper hand to win the fight or escape unharmed.

To destroy the person's balance you must attack their center of gravity. To determine a person's center of gravity, draw an imaginary line down the center of their body from the top of their head to the ground and then intersect it with a perpendicular line exactly in the middle of their body at their waist (see Figure 8-5). Where these lines intersect is their center of gravity. This point is usually a few inches above their belly button and where they're strongest. Attacking this entry point will enable you to keep them off-balance.

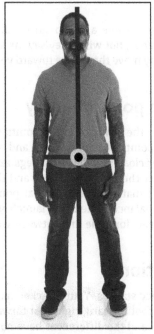

FIGURE 8-5: Find your attacker's center of gravity.

On the other hand, your actual strikes should target parts of their anatomy that are located as far from their center of gravity as possible: specifically, the head and the legs. If you pull, strike, or twist the head, the body will follow. Likewise, tripping or sweeping a leg, kicking a shin, or stomping a foot disrupts their balance, forcing them to shift or adjust.

WARNING

Avoid attacking the body. Attacking the torso or hips isn't effective because it's where the body is strongest. The muscles of the abdomen, hips, and buttocks are very strong, and they're all in the vicinity of the body's center of gravity.

Knowing when to act

After you've established distance and made it clear to your attacker that you don't want to engage, remain prepared to counterattack. If your attacker makes a move in your direction, their intention is clear. Maybe they're moving in for a loving hug, but chances are, they're launching their assault. Now is the time to spring into action!

The position of advantage creates a go/no-go condition that's based on what the threat does, not what they say. As soon as you establish your distance, any move they make toward you solidifies their intent to harm you.

Attacking at the point of entry

If your adversary attacks, the point of entry points you in the direction of their weakest point of balance. Where and how they're standing, how far apart or close together their legs are, how big or strong they are, whether their knees are bent and their center of gravity is lower doesn't matter. Attacking that point of entry will always disrupt their balance. When you launch your counterattack, you want to travel along the line between you and that point of entry.

Ignoring distractions

Don't be distracted by fancy stances. Your attacker can take only three basic stances — left foot forward, right foot forward, or feet parallel (square stance) — and the differences have no impact on how you determine the point of entry. What they do with their hands and upper body is just window dressing and is inconsequential. Whether they're doing the whooping crane, crouching tiger, or hidden penguin, their feet can be in only one of those three positions.

REMEMBER

Taking that initial point-of-entry path disrupts their first move, which is really all you need, because after your counterattack, you're in forward drive. Assaults last seconds not minutes, and those split seconds of balance disruption may be all you need to pause their assault and create enough space to escape or intensify your attack.

Leading with speed and following with power

When you attack or counterattack, your first one or two strikes need to be fast — to disrupt your attacker's balance and make them react defensively. Only after you've caused them to cover and back up should you take a little more time to wind up and put more bodyweight and power into your attack. Imagine you're a boxer throwing a jab to put your opponent on the defensive and then following up with a right cross.

A quick first strike stops the initial attack. The more injury you inflict, the more defensive they become, and the more power you can put into your assault.

REMEMBER

Speed and power are inversely proportional. When you act with speed, you sacrifice power. When you opt for power, you sacrifice speed.

REMEMBER

BE UNRELENTING

Attacking targets is not a one-and-done proposition. Don't stop after just one strike. Unleash a barrage of strikes. This is the real world, and well, sometimes you miss. Your assailant won't just stand there waiting for you to wind up and sock 'em in the jaw. Train to attack target areas in combinations.

Combinations are like opening moves in chess. Chess masters have developed thousands of effective opening combinations. After executing your opening combination, the chess game progresses from there, with your success hinging on the ebb and flow of the game. Self-defense is the same. You execute an opening attack or a combination of attacks, and depending on the outcome, you continue until you've escaped the situation or subdued your assailant.

Whatever you do, don't stop.

Zeroing In on Target Areas

During an encounter with an assailant, focus on the most vulnerable areas of your attacker's anatomy — the neck, head, groin, and lower legs from the knee down (see Figure 8-6). These areas are more exposed and easily exploited compared to attacks to the center mass of the body. Attacking these areas disrupts your attacker's balance and momentum, and may inflict pain, injury, or death.

TIP

In this section, I highlight the most accessible target areas on your attacker that have the highest percentage of causing injury and disrupting their balance and momentum.

KEEP IT SIMPLE

I totally acknowledge the existence of other valuable target areas on the body. The solar plexus, spleen, liver, and kidneys are extremely vulnerable. However, these targets are hiding behind and cushioned by body mass, winter coats, and sweatshirts, which makes them very difficult to exploit.

Now you may be thinking, "But what if I'm in a warm climate?" Doesn't matter. Devastating body shots require more power and training. Consider that your attacker is probably larger and stronger than you, which makes those target areas even harder to strike. Ask yourself, "How much time am I going to dedicate to training?" Your time is better spent practicing something that's 100 percent effective than trying to learn something that's about 25 percent effective.

Always seek to eliminate as much as possible from your bag of tricks because when you're under *real stress,* you're only going to be able to do a handful of techniques, so you'd better make 'em count. Focus on a few methods that have the highest percentage of success and effectiveness.

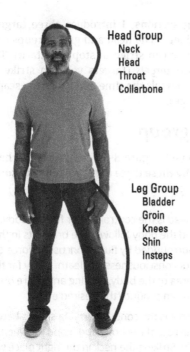

Head Group
Neck
Head
Throat
Collarbone

Leg Group
Bladder
Groin
Knees
Shin
Insteps

FIGURE 8-6: Focus your counterattack anywhere above the neck, in between the legs, or from the knees down.

Grouping high-value targets

Because you'll be operating under extreme stress and in less-than-perfect conditions, think of target areas as groups — target-rich areas that don't require you to be exceptionally accurate. Why? I can give several reasons:

» The target areas are home to the least protected and most accessible parts of the body. Hit anything in those areas, and you're likely to inflict at least some pain and discomfort.

» Larger areas make it easier to hit *something*. For example, if you aim for the chin and your attacker moves their head, you still have a good chance of hitting the jaw, the temple, the bridge of the nose, or some other target in the vicinity.

» The arms can very easily block or fend off attacks to the body, so strikes to the body are almost a waste of effort. Even if you're highly trained to strike torso targets, aiming for them makes self-defense more complicated than it needs to be.

In the following sections, I introduce three target groups: the head, groin, and legs. The head and groin groups contain *primary targets* (targets you can strike to stop an attack). The legs group contains *secondary targets* (targets you can strike to disrupt an attack and give yourself the time and space to escape or intensify your counterattack).

The head group

The head group (see Figure 8-7) comprises the head, neck, and throat. Here's why these three areas are home to some of the most attractive targets:

>> **Head:** The head is the control center for the body. Take out the head, and the body follows. The brain sits in the brain pan and is surrounded by fluid. Concussive force can cause distraction, unconsciousness, or death. It's by far the most vulnerable area of the body. Striking anywhere on the head hard enough can produce the desired effect.

>> **Neck:** The neck is the conduit carrying signals between the brain and the rest of the body and blood between the heart and the brain. Striking the neck in the right place with enough force can short-circuit the connections between body and brain or disrupt the flow of blood to or from the brain, which can result in loss of consciousness or worse.

>> **Throat:** The throat is home to the windpipe, which carries oxygen to the lungs, from which it travels to all parts of the body. A strike with sufficient force can crush the windpipe and cause intense pain and discomfort and possibly unconsciousness or even death.

I cover more specific targets in the head group in the following sections.

Head

Targets in the head group include the following:

>> **Face:** The face is home to many sensitive nerves and delicate bones and features. Any strike to the face is effective to some degree in distracting or discouraging your assailant.

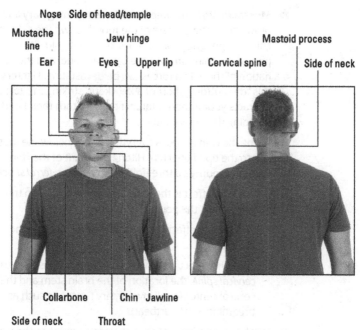

Nose   Side of head/temple
Mustache
line   Jaw hinge   Mastoid process
    Ear   Eyes   Upper lip   Cervical spine   Side of neck

    Collarbone   Chin Jawline
Side of neck   Throat

FIGURE 8-7: Specific targets in the head area.

>> **Eyes:** Simply striking *at* the eyes causes them to shut, distracting your target and allowing you to escape or follow up with a more effective attack. Striking or gouging the eyes can cause shock and blindness.

>> **Ears:** Attacking the ears can cause anything from slight pain and ringing in the ears to severe pain, loss of balance, or hearing loss. Ears can also be torn and ripped as a distraction or used to gain leverage when gouging the eyes.

>> **Nose:** A minor strike to the nose can cause the eyes to water and shut, impairing the attacker's vision. A more severe blow can break the nose and cause unconsciousness or severe swelling and hemorrhaging, which can restrict breathing.

>> **Upper lip:** The area of the mouth just under the nose is a nerve-rich environment very susceptible to pain. A blow to this area can cause anything from minor pain and distraction to a fractured upper jaw, unconsciousness, and hemorrhaging.

>> **Mustache line:** The *mustache line* is the imaginary line drawn from the corners of the mouth down the sides of the chin, designating an area that's knockout gold. Strikes to this part of the chin can twist the cervical spine, and the combination of these two forces can be devastating. Fighters call this "the button." Short of a knockout, striking this target distracts your attacker, forcing them to turn their head and stopping their momentum.

>> **Chin:** The chin includes everything from below the mustache line to the tip of the chin. Hitting the point of the chin hard enough produces a threefold effect called *referral shock:*

- The first effect is the initial damage inflicted on the jawbone at the point of contact.

- The second effect is the rattling of the brain in the brain pan.

- The third effect is the whiplash trauma caused to the *cervical spine* (the location of the brain stem and the control center for all involuntary functions such as breathing and heartbeat).

>> **Jaw line and hinge:** At the very least, a strike to the jaw line or hinge distracts your attacker, causing them to turn their head and stopping their momentum. Striking it on the side or from underneath with enough force produces the triple-threat referral shock that is so devastating. A severe blow can cause unconsciousness or break or dislocate the jaw, impairing breathing, in which case the subject would require immediate medical attention.

>> **Side of the head:** The side of the head is the weakest part of the skull, covering the area of the brain that controls speech, hearing, episodic memory, and vision. A strike to this area can cause severe pain, unconsciousness, and even death. Striking the side of the head hard enough can cause an epidural hematoma, which basically means blood vessels rupture and bleed into the skull. The blood travels through the brain, shutting down function after function.

DRIVING THE NOSE INTO THE BRAIN

Don't believe the myth that you can drive your attacker's nose into their brain. That's impossible. The nose is made primarily of cartilage and breaks easily when hit. Think of it like a crumple zone in your car. If you look at a skull, you'll see a hole where the nose used to be, and the nasal bone remains. The average size of an adult nasal bone is just under 3mm (0.12 inch), whereas the distance from the tip of the nasal bone to the brain cavity is roughly 100mm (4 inches). Oh, and in between is another bone called the *ethmoid* that would impede the nose's journey into the brain. What *is* possible is striking the face hard enough to crush the skull, in which case the nose would go along for the ride.

Neck

Targets in the neck group include the following:

>> **Side of the neck:** The side of the neck is the superhighway for your nervous and circulatory systems. A blow to the side of the neck can cause anything from minor pain and discomfort and a slight loss of balance to vomiting, unconsciousness, brain damage, or even death.

>> **Mastoid process:** The mastoid process is a smooth conical projection of bone located at the base of the skull just behind the earlobe. The muscles that control the head and neck connection are located here, so a blow to this area can impair your attacker's ability to move their head. At the very least, pressure applied to the mastoid process can cause pain and disorientation. At the other extreme, it can cause unconsciousness and serious long-term health complications, such as hearing loss, blood clots, or a brain abscess.

>> **Cervical spine:** The cervical spine is the portion of the spine that forms the back of the neck and connects to the base of the skull. A blow to the cervical spine can cause anything from slight pain and a loss of balance to unconsciousness, paralysis, and even death.

>> **Collar bone (clavicle):** Located at the base of the neck, the collar bone is worth mentioning because it can be broken easily. Any severe force on the shoulder, such as falling directly onto the shoulder or falling on an outstretched arm, transfers force to the collar bone, and it only takes about 25 pounds of direct pressure to break it. Break your attacker's collar bone, and they lose the use of the arm on the side with the break.

Throat

The throat includes the larynx and the trachea down to the jugular notch. A strike to the throat can cause gagging, eye watering, and temporary to permanent loss of oxygen, which can lead to death.

REMEMBER

A severe blow can crush the trachea like a bear can, and because it's lined with mucus, it will literally self-seal, causing asphyxiation.

All the blows you land can range from being moderately effective to deadly, depending on the force and the number of strikes. Any part of the body becomes susceptible to massive injury if struck enough times. No matter how big or strong your attacker is, the level of vulnerability remains constant. There isn't a weight you can lift or an exercise you can do to make your eyes less susceptible to damage. With exception to some parts of the neck, you can exploit all target areas of the head group regardless of your size and strength.

The groin group

The groin area (the location of male and female genitalia) contains a great number of densely packed nerve endings in a small area (especially the testicles). This high concentration of nerves makes the area very sensitive and susceptible to pain. Unlike other organs, which are internal and receive protection from muscles and bones, the genitalia (especially male) are external and more vulnerable to injury.

REMEMBER

As with the head, the effectiveness of attacks to the groin (specifically the testicles) depends on the force and number of blows.

You can attack the groin in two ways: either by striking the groin (regardless of your attacker's anatomy) or by seizing the testicles.

Striking the groin

Striking the groin usually involves kicking or kneeing the attacker between the legs with a firm upward motion. Upward is key. When the attacker is male, you want to drive the testicles directly upward and smash them against the pelvic bone. Most systems teach you to strike *at* the testicles, which is far less effective. At best, you end up striking the bladder, which can be painful and cause injury if full, but it's not nearly as effective as smashing the testicles.

Done properly, a strike to the groin can cause anything from pain and nausea to shock, unconsciousness, vomiting, and internal or external bleeding. Damage to the testicles, spermadic cord, or scrotum will cause hemorrhaging.

TIP

Think of the testicles as a speed bag; when struck, they move and absorb the impact, but when they're smashed, squeezed, or constricted, they have nowhere to go.

Seizing the testicles

Although a strike to the testicles causes an immediate, intense shock to the target, squeezing the testicles subjects your assailant to overwhelming and prolonged agony that can render them powerless. At the very least, a good squeeze can cause pain and nausea. A tight squeeze for a prolonged period can cause shock, unconsciousness, vomiting, and internal or external bleeding.

PICKING THE PEACHES

Many martial art styles include a technique for deftly removing an assailant's . . . um . . . twig and berries with one quick motion.

Ridiculous!

First, attackers are almost always fully clothed, and gaining the access required to achieve such a feat is a monumental challenge in itself. Even the thinnest of linen pants are difficult to penetrate with your bare hand. Combine that with the challenge of getting a firm grip on your adversary's wedding tackle, and having the grip strength to remove them makes this impossible.

(continued)

(continued)

Second, even if you have direct access to your assailant's package, you would need to "grab it by the root" and have the grip strength to remove it from his person.

Third, you're probably going to encounter a "little bit" of resistance as you try to dismantle him. Unless he's unconscious, he'll be moving and thrashing about and probably kicking, punching, and scratching while you attempt to extricate the offending member.

True, when some primates fight, they do attack the genitals in this exact manner, and it's about as brutal as you can imagine. However, even the weakest chimp's grip strength is *exponentially* greater than that of a human. So, let's leave this move for the monkeys.

The leg group

REMEMBER

The leg group (see Figure 8-8) is a collection of secondary targets (as opposed to the primary targets in the head and groin groups). They're secondary because striking them doesn't stop the attack. You strike the legs to stop your attacker's momentum and break their balance, enabling you to escape or inflict more pain. An attacker off-balance can't generate power.

Kicking your attacker in the shin, the instep, or the knee, even without a lot of power, can be effective. It's disconcerting and painful at the very least. Blows to the legs include hand strikes, kicks, stomps, and knee strikes.

Here's a list of specific targets in the leg group:

>> **Inner thighs:** The femoral nerve runs the entire length of the inner thigh. Striking it can cause mild to severe pain and disrupt an assailant's balance.

>> **Knee joint:** This joint includes the sides and back of the knee. You can exploit the knee joint by striking, bending, or twisting it in an attempt to make it collapse. An effective blow to the knee can temporarily slow the attack or disrupt the assailant's balance.

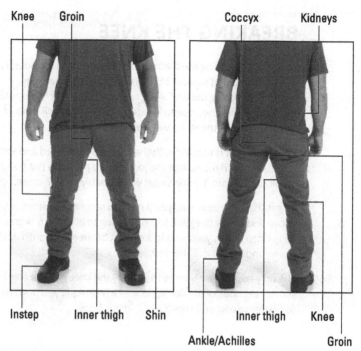

FIGURE 8-8: The target areas of the leg group.

>> **Shin:** If you've ever banged your shin on a coffee table late at night, you know how painful a shin strike can be. The shin has two major nerves, both of which are branches of the sciatic nerve and have multiple branches of their own that carry all signals to the lower leg and foot. They do not like to be struck. A strike to the shin can significantly disrupt an assailant's plans and their balance.

>> **Instep (arch):** The tops of the feet have small bones (metatarsals) and the toes (phalanges), which are very easily broken when stomped. Stomping an assailant's foot can cause anything from a brief and partial loss of balance to a broken foot and complete loss of balance.

After you strike a target in the leg group, escape or follow up with more effective attacks to primary targets in the head and groin groups.

BREAKING THE KNEE

At the risk of ruffling the feathers of martial arts aficionados, I regret to inform you that you can't break or dislocate a knee merely by kicking it or "sweeping the leg." If the target's foot isn't firmly planted on the ground with the knee fully extended, the knee will simply rotate or take the force of the strike without issue.

Even if the foot is planted with the knee fully extended and you kick it with full force, right against the joint, you're probably not going to break or dislocate it. Your target will probably just fall down.

To get that knee to break, you'd need to secure both sides of the joint, above and below the joint. Imagine trying to break a thick tree branch. To get it to break, you need to extend it between two solid anchor points and stomp it in the middle.

The only really effective way to destroy the knee in close combat is with a heel hook or similar leg lock — a technique you don't need for self-defense and one I don't teach in this book.

Chapter **9**
Mastering Basic Empty-Hand Techniques

The keys to surviving an attack or winning a fight are no secret: Strike first, hard, and repetitively the most vulnerable parts of your opponent's body. Offense is the best defense. Your goal is to disrupt your attacker and keep them on the defensive long enough for you to escape or hurt them badly enough that they no longer pose a threat.

In this chapter, you develop a handful of techniques for doing just that. You discover how to launch your counterattack in a way that maximizes your power and speed to shock your attacker while protecting yourself. And you find out how to deliver devastating blows without breaking your hand or causing injury to yourself.

REMEMBER

Keep it simple. The most effective self-defense techniques are the most basic. Don't believe any self-defense "experts" who promote advanced or complicated techniques as "better." Stick to the fundamentals, as I advise in this chapter and throughout this book. When some maniac is trying to kill you, smash you into the ground, or maim you, these basic techniques will save your life. They don't look pretty. They don't look nice. They just work.

COMBAT SPORTS VERSUS SELF-DEFENSE

Combat sports such as judo, karate, tae kwon do, boxing, and mixed martial arts (MMA) are combat sports, not to be confused with self-defense. Unfortunately, many experts repackage these combat sports to sell self-defense versions of them, such as "judo for self-defense" or "boxing for self-defense." This approach has two drawbacks:

- **You need proficiency in the style to learn the "street" modified system.** For example, to learn Brazilian Jiu-Jitsu for self-defense you first need to know Brazilian Jiu-Jitsu basics.

- **Combat sports are bound by rules for safety and require more skill, fitness, and athleticism.** With self-defense, you do whatever it takes to achieve the desired outcome.

Launching a Quick Counterattack to Escape an Assailant

If you're alone and you merely need to escape from an attacker without necessarily causing severe damage, you can do so by assuming the bladed stance and delivering a finger dart and whip kick and then fleeing the scene. In this section, I bring you up to speed on these easy but effective maneuvers.

Assuming the bladed stance

The bladed stance enables you to escape as quickly and safely as possible. It makes you a smaller target and shifts more of your weight to your rear foot (in contrast to the interview stance covered in Chapter 8). In the bladed stance, you're giving up power for increased mobility and defense.

To assume the bladed stance, take the following steps (see Figure 9-1):

1. **Step back so your attacker must shift their weight or take a step to reach you.**

See Chapter 8 for more about setting your distance.

2. **Stand sideways, strong foot forward, strong shoulder facing your attacker.**

   Your chest should be positioned 90 degrees to the threat. See Chapter 8 for more about determining your strong foot or side.

3. **Point your strong foot directly at your attacker.**

4. **Rest about 30 percent of your weight on your front foot and about 70 percent on your rear foot.**

FIGURE 9-1: The bladed stance.

REMEMBER

The bladed stance works best if you're alone and you don't have to worry about the safety of another person. The interview stance is more effective when you need to stop and disable your attacker.

Delivering the finger dart

The *finger dart* is essentially a poke in the eye. Compared to other strikes, it enables you to have the least amount of physical contact with your attacker from the farthest point possible using your upper body.

To execute the finger dart, assume the bladed stance. As your assailant moves forward to attack, whip your lead (front) arm forward, and let your hand snap open convulsively toward your assailant's eyes (see Figure 9-2). Focus on making contact with the pads of your fingers.

FIGURE 9-2: The finger dart.

Don't *attack* the face. Let your attacker impale themselves on your finger dart.

TIP

Executing the whip kick

The whip kick is the finger dart's counterpart, in that it allows for the least amount of contact from the greatest distance using your lower body.

To execute the whip kick, simply flick the toes (the point of your shoe) of your forward foot at your target's groin or lower legs (knee or below; see Figure 9-3).

Don't *chamber* (wind up) the kick. Your foot simply leaves its current position and travels a straight line toward the target, allowing your target to lurch right into it. Like the finger dart, the whip kick is meant to make your attacker pause.

REMEMBER

FIGURE 9-3: The whip kick.

Delivering a combination

The finger dart and whip kick are most effective when delivered in combination. From the position of advantage (see Chapter 8), set your distance, assume the blade stance, and when your attacker shifts their weight toward you, deliver the following combination:

1. **Snap the finger dart with your strong (front) hand.**
2. **Deliver the whip kick with your strong (front) foot.**
3. **Escape, grab a weapon, or continue with a more devastating counterattack.**

REMEMBER

Speed and surprise trump power. Your first one or two strikes need to be fast. Speed enables you to beat your assailant to the punch and pause their attack to give yourself time and space to escape or ramp up your counterattack.

Maximizing Speed, Power, Shock, and Cover

When you need to stop and disable your assailant, instead of merely escaping, you'll need to put much more power into your initial attack. In this section, I focus on how to move your body to maximize speed and power, take full advantage of the element of surprise, and protect yourself while you *get in* — move past your attacker's defenses to deliver devastating strikes.

Drop-stepping into your attack

The *drop step* is a technique that is unique to this system and works hand in glove with the interview stance. Move to your position of advantage, assume the interview stance, and simply lift your front foot and fall forward into your step. Let your rear leg follow naturally. That's all there is to it.

From this point to the end of the chapter, every opening move I discuss begins with the drop step. This technique is the key to putting the most power into your first strike without *telegraphing* (signaling) your intention to attack.

REMEMBER

Telegraphing, such as winding up to deliver a punch, gives your attacker time to beat you to the punch or take a defensive posture. You must deliver your initial strikes with as little advanced warning as possible. After you start, all bets are off, and telegraphing is no longer a concern because, well, it's no secret — you're in a fight now, and after you get your target to react (which they will) you'll have more time to wind up and deliver more powerful blows as long as you remain on the offensive.

When first practicing the drop step, don't think about your hands. You can leave them in one of the three acceptable arm/hand positions for the interview stance: crossed in front of you, folded across your chest, or up by your chin palms facing out (see Chapter 8). When launching your counterattack, though, your lead hand should strike your target before your lead foot hits the ground.

Your first strike *must* land before your drop-step foot touches the ground. This technique is the best way to get most of your body weight and momentum moving into your target without telegraphing your intention.

Stomping your feet

After your drop step, continue your forward drive into your attacker. As you step, always *stomp* your foot — no sliding or smooth steps like you see in many martial arts styles. Why stomp? Several reasons:

>> **Stomping increases your power.** It forces you to bring your knee up sharply and drive your foot into the earth, propelling you forward and putting more power into your forward drive and your strike.

>> **Stomping enables you to traverse any terrain.** Only in the dojo, the ring, or the gymnasium do you have the benefit of a clean, smooth, level surface. In the jungle, on a beach, in woodlands, on staircases, on city streets, in alleyways, the ground has all kinds of obstructions and debris. If you try to slide your feet, you'll eventually hit something and trip. The only way to move effectively over debris is to lift your leg and place it firmly straight down.

>> **Stomping is a loud, aggressive action that may have an unnerving psychological impact on your attacker.**

>> **In a crowd or a riot or when facing multiple attackers, stomping enables you to create space more effectively.**

>> **Stomping carries the potential of delivering ancillary strikes.** Every knee up is a potential knee strike and every step down is a potential stomp on your attacker's foot or other body part. During a fight, you're close to your attacker and you may get the added benefit of simply kneeing them in the groin or crushing their instep.

Stomping plants your weight. Ignore what some experts say about "efficiency of movement." In combat, stomping is the only effective way to move. With practice, it quickly becomes an instinctive, natural way to move.

Tucking your chin

As you step into your attack, tuck your chin (see Figure 9-4). Every boxer and MMA fighter does this for good reason — it protects the nose, mouth, chin, and throat while presenting the forehead (the strongest part of the skull). A bare-knuckle boxer trick is to drop the forehead into the opponent's punch to break their knuckles.

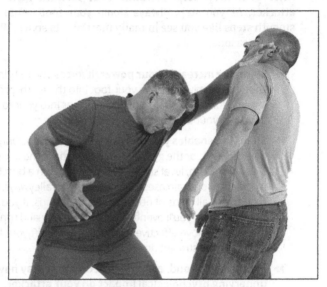

FIGURE 9-4: Keep your chin down.

Protecting your kisser

With chin tucked, move your arm across your mouth and nose as if you're "sneezing into your elbow" (see Figure 9-5). Having your arm across your nose and mouth with your chin tucked behind it presents your elbow and forehead to any strike aimed at your head and neck area and puts your arm in the perfect position to deliver an edge-of-hand or hammer-fist strike.

TIP

At the start of a fight, keep your hands and arms close to your body, like a boxer does. After you've inflicted enough damage to put your attacker on the defensive, you can allow greater distance between your arms and your body as you wind up to deliver more powerful blows.

FIGURE 9-5: Use the elbow cover to protect your head and neck.

Driving forward

With chin tucked and your nose and mouth covered by your elbow, you're ready to drive forward. The forward drive is one of the most important tactics — the "secret sauce" of self-defense. As you drive forward, focus on the following:

>> Move forward forcefully to where your attacker is standing.

>> Try to step through your attacker's center of balance.

>> Bury your forehead in the center of your attacker's chest (see Figure 9-6).

The forward drive gives you the following advantages:

>> Gets you moving off your X — the point of attack chosen by your attacker, the place where they're focusing their power, the place where multiple attackers (the ones you don't see) will ambush you. The farther you are off your X, the better.

FIGURE 9-6: Drive your forehead into the center of your attacker's chest.

>> Puts more power and bodyweight into your attack. Your movement combined with your pushing off the earth and driving into your attacker maximizes your power.

>> Keeps your attacker off-balance. Without balance, your attacker won't be able to deliver a meaningful assault of any kind, be it a strike or even using a weapon.

>> Moves your head out of your attacker's punching range, making it too close to your attacker (and below shoulder level) to hit with much force.

The combination of the elbow cover, drop-step, stomping, and forward drive is the foundation for a brutal, protected attack. If all you did was practice one strike such as the edge of hand, and you got into such great condition that you could run to Detroit and back, you'd have a viable fighting technique. You could hit with a great deal of power and keep your target off-balance while gaining momentum and providing yourself considerable defensive cover.

BUT WHAT IF THEY HIT BACK?!

I don't teach blocking. Self-defense isn't a combat sport. It isn't sparring. Self-defense is fast, violent, and explosive. An attack is over in seconds, not minutes. The outcome is decided almost immediately.

The tactics and techniques I demonstrate in this chapter show you how to execute a cover attack. You're not blocking. You're covering while delivering devastating blows and keeping your attacker off-balance. Your offense is your defense.

This combination of strike and cover, always moving forward and taking ground, will crush their momentum, keep them off-balance, and enable you to attack harder. It's simple, direct, and brutally effective. It's what works.

Exploding with convulsive movement

The drop step begins the process of convulsive, explosive, and ballistic movement that puts power into your attack. Convulsive, aggressive movement is what wins fights because it's how your body is designed to move in fight-or-flight mode. These movements are large and heavy. Let your body do what it's hardwired to do. Don't fight it — embrace it!

REMEMBER

Choreographed moves or those requiring fine motor skills or involving complicated, intricate techniques don't work in street fights. Discard those techniques because you won't be able to perform them no matter how much you practice.

HIT WITH HATE

Surviving an attempted homicide or rape requires a level of brutality that may be outside your comfort zone. Remind yourself that you didn't ask for this. Your attacker had every opportunity to leave you alone but chose to push you to the point of having to use force. Now is the time to unleash your inner beast. When you hit, hit with hate. Train with that mantra: *Hit with hate.*

(continued)

(continued)

> After it's over, after you've survived, when you and your loved ones are safe, you can demonstrate compassion by calling 911 to send an ambulance for your attacker.
>
> Think of yourself as the family watch dog who plays with the kids and sleeps at the foot of your bed . . . then, when sensing an intruder, goes full Cujo in an attempt to dismember your uninvited guest. After settling the score, your faithful dog goes right back to being the family pet.

Delivering Edge-of-Hand Strikes

Edge-of-hand strikes (axe hands) are a core combat technique. They involve swinging an open hand to strike an attacker with the edge of your hand or arm — from the base of the pinky anywhere up to the shoulder.

When delivering an edge-of-hand strike, target the vulnerable areas of the head and neck above the collarbone. You don't need pinpoint accuracy — striking anywhere on the neck, throat, or head will have the desired effect.

REMEMBER

Edge-of-hand is the Swiss army knife of strikes. You can deliver it at a variety of angles to nearly any part of the body — head, neck, throat, groin, *solar plexus* (just below the sternum), or anywhere else on the body. The beauty of this blow is that it's simple and effective, and it carries a low risk of hurting or damaging your hand. These advantages make it a preferred technique for military, law enforcement, and any situation involving a firearm or a weapon. Even if you destroy your pinky and ring fingers by striking, you still have two good fingers and a thumb to pick up a weapon and use it on your attacker.

In the following sections, I present three different edge-of-hand techniques.

The short edge-of-hand strike

The *short edge-of-hand strike* or *short axe hand* involves snapping your hand open, fingers and thumbs straight out, and swinging it like an axe, at your attacker's head, neck, or throat (see Figure 9-7). To maximize its effectiveness, do the following:

>> Deliver your short edge-of-hand strike with the arm used to cover your face. Move in under the cover of that arm and then use that same arm to deliver the blow.

>> Snap your hand open, fingers and thumbs straight. Don't worry about holding your hand and fingers just right.

>> Short-chop from the elbow and shoulder, like you're using a hatchet. (This is where the *short* in *short edge-of-hand strike* comes from.)

>> Keep your elbow up and chin down. Don't block — cover while attacking.

>> Keep your head below your attacker's shoulder level. Bury your face in their chest. If you're taller than your attacker, you may not be able to drop your head below their shoulder level, but your reach will give you an advantage.

Instinctively, your attacker wants to throw a punch at shoulder level. Dropping below their shoulder line and moving in close takes you out of the path of those strikes while your elbow provides additional cover.

>> Strike first with the drop step, and then keep hacking in forward drive, stomping with each step.

>> Target anywhere from the base of the neck up with short, snappy, repetitive blows. If your attacker is taller than you, your blows are likely to strike the neck or throat. If you're about the same height, they may strike the side of the head or somewhere on the face. Doesn't matter. Anywhere you hit the head or neck will hurt your attacker and keep them off-balance.

>> Don't let up. Every time you pull your hand back from your attacker, you provide them an opportunity to recuperate and mount a counterattack. Focus on speed and repetition. Hack the throat, the side of the neck, the jaw, the ear, the temple. No matter how they turn their head, you're going to have a vulnerable target to hit. Continue to hack away, and don't be concerned if your strikes are being blocked. Just keep chopping.

TIP

Keep it simple. Protecting yourself against an attempted homicide or rape is challenging enough. Don't add to the confusion by attempting to learn fancy moves. As a rule of thumb, if a technique doesn't feel comfortable with minimal training (15 minutes max), drop it. Less is more. The less you need to think about, the more you'll be able to do.

FIGURE 9-7: A short edge-of-hand strike to the neck.

The long edge-of-hand strike

The long edge-of-hand strike is identical to the short edge-of-hand strike except that instead of using your arm like a hatchet, you swing it like a sword or bat, engaging your hips and swinging for the fences. It incorporates more of your body weight and strength to deliver a more powerful blow.

TIP

To wield the most power, wind up — throw your hand back to your opposite shoulder, twist your torso in the same direction, and keep your elbow up (see Figure 9-8). Really try to whip the strike, cutting through your attacker. Envision your hand as a sword or saber slicing through your attacker's neck. Let 'er rip! Even if you miss the neck and strike somewhere on the face or side of the head, you're going to do some serious damage.

Deliver short edge-of-hand strikes initially, and long edge-of-hand strikes only after your initial attack has given you the time and space to put more power into your delivery. Because you're not delivering long edge-of-hand strikes during your initial attack, you don't need to drop-step. Just continue your forward drive.

FIGURE 9-8: Wind up to maximize the power of your long edge-of-hand strike.

REMEMBER

Lead with speed, follow with power. Start with short edge-of-hand strikes and follow with long ones.

The short and long edge-of-hand combination

Short and long edge-of-hand strikes can make for a devastating combination. Use short edge-of-hand strikes to disrupt and discombobulate your attacker and long edge-of-hand strikes to inflict more serious damage:

1. **Take the position of advantage and assume the interview stance (see Chapter 8).**

2. **As your assailant moves forward to attack, drop-step and drive your short edge-of-hand to the head target group with three quick repetitions.**

REMEMBER

Drop below your attacker's shoulder line and keep your chin down and elbow up.

3. **Continue to drive forward, stomping, and deliver two long edge-of-hand strikes to the head target group.**

4. Continue to drive forward with two more short edge-of-hand strikes.

5. Set your feet and swing for the fences with two long edge-of-hand strikes.

Adjust accordingly. You have no way of knowing how many blows you'll need to deliver to subdue an attacker. A single blow may end the fight, or you may need to deliver 10 or 20 or more.

REMEMBER

When practicing combinations, train in multiples of five (minimum). This approach conditions you to pursue your target aggressively and unrelentingly. You have no guarantee that your blows will strike your target or have the desired effect, but even if you miss, your aggressive forward drive and cover will keep your attacker off-balance, stop their attack, and enable you to continue your assault or escape.

The vertical edge-of-hand strike

Unlike the short and long edge-of-hand strikes, which travel along the horizontal plane (left to right or right to left). The vertical edge-of-hand strike travels (you guessed it) the vertical plane (top down or bottom up). To deliver a vertical edge-of-hand strike, take the following steps:

1. Bring your hand up to the side of your head with your hand snapped open in the edge-of-hand position (see Figure 9-9).

   You can use either hand, but using the rear hand enables you to put more body weight into it.

2. Slightly rotate and open up your hips to the side of your striking hand.

3. Raise up on the balls of your feet, like you're swinging an axe downward.

4. Drop the full weight of your hand down into the target as if you're splitting a log or breaking a cement block.

   Don't wind up; simply "drop" the vertical edge-of-hand down on your target. Think of it as a short hack with your entire body, snapping at the elbow.

   Optionally, you can twist your torso to add power or turn your hand or adjust the trajectory of your arm to strike a specific target — for example, the neck, jaw, or temple. Following up with a kick to the groin can be very effective.

FIGURE 9-9: Start with your hand to the side of your head.

REMEMBER

If the short edge-of-hand is a hatchet, and the long edge-of-hand is a saber, the vertical edge of hand is a log splitter. Imagine slitting wood with an axe or breaking up concrete with a 5-pound sledgehammer. It's the same motion.

The vertical edge-of-hand strike is versatile. You can use it as an opening strike when you're in extremely close range, as a follow-up strike in a combination, or as a finishing technique. If your attacker is on the ground covering up, you can use it to break down their guard. You can even use it when *grappling* (wrestling) with an attacker.

If an individual assailant is bent over after you kicked them in the groin or in the shin, kneed them in the face, or simply pulled their head down, you can take more time to raise your arm and drop it to deliver a more powerful blow to the base of the skull, the cervical vertebrae, or the kidneys. A short hack is still effective, but when an attacker is bent over or in a prone position, you can take more time and put more of your body behind the strike.

TIP

Striking the cervical spine when your target is bent over can be deadly. Delivering a vertical edge-of-hand strike upward to the groin area can also be very effective.

Combining edge-of-hand strikes

Here's an effective combination that uses all three edge-of-hand strike techniques:

1. Take the position of advantage and assume the interview stance.

2. As your assailant moves forward to attack, drop-step and drive your short edge-of-hand to the head target group with three quick repetitions.

3. Continue to drive forward while delivering two long edge-of-hand strikes.

4. Using your rear hand, deliver two vertical edge-of-hand strikes to your attacker's collarbone.

WARNING

Never rely on a single blow or even a single technique. Deliver a barrage of strikes — edge-of-hand strikes, knees, elbows, head butts, hairpulling, gouging, and whatever else you feel is needed and comes naturally. An attack is a very fluid and unpredictable situation. You can't plan for what's going to happen, but you can, through practice, program yourself to move and strike instinctively in very effective ways.

Delivering Heel-of-Hand Strikes

The *heel* of your hand is the base of your palm, and it's one of the toughest parts of your body — tougher, even, than the edge of your hand. You can strike even the hardest parts of the body with the heel of your hand while exposing yourself to a very low risk of hand injury.

In this section, I explain how to deliver two potentially devastating heel-of-hand strikes — the chin jab and chin-jab uppercut — along with the punch stop, which is effective for preventing an attacker from throwing a punch while keeping them off-balance.

The chin jab

The chin jab is a very effective strike taught by close-combat pioneers William E. Fairbairn and Rex Applegate. It's a great opening strike that you can deliver in place of a short edge-of-hand strike, but it can be very effective anytime during an attack. To deliver the chin jab, take the following steps (see Figure 9-10):

1. **Start with either hand in whatever position it happens to be.**

    You can strike faster with your lead hand or harder with your rear hand.

2. **Bend your hand back at the wrist, fingers clawed.**

3. **If you're delivering a chin jab as an opening strike, drop-step into it regardless of which hand you're using.**

    If you're not delivering it as an opening strike, you can simply snap it out like a jab and snap it back.

4. **As you move forward, drop below your attacker's shoulder level.**

5. **(Optional) Immediately after making contact, drive your fingers into your attacker's face and eyes.**

6. **Follow up immediately with a driving knee to the groin, a short edge-of-hand strike, or another chin jab with your lead hand.**

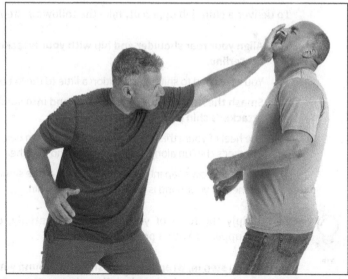

FIGURE 9-10: Delivering a chin jab.

At first, practice the chin jab by itself. When you're comfortable delivering the jab, combine it with the drop step and eye gouge. To deliver with more power, pretend that you're shot-putting a 20-pound ball and let your body follow through. Don't worry about losing your balance. Any time you start to lose your balance, knee your attacker in the groin or stomp on the top of their foot. You won't fall.

Be careful when practicing the chin jab with a training partner. When you do it right, it's difficult to control.

With the chin jab, pinpoint accuracy is not required. It can cause severe pain and damage wherever it lands — the neck, throat, temple, nose, cheek bone, eye, you name it. One effective technique is to get behind the attacker and deliver a chin jab to the base of the skull or the cervical spine.

The chin-jab uppercut

The chin-jab uppercut targets the chin, jawline, or base of the skull with the goal of turning your attacker into a Pez dispenser. It's meant to be delivered at very close range — about 6 inches max from an attacker.

To deliver a chin-jab uppercut, take the following steps:

1. **Align your rear shoulder and hip with your attacker's centerline.**

   You may need to shift your position a little to the left or right.

2. **Smash the heal of your rear hand up and into your attacker's chin (see Figure 9-11).**

   The heel of your striking hand should travel from below your attacker's chin up along their centerline and into their chin.

   Let your elbow snap into their solar plexus at the same time the heel of your hand is smashing into their chin.

To multiply the force of your strike exponentially, deliver the chin-jab uppercut with a post:

1. **As you step in, wrap your opposite arm around your attacker's lower body to lock them in (see Figure 9-12).**

   This prevents them from moving backward so more of your power is delivered into the strike.

FIGURE 9-11: Delivering a chin-jab uppercut.

2. Deliver your chin-jab uppercut.

Now your attacker's body has no means of moving to absorb the tremendous force. All that upward energy, all that force, is transferred to your attacker's chin, jaw, and skull.

The effectiveness of holding an opponent in place while punching them is attested to by the fact that it's not allowed in boxing. A boxer isn't allowed to hook one hand behind their opponent's head while punching them in the face. Why? Because it can cause severe physical damage.

TIP

Here's a perfect combination involving the chin-jab uppercut (the first combination I ever learned):

1. **Take the position of advantage and assume the interview stance.**

2. **As your attacker moves toward you to initiate contact, drop-step and deliver two short edge-of-hand strikes to the head target group.**

3. **Continue your forward drive while delivering one long edge-of-hand strike.**

FIGURE 9-12: Delivering a chin-jab uppercut with a post.

4. Continue your forward drive, shifting a little to one side of your attacker, while delivering a chin-jab uppercut with a post.

5. Lift your elbow and drive your fingers into your attacker's eyes.

6. Drive your knee right into their groin.

TIP

After delivering the long edge-of-hand strike with your lead hand, use that same hand to wrap around your attacker's lower back as you align your rear shoulder with their centerline. With your chin tucked, bury your forehead right into their shoulder and then drive your rear hand right up their centerline into their chin. Lift your elbow, let your fingers find their eyes, and *drive*. Your rear knee will automatically pop up and find a target. This combination should start to feel natural after several minutes of practice.

The punch stop

The punch stop is a variation of the chin jab. You deliver it the same way to a different target — the shoulder instead of the chin (see Figure 9-13). Its purpose is to stop a punch at its source.

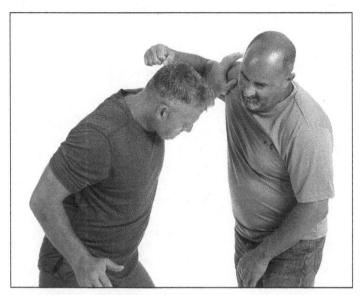

FIGURE 9-13: The punch stop.

REMEMBER

Here are some additional details about the punch stop to keep in mind:

>> **Use the punch stop only in extremely close-range situations.** You can stop a punch at its source only if your hands are already close to your attacker's body. Stay right in front of your attacker, right on them, and below their shoulder line.

>> **Combine the punch stop with dropping below your attacker's shoulder level to temporarily stay out of harm's way.**

>> **Follow up immediately with a strike to one of the target groups — the head, neck, groin, or lower legs.** The punch stop disrupts your attacker's balance and momentum only temporarily. It stops a punch, not the attack.

IN THIS CHAPTER

» **Delivering advanced open-hand, cupped-hands, and hammer-fist strikes**

» **Throwing elbows, knees, and shoulders**

» **Headbutting and hip-butting**

» **Going for the jugular . . . notch, that is**

» **Mastering close-quarter kicking techniques**

Chapter **10**

Adding Advanced Strikes to Your Arsenal

You mastered the basics — the position of advantage, the interview stance, and basic edge-of-hand and heel-of-hand strikes. If you haven't, head back to Chapters 8 and 9 to get up to speed on the fundamentals. Now you're ready to add some advanced strikes to your repertoire.

In this chapter, I introduce you to several additional hand strikes, along with blows you can deliver with your elbows, knees, shoulders, head, hips, and feet, and, for good measure, a simple choke hold, plus some variations on those themes. Feel free to pick and choose your favorites and ignore the rest. Delivering a few basic strikes perfectly is more effective than executing a dozen different techniques sloppily.

REMEMBER

By "advanced," I don't mean better or more effective. These advanced techniques require more training and development. Some also involve targeting more specific areas of the body. They're not intended to replace or supersede the basics, only augment them. Basics always come first.

Delivering Web-of-Hand Strikes

The *webbing* of your hand is the skin between your thumb and forefinger. This area of your hand is very suitable for delivering strikes to the throat, side of the neck, back of the neck, and groin. To execute an opening web-of-hand strike, take the following steps:

1. **Take the position of advantage and assume the interview stance (see Chapter 8).**

   Don't worry about your hand position. You deliver the strike starting from wherever your hand happens to be.

2. **As your attacker moves forward, drop-step, as explained in Chapter 8, and drive the web of your hand directly into your attacker's throat or neck, twisting your body into the blow (see Figure 10-1).**

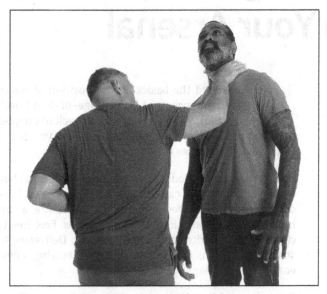

FIGURE 10-1: Deliver a web-of-hand strike to the throat.

3. **Follow through with your forward drive, and smash your rear knee up into your attacker's groin.**

REMEMBER

In any scenario in which you deliver a blow like this, following up immediately with a knee to the groin or another strike maintains your balance as you continue your assault.

The web-of-hand strike is very versatile. Here are some other applications of it that can be very effective:

>> At close quarters, use gouging, ripping techniques, and hair grabs to maneuver your attacker's head and neck into position (say, with an eye gouge to expose their throat), and then deliver a sweeping web-of-hand to the throat. You can do this when standing or on the ground.

>> Deliver a web-of-hand to the face with an upward trajectory, smashing it into the bottom of your attacker's upper lip and nose.

>> Deliver a chin jab to expose the throat, followed by a web-of-hand to the throat and then a powerful knee to the groin.

>> Target anywhere on the neck. You don't have to be in front of your attacker to do it. Hitting the jugular notch or the carotid artery can be very disconcerting to an attacker. A web-of-hand to the cervical spine or the base of the skull can knock the subject out cold.

>> If your attacker is so equipped, drive the web of your hand into their testicles and squeeze with all your might.

REMEMBER

Different target areas require different angles of entry. If you're targeting the throat or back of the neck, you come in straight. If you're in front of your attacker, aiming for the side of the neck, your hand needs to travel in more of an arc. Practice on a training dummy with a head and neck until you feel comfortable delivering the blow from different angles.

Rattling Your Attacker's Skull with a Double Chin Jab

The double chin jab involves smashing both palms right into the point of the chin or jawline and then driving your fingers into the attacker's eyes. This technique is ideal for a smaller person, effectively doubling the power and impact of the basic chin jab (see Chapter 9). To execute the double chin jab, take the following steps:

1. **From the position of advantage and the interview stance (see Chapter 8), begin your drop step.**

2. **As you drop-step, hurl your arms up, bring your hands together into a V, and drive that V into your attacker's chin (see Figure 10-2) and your forearms into their chest.**

3. **Push through your forward drive, keeping your chin down for cover, and continue to drive with all your body weight, digging your fingers and thumbs into your attacker's face and eyes, and smashing your rear knee into their groin.**

   Don't merely scratch the eyes, drive your fingers or thumbs *into* the eyes.

REMEMBER

4. **Use your stomping footwork to deliver knee strikes and stomps to anything in your path.**

You can also deliver the double chin jab at close range. Simply drive your hands straight up and strike the groin with the knee at the same time. A knee to the groin increases the power of the blow, because when you strike the groin, it forces your assailant's chin forward.

FIGURE 10-2: Delivering a double chin jab.

Targeting the Jugular Notch

The *jugular-notch strangle* involves wrapping your hands around the base of your attacker's throat and driving your thumbs into their *jugular notch* (the dip between the throat and the clavicles), as shown in Figure 10-3.

TIP

Immediately after delivering a double-chin jab and driving your fingers into your adversary's eyes, let your hands drop to their throat. Drive your thumbs straight into the jugular notch as you continue to stomp, knee, and headbutt your attacker.

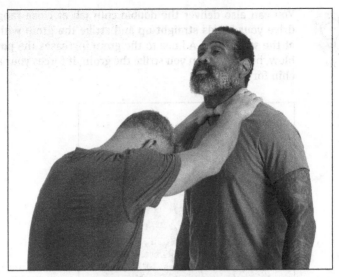

FIGURE 10-3: The jugular-notch strangle.

Pounding with Hammer Fists

Hammer fist is a closed fist covered tightly with thumb over fingers, *not* thumb on top (see Figure 10-4). Just ball the fist and cover it with your thumb, tightening the pinky as much as possible.

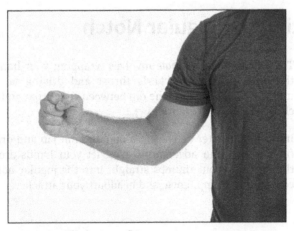

FIGURE 10-4: The hammer fist.

Never, close your fist with your thumb inside the fingers or leave your thumb exposed on the top. The thumb can easily be broken or jammed.

Your hammer fist has two distinct areas you can use to strike your attacker:

>> The L formed by the pinky and the beginning of the edge of the fist

>> The meat of the fist up to the bone of the heel of the hand

Compared to edge-of-hand strikes (see Chapter 9), the hammer fist has two advantages:

>> **Better protection for your fingers:** You're less likely to damage your pinky and ring fingers. If you have small or delicate hands, you may want to start with hammer fists, but with a few weeks of practice, you'll be able to deliver both hammer fists and edge-of-hand strikes with little risk of hurting your fingers.

>> **More concussive force:** Hammer fists carry more force, making them suitable for striking the *solar plexus* (just below the sternum) or skull, or penetrating your attacker's defenses if they use their arms to cover up.

The drawback of a hammer fist is that it isn't a precision instrument. The edge of your hand has a lower profile that can get into tight areas much easier, like the throat, groin, and neck.

Short hammer fist

Deliver the short hammer fist like the short edge-of-hand or vertical edge-of-hand (see Chapter 9) with short, chopping, fast movements, as if you were swinging a hammer:

1. **From a square stance, casually bring your fist up to the side of your face.**

   No big movement is required. Keep your hand close to your body. Don't reach back.

2. **Simultaneously twist your hips and rise up slightly on the balls of your feet.**

3. **Drop your weight and the pinky side of your fist into the target's face or collarbone (see Figure 10-5).**

If you strike in a downward direction, you're likely to hit the chin, nose, or cheekbone.

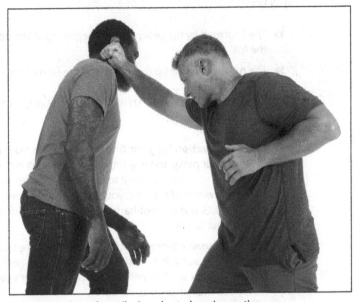

FIGURE 10-5: Drop the strike in a short, chopping motion.

TIP

Try to make contact with the L of your fist (near the pinky knuckle). If you try to make contact with the meaty part of your fist, you'll tend to draw your fist too far back, turning your strike from a short hammer fist to a long hammer fist.

4. **Continue driving forward, delivering follow-up strikes, stomping, kneeing, headbutting, gouging, and anything else that feels right at the time.**

Long hammer fist

The long hammer fist is very similar to the long edge-of-hand and long vertical edge-of-hand discussed in Chapter 9. Use it only after you've injured your attacker and you can take more of a swing. In contrast to the short hammer fist, you need more of a windup, and you deliver the strike with the meat of the fist. Instead of a hammer, imagine swinging a sledgehammer.

To execute the long hammer fist, take the following steps:

1. **From a square stance, bring your fist as far back as comfortably possible.**

2. **Simultaneously twist your hips and slightly rise up on your toes.**

3. **Drop your weight and the meaty part of your fist into the target (see Figure 10-6).**

FIGURE 10-6: Drop the long hammer fist into your target with all your weight.

Long hammer fists are most effective when the attacker is bent over. Target the back of the neck, the kidneys, or the thoracic spine (middle of the upper back).

TIP

Boxing the Ears with the Cupped-Hands Strike

The cupped-hands strike involves sandwiching your attacker's head between the palms of your hands as if you're playing the cymbals with their head in the middle. More commonly referred to as "boxing the ears," this technique can be used anywhere on the head using one or both hands, the latter of which is much more effective.

The cupped-hands strike forces air into the ear canals, causing pain, disorientation, and loss of balance and potentially rupturing the eardrum. But even if you miss the ears, the strike will still "rattle their cage."

To deliver the cupped-hands strike, take the following steps:

1. In the interview stance (see Chapter 8), cup your hands as if you were going to use them to scoop water out of a bucket.

2. Drop-step while bringing both hands in a short arc to your attacker's ears with as much force as possible (see Figure 10-7).

   A short arc is key to not telegraphing your strike.

FIGURE 10-7: The cupped-hands strike.

TIP

Deliver a knee to the groin at the same time.

3. **Drop your head below your attacker's shoulder line, anchoring your fingers behind their ears, and gouge their eyes with your thumbs in a scooping motion.**

TIP

Possible combinations are endless. After striking the ears and eyes, you can headbutt, pull your attacker's head down, drop a hammer fist to the neck, strike the collarbone, smash a knee up into the groin, and more.

You can also use the cupped-hands strike when your assailant starts to *grapple* (wrestle) with you, but you need to use it immediately. If your attacker is larger or skilled, you've got a serious problem. Immediately try to box the ears, gouge an eye, gouge the throat, knee the groin, or break their instep.

The atomic slap

The atomic slap is a variation of the cupped-hands strike delivered with one hand to one side of your attacker's face from a non-threatening position at close range (where your attacker is in your face). Your hand travels outside their field of vision and lands on their ear or jaw or some other area on the side of their head. You can also make contact with the heel of your hand to deliver an extremely concussive strike.

To execute the atomic slap, take the following steps:

1. **Stand close to your target (about a foot away).**

2. **Take a small opening step with the foot opposite the hand you'll use to strike to open your stance for maximum striking power, and step across to drag your arm across the path of the strike with your hip.**

3. **Rotate your hips, using your entire body to swing your hand into the side of your target's face.**

When you make contact, your elbow should be bent slightly.

REMEMBER

To get the most power into your strike you *really* need to engage your hips. Let your hips pull your arm across and try to take their head clean off.

TIP

After the first strike, a great follow-up is a long edge-of-hand with the same arm in the opposite direction. It's already loaded up on the follow-through.

Stopping an attack on someone else

To stop an assailant who's attacking someone other than you, you can use the cupped-hands strike from behind the attacker to stop them in their tracks. Here's how:

1. **Quickly approach from behind the attacker.**

2. **Step in between their legs with your thigh right up under them and cup their ears in one fluid motion.**

   Don't try to do this move from a distance. Your hands can travel a wider arc to strike with much greater force because the attacker won't see what you're up to.

3. **Follow up with a knee to the groin, hammer fists or edge-of-hand strikes to the neck or head, kicks to the lower legs, or anything else that's likely to stop the attack and disable the attacker.**

Delivering a Shoulder Smash

Few people ever consider using a shoulder as a weapon, but it can inflict some serious pain and damage. To deliver a shoulder smash, take the following steps:

1. **Stand about 6 inches (max) from your target, chin tucked.**

   Typically, at this point, you're holding your attacker by the shoulders or hooking or grabbing their neck so you can pull them into your shoulder. Think of your shoulder as an anvil that you're going to smash your attacker against.

2. **Raise your weight up on the balls of your feet while drawing your shoulder slightly back to "cock" it.**

   If possible, push your attacker away from you slightly so you can pull them in with more force prior to contact.

3. **Drop-step with the foot opposite the shoulder you're using while pulling your attacker into that shoulder and driving the point of your shoulder into the target.**

TIP

Locking your arms around your target's neck in a wrestler's grip (see Figure 10-8) enables you to pull them into your shoulder with incredible force. Extend your arms out to create space; you can then move back a little (or your attacker will pull back giving you the space you need).

FIGURE 10-8: Lock your arms around your target's neck in a wrestler's grip.

Using the shoulder smash in conjunction with a knee to the groin, kicks to the shins, or stomps to the top of the feet can be very effective.

The shoulder smash is also helpful for creating distance when you don't have a lot of room to move. Drop the point of the shoulder into your attacker's chest, solar plexus, stomach, face, or head to create space to follow up with a more devastating attack.

Headbutting Your Attacker

Your head can be a formidable weapon, as long as you wield it properly — neck and shoulders stiff, teeth clenched, eyes shut tight, and using your waist and legs to drive the hardest parts of your skull into your attacker and, when possible, your arms to pull your attacker into the headbutt. If you headbutt by swinging your head and neck, you'll injure your neck. If you keep your eyes open when you headbutt, you'll end up with double vision, which will pass after a few minutes, but that's time you don't have.

In this section, I show you two ways to headbutt your attacker — using your forehead or the top of your head to target the soft parts of their skull or their face or chest.

Do not attempt to deploy head butts without practicing on a training dummy or a heavy bag. It's the only way you'll be able to develop proper and safe technique.

Also, don't headbutt forehead to forehead. You may hurt your attacker, but you'll hurt yourself, too, maybe even more.

Forward headbutt

With the forward headbutt, you drive your forehead into your attacker's face, nose, eye orbits, temple, or even the chest (to create space). To perform the forward headbutt, take the following steps:

1. Squeeze your eyes shut, clench your teeth, stiffen your neck, and tighten your shoulders as you prepare to deliver.

2. Drop-step and bend at the waist, driving your forehead into the target (see Figure 10-9).

    Use your whole body, dropping your weight into the strike as you make contact. Your body, neck, and head should move as a single unit.

Grab your attacker's shoulders or lock their neck in a wrestler's grip and pull them toward you as you smash your head into their face, head, or chest for an even more devastating blow. The headbutt can be very useful when you're grappling with an attacker.

Upward headbutt

The upper headbutt involves launching your body upward, like a rocket, to smash the top of your head into your adversary's chin or face. You can combine it with a knee to the groin and a short edge-of-hand strike for added effect.

FIGURE 10-9: Drive your forehead into your attacker's face.

To execute the upward headbutt, follow these steps:

1. **From a low position, with your feet apart and knees bent, tighten your neck and shoulders and shut your eyes tight to prepare for launch.**

You may be face-to-face with your attacker, standing sideways to them, or even standing with your attacker behind you.

2. **Using your legs and entire body, drive the top of your head straight up into your attacker's chin, like a rocket following their centerline (see Figure 10-10).**

3. **Bring your feet together and extend your knees and body to make yourself as tall as possible as fast as possible.**

TIP

Any time you find yourself in a low position, even when grappling, align your head with your attacker's centerline and drive straight up into the chin. It's lights out.

FIGURE 10-10: Drive the top of your head into your attacker's chin.

Throwing Elbows

The elbow is a brutal, powerful weapon you can employ with nearly zero risk of injuring yourself. Almost anywhere you strike on your attacker's body is going to inflict pain and damage. And the elbow is extremely versatile — you can use it to smash, chop, or jab, or you can cover and drive with the point of your elbow.

The elbow spike

The elbow spike involves raising your elbow and thrusting it into your attacker or simply letting them smash into it. It carries the added advantage of providing cover to allow you to move in, it can startle your target because there's no windup, and it can be used at extreme close range from any direction.

To deliver an elbow spike, take the following steps:

1. From the interview stance (see Chapter 8), drop-step and snap your elbow into position, pointing directly at your target.

2. Tuck your chin and drive forward, using your elbow as cover (see Figure 10-11).

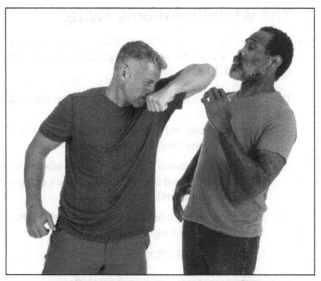

FIGURE 10-11: Drive your elbow forward into your target.

3. **Follow up with a short edge-of-hand or hammer fist.**

You can use the elbow spike in a variety of ways:

>> Thrust your elbow straight into the throat, jaw, or skull.

>> Snap your elbow into position as your attacker charges toward you, letting them smash into it. Drive forward, following up with edge-of-hands, hammer fists, knees to the groin, stomps to the feet, headbutts, and more.

>> Snap your elbow up to cover and block a punch. When a closed fist lands on an elbow, the closed fist loses. Elbow cover provides excellent protection against sucker punches, too. If you sense or anticipate a sucker punch coming in, simply snap your elbow spike into position as you launch your counterattack.

>> In a crowed situation, like a bar or a subway platform, when the threat is right next to you, snapping the elbow spike into their head group creates space and causes them to pause, allowing you to follow up with a more powerful attack. In this application, the elbow spike can be used in all four directions (front, back, left, and right).

The wheeling-elbow swing

The wheeling-elbow swing involves using your whole body to swing your rear elbow at your target, typically as a follow-up to a lead edge-of-hand strike.

To execute the wheeling elbow swing, follow these steps:

1. Stand normally in front of your target (no need for a stance because this is a follow-up technique).

2. Take a step with the foot opposite the elbow you're about to swing and open your hips (think of a pitcher throwing a baseball).

3. Push off your back foot, swinging your elbow horizontally across your target (see Figure 10-12).

   Let your back foot follow through naturally.

FIGURE 10-12: Swing your elbow horizontally across your target.

You can also execute the wheeling-elbow swing at a downward or upward angle.

The rear elbow smash

When your assailant is behind you, you can deliver the rear elbow smash to surprise them, create space, and start your assault.

To execute the rear elbow smash horizontally, take the following steps:

1. Stand normally with your target right behind you.

2. Step out to the side, aligning your elbow with their centerline.

3. At the same time, twist your body, with your striking elbow forward, and torque your hips without telegraphing the strike.

4. Drop your weight and drive the elbow into your target, torquing your body for maximum impact.

5. Follow up with another elbow with a bigger windup.

In a grappling situation, if your attacker's head is bent over, drive the elbow up into the throat or the face. Even if you miss, you can take some other action. Take any opening that presents itself.

TIP

To strike at an upward angle with additional force, bend your knees and align your elbow with your attacker's centerline in preparation for delivery. Drive your elbow along your attacker's centerline into their chin as you straighten your legs.

Hip Butting

Blows using the hips can be very effective, especially in situations with multiple assailants or whenever you need to create room to move. You can deliver a hip butt with either the side or back of your hip:

>> **Side hip butt:** Take the position of advantage, assume the interview stance (see Chapter 8), and drop-step as you turn your foot toward your attacker's centerline and drive your hip into them, like you're doing "the bump" (see Figure 10-13). Make sure your hip strikes the target before your foot lands.

FIGURE 10-13: Delivering a side hip butt.

>> **Rear hip butt:** The rear hip butt can be effective when you're approached or grabbed from the rear. Just thrust your butt back in a convulsive movement while you throw your hands out, bend at the waist, widen your stance, and bend your knees.

Kneeing Your Attacker

The knee strike is one of the most common leg attacks used in close combat, and for good reasons: It works, and it's versatile. Here are a few effective knee-strike applications:

>> **Knee to the groin:** With your foot planted between your attacker's legs, drive your knee straight up into their groin (see Figure 10-14), smashing your attacker's testicles (if so equipped) between your knee and their pelvis. Holding your attacker in place while delivering your knee increases the force.

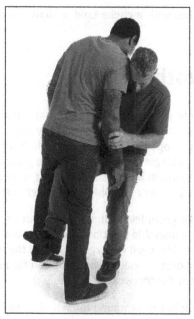

FIGURE 10-14: Drive the knee straight up into the groin as you drive forward.

Don't make the common mistake of kneeing and moving back to your starting position. Continue your forward drive, always taking ground.

>> **Spear the groin:** Drive your knee horizontally into the groin as a diversion, following up with additional strikes. Any attack to the groin will most likely illicit *some* reaction from your attacker or at least cause them to pause.

>> **Repetitive knee strikes:** As you drive forward, lift your knees high and stomp with each step, chin down, delivering knees to the testicles, legs, stomach, and rib cage, and foot stomps to the top of the attacker's feet. You might even deliver a headbutt to the face as a bonus.

>> **Knee to other body parts:** In a grappling situation, if your attacker straightens their arm, drop a knee on their elbow. Use your knee as a stationary "anvil" to smash your attacker's face or other body part against it. From behind, you can strike the kidneys and the spine. You can also drive your knee into the target's hamstring from behind to buckle the knee.

TIP

Combine knee strikes with a choke hold to deliver a devastating combination.

Kicking . . . But Nothing Fancy

Kicking is extremely popular in the martial arts but extremely limited in self-defense. I recommend kicks only to cover distance to your target with an opening strike, disrupt their balance when grappling, or finish a target when they're on the ground. Use your legs primarily to maintain balance. A real fight involves a lot of pushing and shoving on very unstable and uneven terrain.

WARNING

Don't kick above the groin level. High kicks are unnecessary and place you in a very vulnerable position. Also, wear boots or heavy shoes whenever possible, even when going out on the town. I recommend steel-toe boots or shoes, which you can find in a variety of styles. The heavier the footwear, the better.

Following are the kicks I recommend for self-defense:

>> **Direct front kick (whip kick):** Drop-step while kicking straight into the groin, shin, or kneecap (see Chapter 9). Don't chamber the kick; snap it — fling the tip of your foot into your target. And don't do this barefoot!

>> **Saddle kick:** If your attacker assumes a wide stance, a saddle kick can make them regret it. From any standing position, step with the foot opposite your kicking foot to open your hips. Swing your kicking leg so your instep smashes directly up into your target's groin. (Imagine you're kicking a soccer ball.) Your foot's the saddle, and your attacker is now sitting on it . . . very uncomfortably I might add (see Figure 10-15).

>> **Stomping side kick:** Lift either foot slightly and step forward, turning your foot and driving the heel or outer edge of your foot into your target's knee or shin (see Figure 10-16). Avoid lifting your knee or chambering your kick. Follow through by stomping your foot firmly on the ground or on the top of your target's foot.

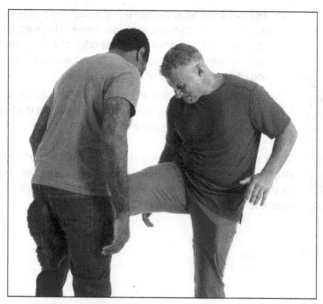

FIGURE 10-15: The saddle kick.

FIGURE 10-16: Drive the stomping side kick directly into your target's knee or shin.

>> **Edge-of-boot kick:** Deliver this kick with the inside edge of your foot. Step forward with your non-kicking foot; lift the opposite foot and drive the inside edge of it into your target's knee or shin. Let it scrape all the way down and smash the top of the foot with your full body weight.

TIP

Deliver a stomping side kick or edge-of-boot kick from behind the target, smashing the calf just below the knee to take the target to the ground.

REMEMBER

Don't worry about executing the perfect kick. You're not going to stop the attack with a single blow. Move like a locomotive. Kick to surprise and disrupt an attack and then immediately escalate your counterattack.

Chapter **11**

Breaking Free of Grabs and Holds

A ttacks often, but not always, begin with face-to-face encounters. However, your attacker may not always be standing conveniently in front of you while you take the position of advantage and assume the interview stance, as described in Chapter 8. They're just as likely to approach from your side or from behind you, grabbing your arm, wrist, or hair, or getting you in a bear hug or a choke hold.

Even if your attacker does show you the courtesy of standing in front of you, and you launch a counterattack, you may end up in a *grappling* (wrestling) situation in which the assailant grabs hold of you and gets you in a headlock or a choke hold. Not surprising — their goal is to control you and make you submit, so they can continue their assault with little or no resistance.

Regardless of how your attacker tries to restrain you, you need to know how to respond effectively, and what's most effective is often counterintuitive. The effective response isn't so much about freeing yourself from the hold as it is about making your attacker pay a high enough price for putting you in that hold that they have no choice but to let go.

Think of this chapter as the street fighter's guide to freeing yourself from grabs and holds.

Attacking Your Attacker

Under real fighting conditions, you won't have the time or the wherewithal to respond to an attack with a *specific defense*. What do I mean by "specific defense"? I'm talking about techniques often taught in martial arts schools. An attacker grabs your wrist, so you respond with a rote memorized counter-defense designed for that single attack. If they get you in a choke hold, you respond with another technique. That approach doesn't work on the street.

What *does* work? When someone grabs you or gets you in a hold, *attack!* Don't overthink your response. If someone grabs your wrist, *attack!* If they grab your collar, *attack!* If they get you in a choke hold, *attack!* What they do doesn't matter nearly as much as your response. As close-combat expert William E. Fairbairn said, "Attack first and keep on attacking, and you can defeat almost anyone, even a highly skilled adversary."

I do recommend a handful of specific techniques in response to specific grabs and holds, and I share them in this chapter, but the focus is not so much on breaking free from the grab or hold. The focus is on maintaining your balance and creating enough space to attack your attacker.

REMEMBER

The initial attack is unimportant. An attacker grabs your wrist to pin you so they can strike you or knee you. They choke you so they can headbutt you or knee you. They grab your torso so they can immobilize you and then strike you, knife you, or club you. If you respond to a wrist-grab by trying a wrist release counter, a joint-lock or a joint-twisting maneuver, they're going to continue to pummel you, and you're going to lose.

WARNING

Don't wait to be attacked. As soon as a threat enters your personal space, *attack!* You can defend against almost any grab with an edge-of-hand blow, a chin jab, or a knee to the testicles (see Part 2). Even if you're grappling, an edge-of-hand to the throat or a knee to the groin is the most effective "defense."

Countering Double-Hand Grabs

Your attacker grabs you with two hands. They grab your wrists, arms, or shoulders; they grab your shirt; they get you in a choke hold. Now what? First, realize that this is only the beginning. Your attacker will probably follow up immediately with a head-butt, a knee to the groin, or something worse, so you need to act immediately, if not sooner. In this section, I reveal techniques for launching a counteroffensive when an assailant has two hands on you.

Breaking free of a double-collar or two-handed choke hold

If your assailant grabs you with two hands by the collar or shoulders or around the neck and is right in your face, here's what to do:

1. As your attacker grabs you, tuck your chin while pulling away from them (if possible), and swing one of your arms over their arms to deliver an atomic slap to your attacker's head group (see Figure 11-1).

FIGURE 11-1: Deliver an atomic slap.

Rotate your body and hips as your strike to deliver with maximum impact. (See Chapter 10 for more about the atomic slap.)

Stepping back protects you from a headbutt or knee to the groin. If they try a headbutt, they're going to hit your elbow and shoulder. If they lift a knee, it will hit the outside of your leg. However, if you're pinned, you won't be able to step back — just deliver the atomic slap and continue to attack. Your violent body rotation is all you need.

If you're facing more than one assailant, pulling back creates an opportunity to strike another nearby assailant.

2. **Use the same arm to deliver a long edge-of-hand or hammer fist to the head or neck.**

3. **Continue your forward drive, claiming ground, kneeing, stomping, and striking your assailant.**

   If you have a weapon, draw it and use it as soon as you have the opportunity.

Breaking free of a double-wrist grab

An attacker probably won't get hold of and pin both your wrists, but it's possible, and it's a scenario commonly addressed in self-defense systems, so here's what to do if you ever find yourself in such a predicament:

>> **Breaking free of a double-wrist grab from the front:**
Ignore your attacker's grip. Drop-step to the side to avoid a headbutt or groin to the knee, while you drive forward to deliver a shoulder smash, knee to the groin, or headbutt (see Figure 11-2). Follow up with front kicks and stomps to their lower legs and feet. Continue your forward drive, delivering more brutal open-hand strikes when your hands are free.

>> **Breaking free of a double-wrist grab from the rear:**
Ignore your attacker's grip. Drive back into your attacker, driving your head back into their face and chin (see Figure 11-3). Rotate your body, kicking and stomping their lower legs and feet, and deliver headbutts and shoulder smashes. Throwing backward elbows can also be effective. When your wrists are free, turn around and continue your forward drive with a more brutal assault.

FIGURE 11-2: When grabbed from in front, drive forward into your attacker.

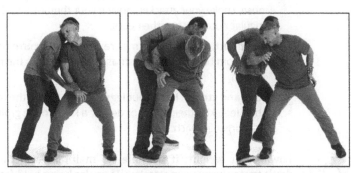

FIGURE 11-3: When grabbed from behind, drive back into your attacker until you can turn around and drive forward.

Escaping a Bear Hug

If an assailant has you in a bear hug, you're in deep doo-doo, so the best defense is to avoid bear hugs altogether. Don't let someone get close enough to you, especially from behind, to put you in a bear hug. If a threat makes a move toward you, launch a preemptive strike (see Chapter 8).

Now, despite your best efforts at avoidance, if you find yourself wrapped in the nonloving arms of an attacker, what do you do? First, be afraid. Be very afraid. Nobody puts you in a bear hug just to hold you there. They're going to body-slam you, break your ribs or back, hold you so someone else can use you as their personal punching bag, or move you somewhere so they can rob, rape, torture, or kill you. I tell you this to make you aware of what really happens and to motivate you to do what's necessary — and it ain't pretty.

When you're in a bear hug, it's time to go medieval, accent on the *evil*. Here's what I'm talking about:

>> **Use a weapon.** If you have a weapon, deploy it at the earliest opportunity and as viciously as possible; a knife, pen, or other pointy object into the neck, ear, or eye can be very effective.

>> **Bite.** Bite the ears, nose, fingers, neck, throat, shoulder, anywhere in reach of your mouth that will cause the most pain and injury.

>> **Claw.** If your hands are free, gouge their eyes; rip an ear or nose; choke your attacker, driving your thumbs into their jugular notch; or box their ears.

>> **Headbutt.** Even if your arms are pinned and you're being held from behind, you can smash your head into their face or chin.

>> **Kick and stomp.** Keep your legs moving. Stomp the tops of their feet, kick their shins, or deliver a knee to the groin or any target in reach.

TIP

Lower your weight, if possible, to maintain your balance, but don't try to throw your attacker. If you're being held from behind, throw your arms forward and your butt back to create space. If they lift you off the ground, run in place, driving your knees or heels into their body (depending on whether they grabbed you from the front or behind). As you continue to fight, bite and gouge. Keep your chin tucked to protect your head because you'll probably be thrown to the ground.

Whether you're grabbed from behind or facing your attacker, whether your arms are free or pinned, stick with those basics. Do the most savage thing possible. As your attacker's grip begins to loosen and you have more space, you'll have additional options to escalate your attack.

No single secret or magical technique will save you. The only effective approach is to know your options and improvise to take advantage of available openings, which change in milliseconds.

WARNING

Don't waste your time and energy with fancy martial arts defense techniques. They don't work on the street, especially with an attacker who's bigger, stronger, and meaner. Those graceful techniques may look great in videos, but they'll get you killed on the street. If you think I'm wrong, approach a big, nasty SOB with no martial arts training and say, "Grab me as hard as you can. Pick me up and throw me on the ground. Let me try my martial arts training." See if it works.

TIP

Train with a training dummy and a live partner — preferably someone bigger and stronger than you. Your training dummy allows you to go all out, while your training partner gives you the experience of being grabbed and moved around against your will.

Countering a Full Nelson

This is another martial arts favorite, so I'll go over it. It's unlikely someone will actually get you in this hold because they would need to sneak up behind you, slip their arms under yours, and lock their hands behind your head (see Figure 11-4). You will stop them by instinctively locking your arms down. There are a plethora of defenses to this move, from the complex to the absurd — just keep it as simple as possible. The best and safest way to deal with a full nelson is to drive your arms down, clamping them forcefully against your core, hard enough to break their grip (if you're stronger or they're not expecting it) and then fight out of it. Heel stomps, rear head butts, and elbows help you create space and pause their initial assault. As soon as you feel them loosen up, turn and continue your attack.

React as you would if you were in a bear hug — maintain your balance and stomp, kick, gouge, claw, rip, headbutt, smash, grab the testicles . . . do the most brutal thing you can, and if you have a weapon, use it. Now *you're* attacking, and *they're* on the defensive.

FIGURE 11-4: A full nelson.

REMEMBER

Here's the difference between a martial arts system and a real close-combat system: Martial arts teach "If your adversary does this, you do this." Close combat teaches "If you have this opening, take it."

Reacting to a Rear Naked Choke

A *rear naked choke* refers to a series of strangles that do not use the jacket (the Japanese martial arts uniform called a *gi*, pronounced "gee"). They consist of one combatant hooking their arm around the other's neck and using their forearm and bicep to constrict blood flow to and from the brain. It can also crush the windpipe. It's a common hold in mixed martial arts (MMA) and other submission fighting, and it can put someone to sleep in less than 10 seconds (and cause brain damage or death if not released after the subject passes out). If a skilled attacker applies the hold with sufficient force from behind, that alone can knock you out immediately.

In other words, if you're in a rear naked choke hold, especially if your attacker knows what they're doing, you're pretty much screwed. However, if you're still conscious, your attacker is probably doing something wrong, and you may have a chance if you act quickly and decisively. Here's what to do:

1. **Immediately pull down on the choking arm while delivering a side or rear hip butt and moving your chin into the crook of their arm (see Figure 11-5).**

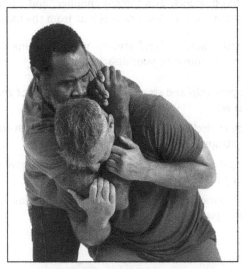

FIGURE 11-5: Create space to relieve pressure and launch a counterattack.

Tucking your chin and positioning it in the crook of their arm can relieve some pressure, protect your windpipe, buy a little time, and create space.

2. **Stomp the tops of your attacker's feet to crush their instep as you deliver rear edge-of-hand strikes to your attacker's groin.**

Your goal is to remain conscious while creating space so you can launch a counterattack and get free of the choke hold.

WARNING

If you're training choke holds with a partner, do so carefully and progressively. You're training only to feel the position and a little discomfort and to practice maintaining your balance and composure. The main point is to trigger yourself to attack them as fast and as hard as possible — follow up with a training dummy for the attacking part.

Freeing Yourself from a Headlock

A *headlock* is a common wrestling hold that involves pinning the head of the adversary between your arm and your body. Many martial arts teach a variety of fancy headlock defense maneuvers, none of which is very effective. In the real world, your attacker will take the headlock in a violent manner, and there's a good chance you may be knocked unconscious from the initial attack.

If you're still conscious and still on your feet, this is the most effective way to convince your attacker to let go:

1. **Tuck your chin and step out toward the front of your attacker.**

2. **As you're circling in front, hack their thighs with edge-of-hand strikes.**

   Striking the thigh muscles tends to open the legs, giving you a clearer path to the groin.

3. **Deliver a modified web-of-hand blow to the groin or testicles (see Figure 11-6).**

FIGURE 11-6: Deliver a modified web-of-hand strike to the groin.

With a modified web-of-hand, you snap your hand open, thumb up, and deliver the strike in an upward motion, making contact with the index-finger side of your hand. If your attacker has testicles, grab hold of them and squeeze with all your might (see the next section for details about grabbing the testicles).

If you have a weapon, now would be a good time to use it.

4. **Continue striking to loosen the hold and create the space needed to deliver more brutal blows.**

Another option, especially if you can't seem to get in front of your attacker, and you're tall enough and strong enough, is to strike the thigh muscles and groin from behind the attacker while reaching up, hooking the attacker's face or neck, and pulling it back (see Figure 11-7).

FIGURE 11-7: Reach up and hook the attacker's face.

Carpe Testiculos: Seize the Testicles

Many of the maneuvers I recommend for extricating yourself from a hold involve attacking the testicles — smashing them with an upward knee or an open-hand strike or seizing them (grabbing and squeezing them). Believe it or not, some methods of seizing the testicles are more effective than others. Here's how to do it properly:

1. Snap your hand open, thumb up, and insert it between the attacker's thighs.

2. Drive your hand straight up into the attacker's groin so your thumb catches on the front of the target's pelvis and the index-finger edge of your hand smashes into the testicles.

3. Turn your hand so the testicles are in your palm.

4. *Squeeze, twist, yank!* Clamp down with your thumb and rip with the fingers. Don't let go.

REMEMBER

The big mistake many people make is that they try to grab the testicles right away. That never works. Your attacker won't just spread their legs and invite you in. You need to use your hand as a blade to force access and then turn it palm up.

Even when you have the situation well in hand, the fight's not over. As you squeeze and yank and twist with one hand, continue your forward drive, kneeing, stomping, and striking your attacker. The fight isn't over until your attacker is incapable of harming you or you've retreated to a place of safety.

IT'S NOT OVER TILL IT'S OVER

A few years back, a visiting soccer player from Italy was accosted by a mugger on the New York subway. Their encounter started with a pushing match. The soccer player was in good shape, so when he hit the mugger, the guy went down. The soccer player figured, "Okay, end of fight."

The guy on the ground had other ideas. He pulled out a .38 snub nose and pumped five bullets into the soccer player's chest, killing him.

Moral of the story: Don't stop until you're sure that your attacker no longer has the means to do you harm.

Reacting to Single-Hand Grabs

After running the gauntlet of two-hand grabs, bear hugs, full nelsons, choke holds, and headlocks, breaking free of a single-hand grab is a stroll in the park. After all, you still have one or both hands free to attack your attacker.

You can defend against a single-hand attack by just chopping with an edge-of-hand. When they grab your wrist, you can drop-step in with a short edge-of-hand and continue your forward drive to pummel the attacker into the ground. If you just want the person to release you, and you don't want to knee them to the groin or deliver a chin-jab uppercut, you can simply chop the forearm of the hand that has hold of you. Even if they grab your throat, you can just chop them. If they go for your gun, hack that arm. It doesn't look like much, but it hurts like hell. Snap your edge-of-hand through a training partner's forearm and see how fast that hand comes off you.

That's only one technique against all those possible attacks, but it's simple and effective. They reach, you hack. In the following sections, I provide some additional guidance on how to respond to more specific single-hand grabs.

WARNING

You never know how someone will react when you hack their forearm. Be prepared to launch an all-out assault. Maybe you'll get lucky, and your attacker will back off at the first hack, but maybe they won't. Maybe they'll feel the need to prove something. Maybe they'll snap. Don't assume that a single strike is the end of it. It could be just the beginning.

Breaking free of a single wrist grab from the front

As much time as self-defense instructors spend on defending against a single wrist grab, you'd think there was a wrist-grabbing epidemic. In fact, over the course of my ten-plus years as a bodyguard and involved in safety and security, I never witnessed or even heard of anyone grabbing another person's wrist in a fight. Regardless, the wrist-grab defense is the first defense everyone teaches, so I'm here to tell you what to do:

>> Suppose your drunk significant other grabs you by the wrist in anger, and you don't want to hurt them — you just want

them to let go. Rotate your hand over their wrist while stepping back to break their grip.

Don't do this with a stranger who grabs you because now they have two hands to attack you and they know you've had some training, so if they persist, they're better equipped to succeed. With a stranger or someone you have no reason to trust, attack immediately and ferociously.

>> If someone grabs your wrist with one hand, attack.

>> If someone grabs your wrist with two hands, attack.

>> If someone reaches across your body and grabs the opposite wrist, attack.

Notice the pattern here? What your attacker does is of little consequence. As soon as they put a hand on you or make a threatening move, attack, and keep attacking until you're safe. And if you have a weapon, use it at the earliest opportunity.

Reacting to a single-arm or collar grab

When an attacker grabs your arm, shoulder, or collar with one hand, they're usually planning to punch or stab you with their other hand. Time to attack:

1. **Drop-step, pull down, and pin the forearm of the hand that's grabbing you; using your other hand, deliver a chin jab or chin-jab uppercut (see Figure 11-8).**

   Be sure to tuck your chin and step to the side to take your groin and centerline out of the line of fire.

   Another option is to deliver the initial chin jab to their striking shoulder (punch stop). This stops the attacker from throwing a punch with their other hand. Follow immediately with a chin jab or chin-jab uppercut.

2. **Follow up with another chin jab and edge-of-hand.**

3. **Continue driving forward, stomping, kneeing, and striking your attacker.**

   If you have a weapon, use it at the earliest opportunity.

But seriously, if you just immediately counterattacked with a barrage of strikes, you probably wouldn't need to pin or trap anything.

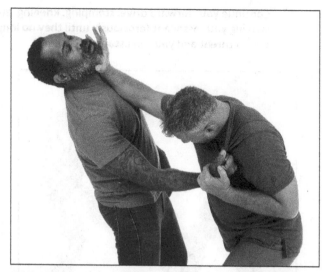

FIGURE 11-8: Pin the grabbing arm and deliver a chin jab with your other hand.

WARNING

Never go to the ground on purpose. Stay on your feet. If you take your attacker to the ground, their friend will kick the living daylights out of you when you're down there. Or you'll end up on broken glass, gravel, a broken brick, or a tree stump. Keep the variables to a minimum. Stay on your feet and continue your forward drive as you pummel your attacker. If they go to the ground, you can stomp and kick them.

Making an attacker let go of your hair

If you have hair long enough to grab and your attacker does so, take the following steps:

1. Grab the arm of the hand in your hair with both your hands, tuck your chin, bend at your waist, and keep your elbows high and pointed toward your attacker (see Figure 11-9).

If they try to punch you in the head, they're going to break their hand on your skull or one of your elbows.

2. **Drive forward, keeping hold of their arm, kicking and stomping their lower legs until they open up and you have some space to do more damage.**

If you have a weapon, now's the time to use it.

3. Continue your forward drive, stomping, kneeing, and striking your assailant ferociously until they no longer pose a threat and you can escape safely.

FIGURE 11-9: Grab hold of the arm of the hand holding your hair and use your feet to counterattack.

IN THIS CHAPTER

» **Avoiding ground-fighting situations**

» **Falling to the ground without getting hurt**

» **Extracting a pound of flesh (or at least a couple ounces)**

» **Driving your attacker into the ground**

» **Getting back on your feet**

Chapter **12**
Down-and-Dirty Ground Fighting

n a street fight, you don't want to be on the ground. But stuff happens.

Don't get me wrong — I love to *grapple* (wrestle). I've done it competitively for the better part of my life. I've wrestled since the age of 7. I wrestled for Lehigh University. I was even inducted into my high school's hall of fame for wrestling. I've studied Brazilian Jiu-Jitsu. I have a second-degree black belt in judo and competed in judo internationally until the age of 39. But I would *never* grapple in the street. And I strongly recommend that you swear it off, too.

Ground fighting is not grappling; it's close-combat survival. When a fight goes to the ground it becomes more complicated, dangerous, vicious, and ugly. Size, strength, skill, and fitness become huge factors. The reality of the terrain and the possibility of your attacker using a weapon, or their friends joining the fray, loom large as you fight for your life.

MOST FIGHTS GO TO THE GROUND . . . *REALLY?!*

When the Gracie family and Brazilian Jiu-Jitsu came on the martial arts scene in the late 1980s, a statistic started circulating that 90 percent of all street fights go to the ground. This statistic was attributed to a study from the Los Angeles Police Department. The truth is, no such study was ever conducted.

Most martial arts statistics cited by instructors are largely made up to support what they're teaching or promoting. I suspect that the study claiming that a huge percentage of fights go to the ground was drummed up to promote Brazilian Jiu-Jitsu.

I'm sure that the debate over the veracity of this claim and others will continue, but one thing's certain: Nearly all fights start on your feet, and you should do everything possible to remain in that position for the duration of the fight.

In this chapter, I offer guidance on the close-combat survival skills you need. This knowledge along with considerable training and practice will increase your chances of surviving and gaining the upper hand.

TIP

Having one or more weapons and knowing how to use them improves your odds immensely and decreases the need to master more complicated tactics and techniques (see Chapter 7 for more about weapons). Unfortunately, your attacker having a weapon and knowing how to use it decreases your odds. Turn to Chapter 13 to find out how to defend against weapon attacks.

Descending the Ground-Fighting Ladder: From Bad to Awful

WARNING

Never go to the ground intentionally or use that tactic as a primary option for self-defense. If, despite your best efforts to stay on your feet, you find yourself on the ground, try to improve your position on the ground-fighting ladder (ranked from bad position to worst):

>> **Position 1:** You're on the ground with your attacker standing in front of you.

>> **Position 2:** You're on the ground with your attacker standing to one side of you.

>> **Position 3:** You're on top of your attacker with your legs straddling them.

>> **Position 4:** You're on top of your attacker with their legs wrapped around you.

>> **Position 5:** Your attacker is on top of you with your legs wrapped around them.

>> **Position 6:** Your attacker is on top of you with their legs straddling you.

If you're anywhere on that ladder, you need to fight to improve your position with the ultimate goal of getting back on your feet. If you're in position 6, fight for position 5 and climb the ladder as quickly as possible. You always want to be the person standing or the one on top. When you're back on your feet, your goal is to escape or render your attacker incapable of harming you.

REMEMBER

The primary goal of ground fighting is to get off the ground. It's not to submit, pin, or knock out your attacker. Always seek to improve your position and escape.

WARNING

Avoid getting close to a threat. Assume that your attacker is armed, trained, and experienced. They can easily pull a knife from a pocket, boot, or around their neck. They know no rules, they don't care about what training you have, and they're not impressed by what you think you're going to do. They also probably have friends nearby who are prepared to beat, stab, club, or shoot you. Your best chance is to follow this street-fighting self-defense formula:

1. Attack the closest target of opportunity with the closest available weapon (your body if no other weapon is available).

2. Continue to attack ruthlessly and viciously until you can safely exit the scene.

Falling Safely

When you end up on the ground during a fight, it's usually because you tripped and fell, lost your balance, or were pushed, shoved, or thrown down. Regardless of the cause, you want to fall in a way that results in as little physical pain and injury as possible.

The general idea is to land on the most cushioned part of your body possible (butt and hips), protect your most vulnerable body parts (especially your skull, spine, elbows, and knees), and roll (to transfer the energy of the fall into motion). In the following sections, I go into more detail about proper falling techniques.

WARNING

Forget what you learned in martial arts class about breaking your fall by *slapping out* (slapping the mat). That works in the gym because it transfers the energy to the mat, but if you slap out on concrete, asphalt, gravel, or a hard floor, you're going to be in a world of hurt; you may even break a bone or two.

TIP

Practice, practice, practice. Proper falling techniques need to be programmed into your muscle memory. Practice progressively from a kneeling position to a low squat to a half-squat and finally to standing position, starting with softer surfaces and working up to harder ones as you're physically able to do so safely. Perfection is not required.

Falling backward

When falling to your back from the standing position, squat to get as close to the ground as possible and transfer as much force as possible to your butt and your back (the side of your back, not your spine). Tuck your chin, hunch your shoulders, and just drop and roll on the side of your butt and the side of your back (see Figure 12-1).

REMEMBER

This technique ensures a *safer* landing, not a *safe* landing. In a street fight, you could be falling on debris — rocks, broken bricks, glass, curbing, tree branches . . . objects that can do more damage to you than your attacker can. And the ground never misses. I tell you this only to stress the importance of doing everything possible to stay on your feet and maintain your balance.

FIGURE 12-1: Squat, tuck, hunch, and roll.

Falling forward

Whether you trip and fall forward or you're shoved from behind, you need to be able to fall forward in a way that minimizes pain and injury. Here are three techniques:

>> **Shoulder roll:** Tuck your chin and roll your shoulder in the direction of the fall, making first contact with the back of your shoulder (upper back), letting your body roll to a stop, and letting the bottoms of your feet slap on the ground to transfer the energy.

You probably won't be able to execute the shoulder roll if you're hit really hard from behind.

>> **Forward fall:** Turn your head to the side (to protect your face), keep your elbows at your sides with hands spread open and palms facing out, land thighs first, and roll forward until your forearms come into contact with the ground. Finish on your toes, so only your toes, thighs, and forearms are in contact with the ground (see Figure 12-2).

Don't land on your elbows, and never straighten your arms out in front of you to break your fall.

FIGURE 12-2: The forward fall.

> **» Forward roll (for future action heroes only):** With your
> right knee up and your left knee on the ground, tuck your
> chin and look at your left knee. Place your right hand, palm
> up, outside your left knee. Hunch your shoulders, round out
> your back, and roll forward, making first contact with your
> right shoulder. Continue to roll and then slam the bottom of
> your boots into the ground (that's your slap out). Reverse the
> instructions and practice rolling in the other direction.
>
> When you're comfortable practicing the forward roll from a
> half-kneeling position in both directions, you can progress to
> a standing position with one leg forward and one leg back.
> Practice from both sides — rolling left and rolling right.

Gouging, Ripping, and Biting

Gouging, ripping, and biting would get you immediately disquali-
fied from any combat sporting event, and for good reason — they
can cause severe and permanent injury. They can also be executed
with a modicum of strength and effort. These reasons make them
an excellent choice for self-defense. When you're up close and
personal with your attacker, chomping on their nose, shoving a
finger or a sharp object in their eye, or ripping off one of their ears
can stop their momentum and create space, improving your position and your ability to escape or escalate your attack.

In this section, I sing the praises of these gruesome self-defense
maneuvers while providing specific guidance on how to execute
them most effectively.

Respectable human beings like you and me don't enjoy inflicting pain or causing permanent physical injury to another being, but when our lives or those of our loved ones are threatened by those who have no conscience, we may need to overcome our reservations and act like savages to survive.

Gouging the eyes or mouth

Gouging is a scooping or digging action. In a street fight, you can use your thumbs or fingers to gouge the eyes or hook the mouth or nose and rip outward. Here are your options:

>> **Finger-gouge the eyes:** Drive your palm or the heel of your hand into your attacker's face and position it so that their nose is pressed against the webbing between your fingers. Dig your fingers into the target's eyes while pushing back their head. If you can't secure their head with your other hand, this may only distract them as they move their eyes to safety.

>> **Thumb-gouge the eyes:** Dig your thumbs into the inner corners of your attacker's eyes, while gripping your fingers behind their ears. Scoop from the inside toward the outside of the skull, driving your thumbs as far back into the eye sockets as you can. For added impact, shake or slam their head against the ground or a wall.

Even in low light, you can smash your hand into your attacker's face and then drive your thumb into an eye. You may not be able to take the eye, but that's not the goal; all you need is to have them react, move their head, and create some space for you to operate.

>> **Thumb-gouge the mouth (fishhook):** Insert your thumb inside your attacker's mouth between their teeth and cheek, hook your fingers behind their ear, and drive the corner of their mouth toward their ear (see Figure 12-3).

In the heat of battle, you can also "gouge" with your chin, driving it into your attacker's eye socket, nose, or temple.

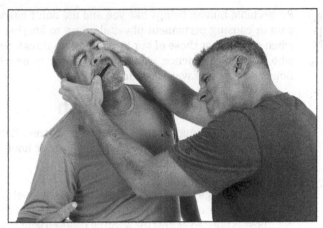

FIGURE 12-3: The fishhook is a classic.

Let 'er rip

Ripping is a rendition of "tearing your attacker limb from limb."
Well, not quite, but you could tear some flesh and break or dislocate some smaller bones. Target the fingers or ears:

>> **Ripping fingers:** Whenever you can get two hands on one of your attacker's hands, you have an opportunity to rip their fingers. Simply grab one or two fingers in each hand as tight as you can, and yank them in opposite directions (see Figure 12-4).

  Blood and sweat can make your attacker's fingers slippery, but if you can maintain your grip and disable a hand, you've made them that much less effective.

>> **Ripping ears:** Drive your thumb inside your attacker's ear, hook your fingers around the outside of the ear, squeeze tight, and jerk. That hurts just writing about it.

Taking a bite out of crime

Biting is vicious and often unexpected, which is why it's so effective. You just need to be careful not to damage your pearly whites. To protect your teeth, use your hands to try to secure the area you want to bite before chomping down on it. However, if your attacker has your arms and legs pinned, you may have no choice but to headbutt and bite unsecured targets.

FIGURE 12-4: Grip and rip.

TIP

The most vulnerable targets are the fingers, ears, neck, throat, and face, but any flesh that comes near your mouth is fair game. The result will be surprise, severe pain, severed veins or arteries, potential loss of blood and flesh, and maybe even breaks or dislocations of small bones.

Fighting from the Ground When Your Attacker Is Standing

When you're on the ground and your attacker is standing, you want to get back on your feet as soon as possible. However, moving from a prone to a standing position at the wrong time can prove fatal. As you're trying to get up, you reach a point at which you're completely off-balance and unprotected — when your attacker or one of their buddies can step forward and penalty-kick your head into next week.

You know *what* you need to do:

1. **Stop the momentum of their attack.**
2. **Create space.**
3. **Improve your position on the ground-fighting ladder.**

In this section, I explain *how*.

Getting off the ground

When to get off the ground is a decision you need to make based on conditions on the ground. All I can tell you is to stand up as soon as it's safe to do so. If you're on your back, take the following steps:

1. Sit up and bring your knees in.

2. Put one hand and your opposite foot on the ground.

3. Lift yourself up slightly with the hand and foot on the ground and bring your other leg underneath and put that knee on the ground.

4. Stand up.

If you're face down, take the following steps to stand up:

1. Crawl your hands back toward your hips, bringing your knees up under your body.

2. Stand up.

Fighting an attacker who's standing in front of you

You're on the ground and some maniac is about to stomp you into the earth or drop down on top of you and pound you into dust. Fight from that position until you can get back on your feet safely. As soon as you land on the ground, assume the following *ground-fighting position* (see Figure 12-5):

1. Turn a little bit on your side to protect your groin and improve your ability to strike with your feet.

2. Tuck your chin.

3. Bring your feet directly toward your assailant.

   You always want your legs pointing in the direction of your attacker because your legs:

   - Are the strongest part of your body

   - Create distance between you and your attacker

   - Keep your attacker off your center of gravity and eliminate their ability to impose their size on you

   - Distance and protect your vital target areas

4. **Hold your bottom leg back a little and your top leg forward a little.**

You'll use your top leg to "jab" and your bottom leg to deliver a more powerful blow.

5. **Raise your hands to protect your head and flanks.**

FIGURE 12-5: The ground-fighting position versus a standing attacker.

From this position, foot-box your attacker until you can stand up safely. Use your top leg to stop your attacker's forward advance and to jab, kicking at the knee, shin, or groin. Use your lower leg as a piston to slam your opponent — this is the power "punch" for causing serious damage. Jab with your top foot and drive with your bottom foot, thrusting your legs like two pistons back and forth.

WARNING

Never kick with both legs at the same time. Always keep one leg back so if they get past your kick, you have a chance to push them off with your non-kicking leg.

Maintaining an advantageous position

To maintain the ground-fighting position as you're foot boxing, use the following maneuvers:

>> **The slight turn:** Keep your torso at a slight angle to the ground, not flat on your back. If you're flat on your back and you start to kick, you leave your groin unprotected.

>> **The rotation:** If they try to circle you, push off the ground with the forearm nearest the ground to keep your feet pointing in the direction of your attacker.

>> **The roll:** When your attacker moves from one side to the other, roll over to your opposite side to keep your feet pointing in their direction. Keep your lead (top) arm up to protect your head.

>> **The crab:** Place your feet and hands, palms down, on the ground, and raise your body off the ground to move in any direction as you transition to a standing position.

REMEMBER

Don't fight from the crab position. It's merely a safer position for standing up. If you have the space to stand, stand. If your attacker continues to press, quickly return to the ground-fighting position to foot-box until another opportunity to stand presents itself.

>> **The stand:** From the crab position, tuck one leg under yourself and stand. If your attacker or their friends rush you, drop back down into the ground-fighting position.

Tossing your attacker

If your attacker rushes you and dodges your foot jab, drive your power foot into their midsection, grab their arms, and help them sail over you onto their face or back (see Figure 12-6). You have a poor chance of executing this move, especially if your attacker is large. Practice with a partner to improve your chances.

Taking down your attacker

If your attacker is weak and tired, you can try taking them down to the ground with the hook takedown. Hook their ankle with your bottom leg while smashing their knee with your top leg to knock them down or off-balance (see Figure 12-7). Then stand up *immediately* and either escape or attack.

FIGURE 12-6: Toss your attacker.

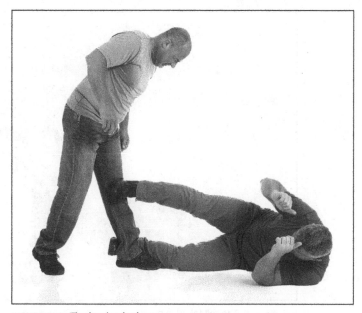

FIGURE 12-7: The hook takedown.

Don't try to take down an attacker who's fresh. If you do, you're likely to end up in a worse ground-fighting position.

Fighting an attacker who's standing to your side

If the attacker gets past your legs and attacks you from the side, roll up into the fetal position — chin tucked, knees up to protect your groin and stomach, arms up around your head. Try to absorb any kick or stomp (they're coming) as you look for an opportunity to execute one of the following takedown maneuvers: the roll takedown or the hook and roll.

Roll takedown

The roll takedown can be very effective when your attacker is one or two steps away. As they move in to kick you, cover your head and roll hard into the kick to catch the leg in your armpit (below the knee), pin the ankle inside your armpit, and continue to roll, bringing your attacker to the ground (see Figure 12-8).

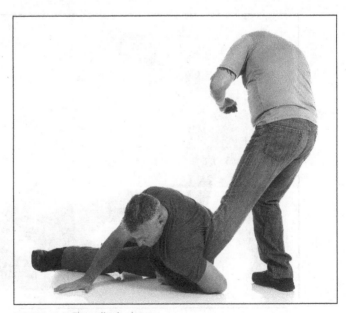

FIGURE 12-8: The roll takedown.

After they hit the ground, continue rolling and smash your elbow (opposite arm), an edge-of-hand blow, or a hammer fist into their groin and lower body. Roll back out and get off the ground . . . quick! Then escape or continue to attack.

Hook and roll

The hook and roll can be effective when the attacker steps in to stomp you. They're too close to roll into, so you just wrap an arm around the nearest leg and roll in the direction they're moving, forcing them to trip over you (see Figure 12-9).

FIGURE 12-9: The hook and roll.

REMEMBER

Really drive your arms and toque your body. If you lie there without any momentum, they'll just fall on you or continue to kick and stomp you. You need to move them to take them down.

As soon as they hit the ground, put your feet between you and them, kick, and scramble to get to your feet. If you're unable to stand, swivel on your hip to point your legs at them. Drive a heel into their heart or ribs, or kick their jaw. After you've injured them severely, get back on your feet and *attack!*

ADAPTING COMBAT SPORTS FOR SELF-DEFENSE

Many self-defense systems use adaptations of combat sports like mixed martial arts (MMA), judo, karate, or wrestling. Adapting these systems for self-defense has two important limitations:

- They're based on rules designed to prevent injury.
- They require a working knowledge of a fundamental skill set.

Street fights have no rules or referees, and you don't need to know a lot of complicated moves. All you need to do is attack more viciously and relentlessly than your attacker. And if you have a weapon and your attacker doesn't . . . well, too bad for them. Self-defense isn't a game. It isn't a sport. It's survival.

Fighting an Attacker When You're Both on the Ground

When you and your attacker are both on the ground, either you're on top or they are. You need to know how to fight from either position.

Fighting from the top down

When you're on top and your assailant is on the ground, you're in one of the following three positions:

>> **Top mount:** You're on top with your legs straddling your attacker (see Figure 12-10).

>> **Guard:** You're on top with your attacker's legs around you in one of the following three positions:

- **Closed guard:** Their legs are wrapped around your waist with their feet hooked behind you (see Figure 12-11).

- **Open guard:** Their legs are wrapped around your waist with their feet unhooked.

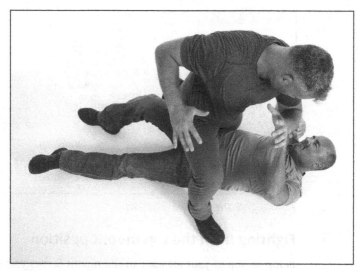

FIGURE 12-10: Top mount.

FIGURE 12-11: The closed guard.

- **Half-guard:** One of their legs is wrapped around your waist while the other is pinned under yours. You both have the same hold on one another but you're on top.

>> **Modified scarf hold:** You're sitting alongside your attacker with one arm wrapped around the back of their neck and your other arm gripping their tricep (see Figure 12-12).

FIGURE 12-12: The modified scarf hold.

Fighting from the top-mount position

Being on top of your attacker in the mount leaves you vulnerable to another attacker, but as far as ground positions go, top mount provides you the following advantages:

>> **Mobility,** which makes it easier to stand up. Keep one knee up and one knee down to improve your mobility and enable you to quickly pin an arm.

>> **Gravity,** enabling you to put your full body weight behind your strikes.

>> **The ground,** which multiplies the force of your attack.

When you're in the top-mount position, you can do the following:

>> **Get up.** When you can stand up safely, push off your attacker, preferably their chest, face, or throat, not the ground. If you can, drop a knee or stomp their arm on your way up.

>> **Pin one or both arms.** Pin one or both of your attacker's arms to the ground using your knees or feet.

>> **Ground and pound.** Hack your attacker's neck and collarbone with edge-of-hand strikes, smash their face with the heel of your hand, drive your fingers into their eyes, drive your thumbs into their throat, and smash with your elbow. Eye-gouge while slamming their head into the ground.

Don't throw closed-fist punches. If you miss and strike the ground, especially a hard surface like concrete or asphalt, you can destroy your hand.

>> **Do a chest smear and chest bounce.** If your attacker wraps their arms around you, place your hands, palms down, against the ground to brace yourself; drop your chest into their face; and smear their face with your chest while smashing their skull into the ground. When they relax their grip, push off using your knee or foot and resume your ground and pound. Deliver chin jabs to their face (nose and eye sockets), fishhook their mouth, rip their ears, smash their nose, crush their windpipe. Be as nasty as you can be, and then multiply it by ten.

>> **Hack their arms.** If your attacker has a free arm to strike or maul you, hack into their bicep, forearm, or collarbone. If they hold you tightly, keep striking. Grab one of their fingers and break it.

>> **Use a reverse Japanese strangle hold.** If you're being overpowered and there's nothing else you can do, use a reverse Japanese strangle hold (see Figure 12-13). Drive one arm behind their head or neck, place that hand on the bicep of the opposite arm, and place your opposite hand on the attacker's forehead and shove their head back. Use your shoulder to lock their head against your grip. Try to move their chin so their mouth isn't in a position to bite you. Stabilize your top position with your feet and knees. This hold is great for immobilizing an attacker and protecting yourself while you catch your breath.

FIGURE 12-13: Reverse Japanese strangle with a grapevine.

From this hold, you can work your fingers into one of your attacker's eyes or a cheek and gouge, or grind your chin into their temple, eye, or nose. As your attacker grows weak and tired, you can release your grip and resume your ground and pound.

>> **Grapevine:** If you're in the top mount or bottom guard positions, wrap your legs under your attacker's thighs, hook your feet over their shins, and spread their legs. The sheer pain will drain your assailant's energy as you take a breather. Combine the grapevine with the chest bounce/smear or the reverse Japanese strangle hold (refer to Figure 12-13).

Fighting from the top when you're in their guard

When you're in your attacker's *closed guard* (your attacker's legs are wrapped around your waist and their feet are hooked together behind your back), they can use their legs to push you to the side or back. In the closed guard, they can squeeze your organs and restrict your breathing. If their legs are squeezing you and pushing you back, smash or punch their groin and drive your elbows into their thigh muscles to open their legs. Use your elbows to attack their thighs, knees, shins, and ankles and loosen their leg grip. Lean back to get away from their hands and put stress on their hold. Use your free hand to deliver edge-of-hand strikes into their pubic bone and bladder. Hack and elbow-smash over and over again.

Grab your attacker's belt or the waistline of their clothing for added support and leverage and to prevent them from reaching your head.

As soon as possible, stand up to escape and then continue your assault from a standing position or, as their legs open, crawl up into the top mount to improve your position, elbow-smashing their *solar plexus* (just below the sternum) and kneeing their groin on the way up. Keep hacking, smashing, kneeing, gouging . . . you know the drill.

If you stand up when you're in their closed guard and they come up with you, immediately *slam* them to the ground. As you drop, sprawl your legs back to avoid smashing your knees on the ground, and put all your body weight on them.

Fighting from the modified scarf hold

The modified scarf hold is the combat adaptation of the sport version (judo and wrestling) with the following important differences:

1. **When you move, use the hand of your arm that's behind your attacker's neck to grab the muscle cord beneath your knee to lock in the hold.**

2. **Lean on their head, driving your shoulder into the side of their head or under their chin.**

3. **Use the arm that's securing their arm to jerk their arm.**

   Don't apply steady pressure on their arm; grab the wrist and use "jerk strength," quickly pulling the arm toward you and then snapping it in the other direction.

4. **Bring your *base leg* (the same leg you grabbed to lock in the hold) over that arm (see Figure 12-14).**

   Figure-four their arm with your legs to lock it in.

FIGURE 12-14: Dislocating your attacker's shoulder.

5. **Grab their head with both hands and rip it up while pushing down with your base leg, destroying their shoulder and elbow.**

6. **Continue to hold their head while you drive your free elbow into their groin.**

   Drive heel-hand blows to their face. Strike their temple and jaw with edge-of-hands. Thumb-gouge their eyes.

If they start to hit you with a free hand, distract and attack: Gouge an eye, continue to hack away, or just lift their head up and twist it. Smash their testicles with your arm that was holding their tricep, slam the heel of your hand into their face. It's a fight — don't let up.

Battling from the bottom up

When you're on the bottom and your assailant is on top of you, you're at a very real disadvantage. Your attacker can do everything to you that I told you to do to them in the earlier section "Fighting from the top down." Skip back to that section if you need to review the specific positions you could be in — mount, guard, or modified scarf hold — except that now you're on the bottom.

In the following sections, I offer guidance on how to fight from these disadvantageous positions.

In a way, fighting from the bottom is no different from fighting from the top. You attack your attacker ruthlessly and relentlessly.

Fighting from under the mount

When your attacker mounts you from the top, they're looking to pin both your arms, ground and pound, chest smash and smear, and even grapevine you. In addition to attacking them with all means possible (including with a weapon if you have one), here are some maneuvers that can help you escape your current predicament:

>> **Ground cover:** Tuck your chin and cover your face with your arm. Grab your opposite shoulder and tuck your thumb into the collar of your shirt or jacket. Reach your other arm to the opposite shoulder, and grab it from behind to protect your neck. You're basically building a shield with your elbows and skull.

You can't stay in ground cover forever. Escaping the mount is urgent.

>> **Rock and roll:** Twist your body from side to side to make your head group a moving target and create opportunities for your attacker to smash their hands on your elbows, your skull, or the ground.

>> **Crossing edge-of-hands:** As soon as you feel you can, deliver edge-of-hand strikes in a crossing pattern — left, right, left, right — aiming for their head but striking any part of their body you can reach. The goal is to get them to stop hitting you and possibly cause them pain and injury. The crossing blows maintain your rocking-and-rolling motion so you remain a moving target.

>> **Hip buck:** Extend your legs and then drive them up forcefully into your attacker's back, slam your heels into the ground close to your butt, and explode upward with your hips, pushing off your heels, to buck your attacker off you. Even if it doesn't throw them off, it disrupts their balance, moves their weight off your center, and creates some space.

WARNING

Don't let your attacker stand up. Continue striking your attacker to keep them off-balance. You may need to return to cover and deliver crossing edge-of-hands and hip bucking until you have an opening or create an opportunity to get back on your feet safely.

>> **Rest:** Wrap your loving arms around your attacker's waist and pull them on top of you. As you catch your breath, you can still try to bite or seize their testicles, drive a knee into their groin, chin-gouge an eye, or get them in a reverse Japanese strangle hold (see the earlier section, "Fighting from the top-mount position").

>> **Escape:** To escape the bottom mount, use one of the following techniques:

- **Roll 'em:** Hip-buck and knee them in the groin repeatedly. Gouge their eye, nose, and cheek, inflicting as much pain and injury as possible. Hook one leg to the outside of one of your attacker's legs to pin it; then push off the ground with your opposite leg to roll them over in the direction of their trapped leg. Having your attacker in a Japanese strangle hold makes this move easier because you can clamp down on them and move them in the direction of your roll.

REMEMBER

  If your attacker is much heavier than you, rolling them may not be an option. Your only option is to shrimp out (see the next bullet).

- **Shrimp out:** Using your hands, keep your legs straight and scoot your body out from under your attacker, pushing off their hips and upper body. As soon as you're far enough out, piston-kick them off you. Assume the ground-fighting stance, and foot-box them until you have a chance to stand up safely.

Fighting from your guard

WARNING

First things first: *Never* spread your legs to invite your attacker into your guard the way mixed martial arts (MMA) and Brazilian Jiu-Jitsu fighters often do. By doing so, you leave your groin wide open and give up your ability to use your powerful legs to attack. Instead, assume the ground-fighting position — shift your hips to the side (so you're on one hip), place one hand over your groin, keep your legs together, and piston-kick the snot out of them.

If they breach your guard, grab your groin with your hand to protect it and use your free hand to *attack!* Get them to cover up. Don't focus on squeezing them in your closed guard. Drive your groin deep into your attacker's belly to keep it outside their reach and attack their head group. Use the same rock-and-roll and crossing edge-of-hands as you did when your attacker had you in their top mount. Keep bashing your assailant. Bite, gouge their eyes, rip their ears or nose, grab their hair or head, and smash their face into your forehead repeatedly. Attack their head, face, neck, and throat with short, sharp, concussive blows. If you have the chance, raise yourself forcefully, grab their neck and head, and get them in a reverse Japanese strangle hold or wrap your hands around their throat and drive your thumbs deep into their jugular notch.

TIP

To really squeeze them in your closed guard, concentrate on extending your legs and pushing your feet away from you. Your legs should be under their rib cage and above their hips to crush their organs.

Use your legs to kick and push them off you or at least create some space to deliver a more brutal attack. At the earliest opportunity, get back on your feet and either escape or continue your assault. Assume they have a weapon and will use it as soon as they're able. Getting free is urgent.

Attacking from the modified scarf hold

When you're on the wrong end of a modified scarf hold, your attacker has your head locked, with one free arm to pummel your head and a free leg to dislocate your shoulder. Here's what you need to do to extricate yourself from this very dangerous predicament:

1. Tuck your chin, bring your hands together in a wrestler's grip (hands crossed, palms together), and cover your face and throat.

2. Drive your elbow nearest your attacker into their ear, their neck, or the side of their head.

3. Reach your outside arm over to bring your hand to their face and gouge or rip their eyes, nose, mouth, cheeks, and ears, as you shove their head back.

4. As you drive their head back, hook it with your outside leg and take it clean off (see Figure 12-15).

   Just rip it. This will break the hold and allow you to put your legs between you and them and get back on your feet.

FIGURE 12-15: Escaping from the scarf hold.

4

Neutralizing Weapon Attacks

Chapter **13**

Clearing the Weapon and Attacking the Attacker

I n a street fight, the person with the better weapon generally wins — assuming, of course, they know how to use it and don't hesitate to do so. If you're unarmed facing an armed assailant, you're at a distinct disadvantage. To improve your odds, you need to be smarter, more determined, and more vicious than they are.

In this chapter, I present techniques for responding to weapon attacks effectively. The overall approach is no different from how you would respond to an unarmed attacker — strike first and attack ferociously and unrelentingly, striking with edge-of-hands and hammer fists, kneeing, stomping, gouging, biting, ripping, headbutting, and so on. Slight variations on that theme can be applied specifically to knife, club, and handgun attacks. In this chapter, I reveal those techniques. But first, I offer some general insights and recommendations.

Weapon Attack Basics

Before I provide detailed guidance on how to defend yourself against specific classes of weapons in specific situations, in this section I share some words of wisdom that apply to all weapon attacks regardless of the weapon and how you're being threatened or attacked with it.

TIP

A little 4-ounce can of pepper spray can quickly end a knife, club, or gun attack before it starts. As soon as you're approached, *juice 'em*, and hightail it out of there. (See Chapter 7 for more about pepper spray.)

PLAYING THE ODDS

Every year, law enforcement agencies submit reports on the types of weapons used to commit violent crime. I've been studying these for years, and the numbers remain fairly consistent:

- **Unarmed:** 31 percent
- **Impact weapon:** 28 percent
- **Firearm:** 27 percent
- **Edged weapon:** 14 percent

Here are the statistics for homicides:

- **Handgun:** 45.7 percent
- **Unknown firearm:** 23.9 percent
- **Impact weapon:** 11.4 percent
- **Edged weapon:** 10.6 percent
- **Unarmed:** 4.3 percent
- **Rifle:** 2.6 percent
- **Shotgun:** 1.4 percent

Based on this data, you can draw the following conclusions:

- You're most likely to get attacked by someone without a weapon or a handgun.

- You're more likely to be killed by a handgun than any other weapon.

- You're more likely be beaten to death than killed by an AR15 or any other type of rifle.

Use these stats to guide your training regimen. Prioritize your time training for unarmed assailants, and then adapt that training for attacks involving impact weapons, firearms, and edged weapons.

Putting it in perspective

First, the bad news: If you're unarmed facing an armed assailant, chances are good that you're going to be shot, bludgeoned, or stabbed. Now the good news: You'll probably survive and still be able to fight. You may not even notice it. (See the nearby sidebar about my friend Jeff.)

More good news: Any resistance you put up diminishes your attacker's accuracy and the amount of force they can put behind their attack. Shots are more likely to miss; instead of getting stabbed in the gut, you're more likely to suffer only a minor cut to the arm; instead of getting bashed in the head, you're more likely to suffer only a glancing blow to an arm, a leg, or your torso.

The point of all the good news is that, regardless of the weapon, and even in the event that you're injured, keep fighting. When you're training, don't stop when you're stuck with the tip of your partner's training knife or when your partner pulls the trigger of their training gun. This isn't a kids' game of "bang-bang, you're dead." When someone shoots you, clubs you, or stabs you, get furious and go ballistic — that's what you need to do when attacked, and it's what you should train for. Train to ignore injury and fight through it.

Attack the attacker

You can search the web for "gun defense" and find hundreds of videos showing how to disarm your assailant with some convoluted joint manipulation technique. Trouble is, these techniques require lots of practice, and when you're in a high-stress situation, you don't have the fine motor skills to even execute them. The more complicated the technique and the more stressful the situation, the less likely you'll be able to execute it. I recommend a simpler and more effective technique: *Attack the attacker!*

MY FRIEND JEFF

My friend Jeff was filling up his Jeep at a gas station in Atlanta, Georgia. It was 5 p.m. on a Tuesday. The station was packed when he was approached at the pump by two teens. One put a gun to his chest and demanded the keys to his Jeep.

Jeff had other plans. He grabbed the gun and pointed it away from him. When they were wrestling over the weapon, the kid pulled the trigger and a round went into Jeff's thigh. The teens fled.

Jeff didn't realize he had been shot until after the attack, when he felt a burning sensation in his thigh. He didn't even remember hearing the gun go off. Jeff drove himself to the hospital. Jeff is a tough SOB.

During an attack, you're likely to be so jacked up on adrenaline and focused on survival that you probably won't feel any injury you suffer . . . at least until the adrenaline starts to wear off.

If I put my SIG Sauer P365 9mm pistol on the ground with a round in the chamber, it could sit there for a thousand years and not harm a single soul. It poses a danger only when someone comes along, picks it up, and shoots somebody. Which brings me to my point: *A weapon is only as dangerous as the person holding it.*

The sooner you disable the attacker, the sooner you'll be safe. When facing an armed assailant, I have a very simple formula:

1. Clear the weapon.

Strike or grab the arm holding the weapon to move it off target. If you knock the weapon out of their hand, all the better, but what's most important is to take the weapon off target (you) as you proceed immediately to Step 2.

2. Attack the attacker.

Wail on your attacker using all the close-combat techniques presented in Part 2. If you have a weapon, now's the time to use it.

Distinguish dynamic attacks from static attacks

Weapon attacks can be categorized as dynamic or static:

>> **Dynamic:** A dynamic attack involves an attacker who's actively trying to use the weapon (for example, trying to stab you with a knife).

>> **Static:** With a static attack, the assailant is threatening you with a weapon to coerce you to do what they want — give them your money, rape you, kidnap you, give you information, whatever.

WARNING

No matter how convincing or reasonable they sound, never trust your attacker or go anywhere with them. The *only* reason they want you somewhere else is because they can't do what they really want to do to you here and now. This is where you must stand your ground and fight.

Responding to Dynamic-Impact and Edged-Weapon Attacks

Your attacker is coming at you prison-style with a club or a knife. They're not just threatening you; they're coming at you to beat or stab you. Respond to both types of attacks the same way — keep moving, look for an opening, and *attack!* The body mechanics of someone trying to hit you with a club are similar to those of someone trying to stab you.

Fleeing and dodging

Every martial artist practices the same weapon defense — they stand there, unarmed, preparing to take on a knife-wielding assailant. That's just nuts.

What's most important is that you move. Make yourself a moving target. Escape if you can, and if you can't escape, stay in motion, attacking as soon as you sense an opening. In the following sections, I explain how to move.

Run

If you're completely unarmed and someone comes at you with a knife, *run!* If you can't outrun them, try dodging around furniture, lampposts, cars — anything you can get between you and them. Use your environment to slow their momentum or trip them up. Grab something to use as a weapon or throw at them. As soon as they're off-balance and they can't set their feet to use their weapon, attack with a barrage of hacks, strikes, knees, and stomps.

REMEMBER

Stabbing someone effectively and repeatedly is difficult. You need to set your feet, wind up, and drive, and then if you do get the knife in, you need to pull it out. Not so easy. Now imagine doing that to someone who's dodging you, throwing stuff at you, or steamrolling you while beating the snot out of you . . . again, not so easy. Don't make it easy for your attacker — keep moving, keep attacking.

Move in all four directions

In retreat mode, you're moving away from your attacker. In attack mode, you're driving forward, into your attacker. During a dynamic club or knife attack against a single attacker, move in all four directions (stomping, not sliding your feet):

>> **Forward:** Drop-step with your lead foot; rear foot follows.

>> **Backward:** Step first with your rear foot; front foot follows.

>> **Left:** Step first with your left foot; right foot follows.

>> **Right:** Step first with your right foot; left foot follows.

Moving in these four directions (and in variations of these four) can put you in a better position to attack, especially in the case of a weapon assault. When an armed attacker is bearing down on you, you may need to step out of the way to avoid the first onslaught.

REMEMBER

Train to attack from a *dynamic* (moving) situation. Practice taking a step in each direction and immediately delivering your favorite combination — driving into your attacker and always taking ground to keep them off-balance.

Using a chair to your advantage: The lion tamer

One of the best improvised weapons is a chair. Hold the top and front edge of the chair and point the legs at your attacker as a lion tamer would do (see Figure 13-1). Hold the chair so the four legs form a diamond in front of you with the top leg pointed at your attacker's face, and keep jabbing it, driving it forward into them. The length of your arms, combined with that of the chair's legs, protect you from any forceful jab or serious harm.

FIGURE 13-1: Use a chair as a lion tamer would to jab your attacker.

Keep driving until your attacker trips and falls or grabs a leg of the chair. If they fall down, keep stomping and smashing or take the opportunity to flee. If they grab a leg of the chair, no problem — just keep jabbing and driving it into their face and body. Don't stop. Kick their legs, stomp their feet, and keep attacking.

Neutralizing a club attack

When an attacker comes at you with a night stick, blackjack, baseball bat, hammer, lead pipe, axe handle, or similar blunt instrument, they're going to use it to attack you in one or more of the following ways: swings, butt strokes, or crossbar smashes (see Chapter 7). These techniques cause the most serious injury when the club is at the desired point of impact — this is when the attacker's feet are set and the blow is about to land at its intended target. Think of hitting a baseball. Too soon or too late, it goes foul or you miss.

You have three ways to neutralize a club attack:

>> **Keep moving.** When your attacker is chasing you, they can't set their feet, strike accurately, or put much force behind the club. Escape, if possible. Don't try to block or grab the weapon. Keep moving, look for your opening, and escape or attack.

>> **Close the distance.** A club increases your attacker's reach and is most dangerous when they're swinging it, so if you can't escape and you need to attack, get inside the range of the weapon to unleash your own attack. You can get inside by kicking and throwing things at your attacker and then rushing them between swings, butt strokes, and crossbar thrusts.

>> **Attack when your attacker is winding up or after they've swung the club or tried to deliver a butt stroke or crossbar smash — when the club's kinetic energy is lowest.** Ignore the club. Your assault and forward drive will destroy their ability to use it effectively. In fact, the fact that they're holding a club will be to your advantage at this point because instead of attacking you, their hands will be clinging to the club, and they'll probably still be trying to use it.

WARNING

Don't attack a club-wielding assailant with only your hands unless you have no other option — when you can't evade or escape the attack, and you can't find a chair, garbage can, or other object that you can pick up and use to your advantage.

Countering a knife attack

When you're unarmed, the most effective approach to a knife attack is to escape. If that's not a possibility, respond the same as you would to a club attack:

>> Keep moving, using the environment to create distance and disrupt your attacker's momentum and balance.

>> Throw things at your attacker or in their path to distract or trip them.

>> When you see an opening, attack ruthlessly.

>> If you need to close the distance to attack, deliver front kicks to their lower legs and groin and move inside the range of the weapon or "behind the knife."

>> Drive forward, kneeing, stomping, and striking repeatedly with edge-of-hand and hammer-fist blows. Maintaining a brutal forward drive is critical for neutralizing the knife attack.

>> If the knife hand becomes available, pin it and keep attacking. Don't try to disarm them — it isn't necessary and will only distract you from your main goal of attacking the attacker.

WARNING

Don't try to "control the weapon" or "disarm the attacker" as many self-defense experts advise. Methods for doing so range from the ridiculous to the bizarre, and all are most likely to fail. First, in a stressful situation, you won't be able to execute any of the fancy moves they recommend. Second, as you're wrestling for the knife, your attacker will be kicking and punching your lights out . . . or their friends will.

REMEMBER

The only effective way to disarm an attacker is to knock them out and then pick up the weapon as it falls from their unconscious grip.

Interrupting Static Edged-Weapon Attacks

If an attacker is holding a knife or other edged or pointed weapon to your neck, throat, face, stomach, back, or any other part of your body to coerce compliance, you have a much better opportunity to clear the weapon than in a dynamic attack. In this section, I explain how to counter a static knife attack when the assailant approaches you from in front or behind and what to do when you're accosted by two or more assailants, one or more of whom is holding an edged weapon.

REMEMBER

The techniques and tactics in the static defenses employ the same primary tactics and body mechanics used against grabs and holds (see Chapter 11).

Attack from the front

Edged-weapon attacks often begin with the attacker approaching from in front. They never begin with the attacker standing 3 feet away, arm extended, pointing the weapon at the victim. That only happens in martial arts demos.

Realistically, the threat is likely to be up close and personal. Your attacker will get in your face and probably try to conceal the situation by putting an arm around you, pretending like you're best friends engaged in casual conversation. The arm around you locks you in while their other arm points the weapon at your midsection, throat, neck, or face.

How to counter a static edged-weapon attack coming from the front varies depending on whether the weapon is low (stomach level) or high (neck, throat, face region).

Weapon low (stomach)

When the weapon is pointed at your midsection, pivot your body away from the weapon while smashing the weapon (or the hand/arm that's holding it) with the forearm of your outside arm (the arm on the opposite side of the hug), as shown in Figure 13-2. Your rotation moves your body away from the weapon, while the smash moves the weapon away from you and toward your attacker.

FIGURE 13-2: Rotate away from the weapon while smashing it with your forearm.

Immediately (if not sooner), follow up with a barrage of strikes — chin jabs, heel-of-hands, edge-of-hands, knees to the groin, stomps to the feet and legs — always driving forward and claiming ground. You must keep them off-balance and just hammer them. You don't want them to set their feet and come back at you with that weapon.

At any time during your attack, if you see an opening to escape, take it. Self-defense is about improving your position and situation step-by-step.

Weapon high (neck, throat, or face)

In this scenario, your attacker is likely to grab you by the shirt, jacket, or collar and hold the weapon to your throat or point it at your neck or face.

Clear the weapon by hooking it with the hand that's on the same side as the hand that's holding the weapon and pin it to your body. Rotate your body hard in the opposite direction and come over the top of the arm that's holding you to deliver a heel-of-hand strike to your attacker's head (see Figure 13-3). Even if the knife is across your throat, your body rotation combined with the hook prevents them from cutting you.

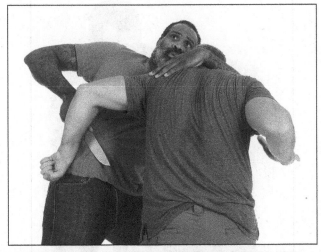

FIGURE 13-3: Rotate away from the weapon while smashing it with your forearm.

After you clear the weapon, keep it pinned to your body as you explode all over them. Just keep hacking, smashing, kicking, stomping, gouging, ripping. If you have a weapon or access to something you can pick up and use as a weapon, what are you waiting for?!

Get your attacker talking. When they're talking, they're not thinking you'll attack. Ask them a question (have one ready) like, "Didn't I see your mom at church?" When they start to answer, *attack!*

Attack from behind

Your attacker approaches from behind, pins you with a body grab or hammer lock, and is holding a knife to your throat. How they have you pinned and how they're holding the knife don't matter — respond the same way:

1. Grab the arm holding the weapon, jerk it down hard, and hold it down, pinned to your chest (see Figure 13-4).

2. Hip-butt backward and rotate hard in the direction of the hand with the weapon.

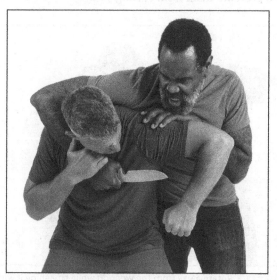

FIGURE 13-4: Pin the hand holding the weapon while smashing your attacker.

WHAT TO DO WHEN THEY DROP THE WEAPON

One reason self-defense experts stress the importance of controlling the weapon is because they're afraid that the attacker or one of the attacker's friends will pick it up and use it. Don't be concerned about that.

First, so long as you're on the attack, your assailant has no opportunity to pick it up. Second, if your attacker has a buddy who's willing to pick up a weapon and use it, chances are, they're already armed and attacking you. Third, eliminating the immediate threat first is always a priority. Remember to always move forward. Your forward drive not only keeps your attacker off-balance but also gets you off your X (where you're currently standing) and provides you with an opportunity to escape, which will help you escape multiple attackers (even if you don't see them).

3. **Keep the weapon arm pinned to your chest as you start hacking and elbowing them along their centerline.**

   Start by smashing the groin and then work up the body with an elbow to the throat or head (or both).

4. **Keep driving into them to keep them off-balance.**

   As they loosen up, you can forget about pinning the arm and just finish them or escape.

REMEMBER

This reaction is the same as when you're in a rear naked choke hold (see Chapter 11). The only difference is that you're clearing the weapon and pinning the arm.

Multiple edged-weapon attackers

When threatened by two or more attackers, at least one of whom is brandishing an edged weapon, you're likely to lose; it's just a matter of how badly. Your goal, even more than ever, is to escape. Focus on the two assailants you sense pose the biggest threat, and then take the following steps:

1. **Grab the hand holding the weapon or grab the blade (see Figure 13-5).**

FIGURE 13-5: Grab the blade or the hand holding the weapon.

TIP

If you grab the blade, use only your fingers, not your thumb, so it remains operational — any cuts will be to your palm or fingers.

Grabbing the blade sounds crazy, but you need to keep that blade from being plunged into you while you fight your way out. Getting cut is usually less injurious than getting stabbed.

2. **Immediately attack the secondary threat to make them pause.**

3. **Attack the primary threat and escape.**

TIP

Here are a few tips to improve your odds:

>> The person threatening you with the weapon will distract you. The one without the weapon, who's not talking, will attack first.

>> When approached by two people, one will talk and the other won't. Attack the silent one first; the talker is just distracting you. The silent one is getting ready to knock you out.

>> After you grab the arm holding the weapon or grab the blade, attack the unarmed threat as fast as possible because they're already moving in. Then strike the armed assailant and fight whatever is immediately in front of you as you escape. You won't be able to fight multiple threats at the same time. Your mind doesn't work like that. Humans are serial processors not multitaskers.

Whenever the threat is one and a half times greater than you, you'll lose. Don't think for a second that you're going to stand in the center of a circle of attackers and defeat all of them — that only happens in the movies, not in real life.

Surviving a Firearm Attack

Firearms are the deadliest weapons and the most common weapons you're likely to encounter on the street. The good news is that, from a self-defense standpoint, a gun is simple. Unlike a knife, which has a point, one or two edges, and considerable surface area, a firearm has only one small area you need to worry about: the muzzle. Keep out from in front of the muzzle, and you're safe.

The general approach to surviving a firearm attack is to make yourself a difficult target — run or *clear the weapon* (move the muzzle of the weapon away from your body, taking you out of the line of fire). To clear the weapon, you grab the hand holding it and move the muzzle off of you, while attacking the attacker.

The specifics of how to respond to a firearm attack vary depending on the situation — whether the shooter is at some distance and not firing, you're in an active-shooter predicament, or the assailant is right next to you threatening you with a gun. In this section, I cover all three situations.

When you clear it, you need to *stay behind the weapon,* so the shooter needs to redirect their aim to fire at you, which is nearly impossible, especially when you're pounding their face. Your forward drive is critical for staying behind the gun.

Dodging bullets: When the firearm is distant

If someone is pointing a firearm at you, even from only a few feet away, running away is a great option. Your odds of getting shot at are only 10 percent. Your odds of getting hit are 1 percent. And your odds of being fatally wounded are only 0.5 percent. I don't know about you, but that's a chance I'm willing to take. Not everyone is a crack shot. Combat shooting is 100 times harder than target practice. Hitting a moving target, even at close range, is a challenge for even the average trained shooter.

In most areas, you can run and find cover fairly easily. Cars, corners of buildings, and other concrete and steel obstacles provide all the protection you need. Look around you right now, and I'm sure you'll spot something you can hide behind. Even if it's a Sheetrock wall, it may not stop the bullet, but at least the shooter won't be able to see you.

If you're in an open area and not close to cover, run away on an angle. Don't run directly away, and don't serpentine — it's not necessary. Plus, it makes you cross the path of the barrel, which increases your odds of getting hit. When you're moving away on an angle, the shooter must adjust for position and distance. Forcing them to move their weapon laterally flushes their accuracy down the toilet.

Distracting an active shooter as you move in

When you're forced to deal with an active shooter and you're unarmed and unprotected, distract the shooter to create an opportunity to move in close and attack. Here are a few ways to distract an active shooter:

>> Pick up and throw anything at them to disrupt their aim.

>> Duck inside places of ambush, like doorways, to close the distance.

>> Discharge a fire extinguisher (pop smoke) to obscure their vision.

>> Break out a firehose reel (built into many buildings including schools and malls), open the valve, and spray the shooter — nothing like 100 pounds of pressure to get the job done.

All you're doing is disrupting the shooter's accuracy so you can get past their weapon and attack them. Clear the weapon by grabbing or striking the arm holding the firearm, and attack.

Resisting firearm threats and muggings

Few experiences in life are as scary as someone pointing a gun at you and demanding that you give them your money or come with them to who knows where. The assailant may even have an arm around you and be pointing the gun right at your head or have both hands pointing a gun directly at you. The good news (if there is any) is that they don't want to shoot you immediately, so you have an opportunity to do something.

By now, you know what you need to do — clear the firearm and attack. But how? The techniques I recommend you already know. The body mechanics are the same — you're just adapting them to these situations in which the assailant is pointing the gun with one hand and doing something (or nothing) with their other hand. In this section, I explain how to respond in several common scenarios.

WARNING

Ignore the advice of many martial arts instructors to "control the weapon." When you're dealing with an armed and violent offender, trying to keep the weapon pointed at the sky or the ground will only make an extremely difficult task that much harder and more dangerous. The smartest and safest course of action is to end the threat as quickly as possible. The chance that someone (you or a bystander) will get shot is greater if you're wrestling over the gun.

TIP

You can adapt any handgun defense that doesn't have a grab or a hold associated with it to a long-gun defense. A *long gun* is any weapon that requires two hands to operate (a shotgun or any rifle — even an AR15 or AK-47 — it doesn't matter).

Handgun from in front to your midsection

When your assailant approaches you from in front, keeping the weapon low and out of sight, they're a bit reluctant because you're probably not in an ideal location for an assault. Their reluctance can work to your advantage. Respond as you would to a static edged-weapon attack from the front.

The technique varies depending on whether your attacker grabs and holds you. If you're not in your attacker's grasp, take the following steps:

1. **Rotate your body out of the line of fire while smashing your arm closest to your attacker into the arm holding the firearm.**

2. **Check the weapon hand with your opposite hand and move in, staying behind the gun.**

   By "check the weapon," I mean hold the arm that's holding the gun to keep it pointed away from you and stay behind it.

3. **Attack immediately with a barrage of strikes, driving forward into the attacker, kneeing, stomping, and relentlessly claiming ground.**

    Maintaining your forward drive is critical for staying outside the line of fire.

    Maintain contact with your "check hand" on the weapon arm until you've disabled your target. You're going to do this instinctively, and it's as close to "controlling the weapon" as you'll ever get.

When your attacker is pinning you and holding you close with one arm (an arm around you, or a shoulder or collar grab) and pointing a gun at your stomach, take the following steps:

1. **Clear the weapon by smashing your forearm (on the side nearest the weapon) into the arm that's holding the gun, driving the weapon across and into your attacker's body.**

2. **Continue to check the weapon with the arm you just used as you hack away at your attacker's head group with edge-of-hand strikes or hammer fists.**

3. **Forward drive into your attacker, continuing your assault with a barrage of blows, while keeping the weapon arm in check until you've disabled your target.**

    Maintaining your forward drive is critical for staying outside the line of fire.

You're in a fight for your life — it won't be clean and tidy. They're going to move and react, and that creates space for you to attack.

Handgun in front pointed at your head or neck, arm extended

If someone is standing in front of you, at extreme close range with a firearm pointed at your head, arm extended, one of two things is happening:

>> They know what they're doing and just want to intimidate you because anyone who has shot anything at close range knows it's going to make a mess, and they're going to walk out of there covered in nastiness (a friend told me this).

>> They don't know what they're doing or don't mind getting maple syrup all over their Sunday-go-to-meetings.

Either way, you have to deal with them.

The gun may be pointed at your head or your neck — doesn't matter. What does matter (a little) is whether the assailant has a hold of you (grab or no grab).

If the assailant is standing in front of you, arm extended, pointing a gun at your head or neck, here's what to do:

1. **Put your hands up — not straight up, just by your ears.**

   The fact that they're extending their arm and pointing a gun at your head in public probably means they don't think (or don't care) about witnesses. But they still may not want you to put your hands up. However, everyone puts their hands up — it's a natural act of submission that people have been conditioned to do, so it's not unusual.

2. **Get 'em talking.**

   Ask them if they've ever been to Bali, so they're thinking about anything other than the fact that you're going to smash their face in.

3. **Clear the weapon by striking the hand holding it or the weapon with a heal-of-hand strike across the assailant's body as you move your head in the opposite direction (see Figure 13-6).**

4. **Immediately use the same hand to attack with an edge-of-hand and use your other hand to "check" the weapon arm.**

   You can even contact the shoulder with your check hand — it doesn't matter, so long as you don't allow them to turn toward you to put you in the line of fire.

5. **Continue to pin that side of their body if you can, and just go ballistic with edge-of-hand hacks as you drive forward.**

   If you can't pin the weapon arm, no worries — don't search for it. Your focus is to attack the SOB holding the gun.

FIGURE 13-6: Clear the weapon and check the arm holding it.

If your assailant grabs you by the throat or collar and points a gun at your head or neck, respond with the same technique for when an assailant holds an edged weapon to your throat, which happens to be the same thing you'd do in response to a two-hand collar grab or two-hand front choke (notice the pattern?):

1. Clear the weapon by hooking it with the hand that's on the same side of the hand that's holding the weapon, pull the weapon hand down, and pin it to your chest.

2. As you rotate toward your attacker, come over the top with a heel-of-hand to the face.

3. Follow through, and then come back with an edge-of-hand to the face in the opposite direction.

4. Keep the weapon hand pinned, and continue to attack until the assailant can no longer pose a threat.

REMEMBER

If these weapon defense techniques seem redundant, good. They're all similar if not identical for a reason — the less you have to recall, the greater your chance of success. Through training and practice, you program these simple moves into your muscle memory. That's why this system works.

Any weapon to your back

If your assailant approaches from behind and is pointing a weapon at you, maybe poking you with it, all you need to know is the height of the weapon — whether it's above or below your shoulder line. Whether it's a knife or a gun, whether they're holding it in their left or right hand or both hands doesn't matter. The technique you choose depends only on the height of the weapon.

REMEMBER

I get a chuckle when "experts" advise to turn around and take a peek. Turning to look behind you may be a natural reaction, but turning in a nondominant direction under extreme stress is not. Fact is, which hand they have the weapon in doesn't matter.

Unless you feel the weapon, you can try to turn around to take a quick look or act unresponsive, forcing them to prod you with the barrel of the gun or the tip of the blade. When you know the height of the weapon and that they're close, use one of the following techniques to clear the weapon:

>> **Weapon low:** Rotate in the direction of your strong side and clear the weapon with a low edge-of-hand, clearing the weapon with your strike. You can clear it with your forearm or upper arm — it doesn't matter as long as you rotate your body and clear the weapon.

>> **Weapon high:** From the "hands up" position, rotate in the direction of your strong side and clear the weapon by striking it with the edge of your hand or your outer forearm.

After clearing the weapon and rotating your body out of the line of fire, check the weapon arm with the hand you used to clear the weapon, drive into your attacker, and start striking with your other hand. Continue the assault until the threat is over or you can escape safely.

Hostage situation

You've seen this situation dozens, if not hundreds, of times in the movies. The bad guy has a single hand grab on the victim and is holding a gun to their back, head, or neck using the victim as a shield.

Treat this like a knife to the throat from the rear or a rear naked choke hold (see Chapter 11):

1. **Put your hands up slightly, regardless of whether you're told to do so.**

   You need to get your hands in a position to clear the weapon.

2. **Hook the hand holding the weapon and clear the weapon by pulling the weapon hand forward and down as you move your head back (see Figure 13-7).**

FIGURE 13-7: Hook the weapon hand and pull forward while driving back into your attacker.

3. **Keeping that weapon hand pinned, hip-butt back into your attacker while rotating into them and hacking their groin and midsection.**

4. **Work your way up their body, finishing with an elbow to the head.**

5. **Continue to pin the weapon and exit (as discussed in the next section).**

6. **Continue your assault until your assailant can no longer pose a threat.**

Exit your grip

Unlike a knife, a firearm can be fired from any position without any windup, so don't just let go of the weapon arm while your attacker is still on their feet. You need to exit to a position of advantage.

To exit, clear the gun and launch your counterattack, as explained in the previous section. When you're ready to exit, duck your head under that arm and come out on the other side (see Figure 13-8), pinning the hand holding the gun. This puts you out of harm's way and in a position of advantage to end the attack.

FIGURE 13-8: Duck under the arm holding the weapon and come out the other side.

REMEMBER

Even though you're facing a weapon and the odds are stacked against you, you still have an advantage: the element of surprise. Use it!

REMEMBER

After seeing me demonstrate a defensive tactic, someone will invariably step up and ask, "What if they do *this*?" and then demonstrate a countermove to my defense. This is preposterous. The fact is, if an attacker thinks you might resist, they will pick someone else or try a different approach. In the time it would take them to counter your defense, their opportunity to do so has already passed.

Protecting Yourself with Body Armor

The easiest and most effective way to avoid getting fatally shot or stabbed is to use *body armor* (protective clothing or accessories — such as backpacks, jackets, bulletproof vests, and plate carriers — designed to absorb or deflect weapon attacks). With the increase of active-shooter incidents and gun violence, more and more people are incorporating body armor into their everyday ensemble, especially in areas of exposure like work, school, parades, concerts, and festivals.

Body armor is generally divided into two categories:

>> **Ballistic:** To protect against bullets. Ballistic protection is designed to absorb energy and disperse that energy over the surface area; like a trampoline, it bends but doesn't break.

>> **Stab/spike:** To protect against knives and other pointy weapons. Stab/spike protection allows the point or edge of the weapon to penetrate and then catches or snags it to prevent it from penetrating deeply enough to cause serious injury.

REMEMBER

Ballistic protection and stab/spike protection are the exact opposite technologies and are not interchangeable. However, I have to mention, that a rifle plate (level 3 or above) is extremely difficult, if not impossible, to stab through.

Body armor is also categorized as either *hard* (rigid) or *soft* (anything that's flexible). Hard armor is made with ceramic, steel, aluminum, plastic, or aramid fibers like Kevlar and Twaron. Soft armor can be made of plastic or aramid fibers as well. What matters most is the armor's rating and how light or comfortable it is. Soft armor is much lighter and easier to wear than hard armor.

TIP

I could go into some detail about types of body armor and ratings, but for most people I recommend soft body armor with a Level 3A rating, which provides sufficient protection against most handgun and edged-weapon attacks like slashes or deflected stabs and is relatively light and comfortable. Here are a couple of additional considerations to keep in mind:

>> Soft armor doesn't protect the head from blunt-force trauma, so skip the sweatshirt with the soft armor sewn into the hood — it won't do you much good.

>> Body-armor ratings apply to adult (post-puberty) bodies, not children. Much of the armor (especially soft armor) that people purchase for their kids will not protect them against the blunt-force trauma of a bullet, especially a 9mm, which is the most popular caliber of round used.

>> Soft armor won't protect against rounds fired from rifles like an AR15, AK-47, or NATO .308 battlefield rifle, or protect against armor-piercing ammunition. This kind of ammo will pass through Level 3A armor like a hot knife through butter. However, these firearms are less likely to be used in street crimes.

Wearing body armor as you go about your daily business or spend a night out on the town can be inconvenient and uncomfortable. Strapping on a bulletproof vest just isn't practical for the average person. However, you may want to consider the following options:

>> Clothing with body armor built into the garment. Jackets are great if you live in a colder climate, but they're not very practical when you're in Florida in July.

>> Bulletproof backpack inserts are available. I've seen demos where a standard backpack with a thick textbook in it can stop a bullet fired from a handgun, but for a rifle you would need to carry a pretty thick stack. To be safe, using a ballistic backpack insert is better than nothing, at least when you're running away.

>> Bodyguard armored backpacks and jackets, made by the Self Defense Company (the company I founded), have a patented deployment system that enables you to instantly pull the front protection out from a concealed compartment while you're wearing it, giving you full front and back protection.

Chapter **14**

Surviving the Horror of an Active Shooter

N o doubt about it, firearm violence is on the rise, and the perfect solution, so far, has been elusive. Economist Thomas Sowell may have been right when he said, "There are no solutions, only trade-offs." Although the problem isn't likely to be solved any time soon, you can act to minimize loss by taking reasonable precautions and responding quickly and effectively to neutralize active shooters wherever and whenever they strike.

In this chapter, I explain how to protect yourself and those you care about from an *active shooter* (anyone attempting to kill people in a populated area). I detail tactics, self-defense weapons to include in your everyday carry, and techniques for seeking cover and even distracting and rushing the shooter. My hope is that you'll never face an active-shooter situation — but, if you do, I hope you'll put this information, insight, and guidance to good use and join the ever-growing army of brave souls committed to protecting themselves, their loved ones, and their communities.

Recognizing the Characteristics of an Active-Shooter Event

Shots fired! That's typically the first sign of an active-shooter event. First, you'll hear pops and cracks, making you think someone's setting off fireworks. Then you'll see people running and screaming. You may never see the shooter, or you may see them only when you're staring down their barrel.

The following statistics provide you with some idea of what to expect and can inform your decisions about how to prepare for and respond to an active shooter:

» **Most mass shootings occur in the workplace, at retail locations, at schools or universities, and at any places where people gather.** Although school shootings get the most media attention, most active-shooter events take place at retail businesses (including grocery stores).

» **Nearly 80 percent of mass shootings are committed with a handgun.** This statistic makes sense because handguns are much easier to carry and conceal. Rifles and shotguns account for the other 20 percent of mass shootings.

» **Police response times average about 10 to 15 minutes.** By that time, much of the damage is done, and the event is over. According to a recent report in the *New York Times,* out of 438 attacks, 249 ended *before* police arrived. In other words, expect to be on your own for at least ten minutes.

RUN-HIDE-FIGHT OR FIGHT-RUN-HIDE?

Many experts recommend the run-hide-fight response to an active shooter: Run to create some distance between you and the shooter; hide to take cover; and then fight the shooter only when you've run out of other options.

That's fine, but I recommend *fight-hide-run* because the intent should be on stopping the threat as soon as possible. The sooner you stop the threat, the less loss of life. I want to help empower and prepare those of us who refuse stand by and wait, hoping and praying that they don't get killed.

If the opportunity presents itself for you to close the distance and end the assault, consider taking it.

Packing in Anticipation of an Active-Shooter Event

If you're going somewhere that could be targeted — for example, an airport, your school or workplace, the local mall or supermarket, or public transportation — pack accordingly (see Chapter 7 for details):

>> **Concealed body armor (jacket or backpack):** These are Transportation Security Administration (TSA) approved and you can take either of them anywhere. Places that won't let you bring a backpack inside will let you take a jacket.

>> **Firearm:** Check the rules and regulations for each place you plan to be in order to determine what's permitted and prohibited.

REMEMBER

Armed civilians stopped active shooters up to four times more than law enforcement. This stands to reason, because an active shooter is less likely to engage if police are present, and law enforcement agencies can't patrol every inch of the country.

>> **Pepper spray:** I generally recommend carrying a 4-ounce can for convenience but for an active shooter, pack bear-spray size, if possible, for longer and wider range.

>> **Edged weapon:** A switchblade or fixed-blade knife. If you're traveling by plane, pack a tactical pen instead.

>> **First aid kit and tourniquets:** Make sure your kit contains blood-clotting trauma pads.

TIP

Use a bulletproof backpack with front and back ballistic protection, so you can carry everything with you wherever your go — work, school, bus, train, shopping, and so on. My company, The Self Defense Company (https://bulletproofbodyguard.com), carries patented backpacks with built-in body armor that you can pull from the backpack and into position in a fraction of a second.

Seeking Cover

Whether you decide to flee the scene or stay and fight, you probably need to seek cover — for the duration of the shooting, temporarily, or intermittently as you position yourself to ambush the shooter.

The first level of cover is visual concealment — hiding behind a Sheetrock wall, table, or trash can. This type of cover may not stop bullets, but it obscures you from the shooter's view, which can give you enough time to formulate a plan or move to a better position to ambush the shooter.

The next level of protection is anything that's made of steel or concrete, such as a vehicle, a concrete wall, or a steel beam.

Attacking the Active Shooter

Assuming you haven't fled the scene or gone into hiding to save your own bacon, you need to stop the attacker or at least slow them down 'til the cavalry (police) arrive. In this section, I cover your options, which vary depending on the weapons you have at your disposal, if any.

Shooting it out

A firearm is your best defense against an armed assailant. Even if they're wearing body armor, the impact from your bullet will slow them down enough for you to deliver more rounds on-target. I assume that if you carry a firearm, you're training with it. Make sure you get some tactical training, like how to *pie corners* (move around a corner while maximizing your cover and keeping your muzzle in line with your line of sight).

Body armor typically covers only the vital target areas and generally doesn't protect the arms, legs, head, and lower torso. Yes, there are products you can purchase to protect those areas, but most active shooters wear a plate carrier that protects the vital target areas of the upper torso. Body armor prevents bullets from penetrating, but it doesn't stop all the blunt-force trauma your bullets inflict, so even if the shooter is wearing body armor, continue to advance and attack. Assuming your bullets are striking the shooter, they won't be able to shoot straight, if at all, at least for the moment.

Pop smoke

If you need to move and don't have cover to hide behind, do what soldiers do on the battlefield: *Pop smoke* (toss a smoke grenade). Because you probably don't have one in your backpack, you'll have to improvise by using a fire extinguisher, assuming one is available nearby. Aim it in the direction of the shooter, and discharge it as you move to keep yourself hidden. When you get close, you can bash the shooter over the head with the empty can.

Blast the shooter with a fire hose

Law enforcement and security professionals commonly refer to the fire hose as "the continuously fed, short-range weapon." If you're in a building with a stand pipe fire-suppression system that has fire hoses attached to a sprinkler system, you have a weapon with 100 pounds per square inch of pressure and an unlimited supply of "bullets." Blasting the shooter with a fire hose will knock them off their feet.

If you work in a building with a standpipe fire-suppression system, make sure it's:

>> **Current with its inspection (check the tag).** If it's neglected, the hose will most likely fail.

>> **Charged.** Check the standpipe system to make sure it's charged (some systems are dry and require fire department connection). The only way to know if it's charged is to turn the valve *slowly*. If the hose fills with water, it's charged. Make sure to open the nozzle slowly when you start to spray to get used to the force. I realize that doing this in this situation might be impossible, but I have to mention it.

Move into ambush position

As you close in on your attacker, duck into doorways, sneak around corners, hide behind cars . . . anywhere that conceals you from the shooter's view as you improve your position. As you close in, try to get into a position from which you can ambush the shooter — where you're hidden from the shooter's view but close enough to pounce without getting shot.

REMEMBER

In Chapter 5, I point out common places attackers hide to ambush victims. All the places I tell you to avoid in that chapter are the places you can now use to close in on your attacker and ambush *them!*

Rush the shooter

An active shooter can kill and injure a lot of people in very little time, so as soon as you sense an opening, rush the shooter. As the attacker passes close to your ambush position, pounce, striking the hand(s) holding the weapon to clear it (see Chapter 13). Your goal is to get behind the weapon and attack the attacker. As you keep the weapon in check with one hand, forward drive into your attacker, kneeing and stomping and striking the attacker with the other hand.

If you're facing the shooter and unable to move to a position of ambush, and you are unarmed and have no body armor, you have no other option but to rush the shooter — close the distance and attack. If you hear a break in the shot pattern, time to attack! The shooter is probably reloading, or their weapon jammed. You can distract them by throwing anything you can pick up — chairs, books, computers, anything to disrupt their ability to aim and fire.

REMEMBER

Rushing the shooter is difficult. This is a horrifying situation that I wish no one had to face, but stopping the shooter is the only way to minimize the loss of life, and it's the best chance for your own survival.

Letting the Police Do Their Job

When you see a police officer with gun drawn, shelter in place or, if you're in a common area like a hallway, lay flat on your stomach unless you're told to do something else by the officer. You want to leave the officer a clear line of fire to the threat . . . and not get shot accidentally. This is an extremely stressful situation, and humans make mistakes. The less threat you present, the less likely this is to happen.

Until you have sight of a police officer, keep improving your position and looking for an opportunity to stop the shooter. When you see the officer, lay flat on your stomach, hands above your head, if you have a weapon, place the weapon on the floor. If the officers tell you to do anything different, do what they say. Don't talk, just do. The only thing you should tell them is how many shooters and where they're located. They may ask for more intel; answer as best you can, but be brief. If you don't know, tell them "I don't know."

REMEMBER

In every training I've ever been a part of or even heard of, the first officer on scene goes in, period. There's no waiting for backup, no waiting for an order, it's *go!*

Knowing What to Do as a Parent

School shootings are rare in the context of other violent crimes, but they do happen and seem to be on the rise. As a parent, you should be aware of the possibility, know what you can do to make your schools reasonably safe, and know what to expect and how to respond if you're notified of an active-shooter incident at your child's school.

Working the system

The first step you can take as a parent is to start asking questions to find out what the school board and administration are doing to protect the schools in your system. Here are some questions to ask to start the conversation:

>> What preparations has the school taken (for example, doors, alarms, cameras, protocols, armed security)?

>> How often do the local police department and first responders drill for active-shooter incidents?

>> What should you do, as a parent, in the event of a school lockdown?

>> Where should you go for more information on the safety of your child during a lockdown?

If you think something is lacking, let school board members and administrators know, in writing, what you expect. Introduce the topic at a school board meeting, so your concerns become part of the public record. If they fail to address your concerns in a reasonable amount of time, let them know (again, in writing) that you will hold them personally responsible in the event that your child or others are injured or killed as a result of their negligence.

Preparing your child

The best way to prepare your child for the possibility of an active-shooter situation is to talk with them about self-defense and reinforce what they're learning at school. Approach the topic in a casual, matter-of-fact manner. Don't alarm, don't shock, just talk and listen. Children are incredibly resilient.

Ask their teacher when they're going to have an active-shooter drill so you can ask your child what happened that day. Listen to what they have to say, and get their thoughts (teenagers may be reluctant to share their thoughts, but ask anyway). Reinforce what they've been told to do (listen to the teacher, stay under the windowsill, remain quiet, and so on). This conversation gives you insight as to where your child will be during an incident and what they'll be doing.

TIP

Don't go directly to the school or call them directly during a lockdown. The first responders are handling the situation. Calling your child or going to the scene will cause unneeded congestion and slow response time. Instead, establish a rendezvous point with your child on the edge of the school grounds outside the hot zone, about a half-mile from the school. Pick a place that has plenty of parking and easy access. It could be a park or a train station parking lot.

The only other suggestion I would make for teenage students is to carry a bulletproof backpack. With these backpacks, the wearer reaches back and pulls the front panel from the backpack and down over their head in a fraction of a second to move it in place. If your school doesn't allow backpacks in class, take it up with the school board.

REMEMBER

Body armor is rated to protect adults, not children. Soft armor provides insufficient protection against the blunt-force trauma of a bullet, and hard armor tends to be too heavy for them to carry.

Staying informed when your child's school is in lockdown

Schools often lock down in response to any threat in the area. A lockdown doesn't mean that the threat is inside the school or even on school grounds. It could be in response to an armed robbery several miles away.

You're not going to get any real information while the event is happening. You'll only know when the event is over. The reality is, the average police response time is 15 minutes. So, by the time you hear it's happening, it will most likely be over. If the perpetrator is still at large, your child, sheltering in place in their classroom, is in one of the safest places they can be. You can try to gather information from group chats (and even your kid), but it will most likely be wrong.

REMEMBER

You're going to freak out, and you won't be able to reach your kid because cellphone networks tend to get overloaded during these incidents, which typically end in minutes.

Responding to a credible active-shooter event

If you receive any credible information about an active-shooter event at your child's school, you're not going to want to stand and wait. The best thing I can tell you to do is go to your rendezvous location you set up about a half-mile off-campus. Any emergency event, especially an active shooter, is chaos — don't add to it.

REMEMBER

I know there have been instances in the past where first responders and security failed to do their jobs, but you're probably going to cause more harm than good if you show up at the school.

At the end of the day, you can only hold your school board, local police, and security accountable and hope the school security, teachers, staff, and students are prepared. The best thing you can do is get involved now to ensure the right measures are in place.

TIP

Here's what to expect during an active shooter-event:

>> **You won't be able to park near the school.** By the time you hear that there's an active shooter at your child's school, almost every first responder within 50 miles will already be there. Nearly every parent will be there, too.

- >> **You won't be able to get near the school.** It's a crime scene.
- >> **You won't be able to get through on your phone.**
- >> **You won't get an answer from any uniformed officers.** They won't talk to you — they're busy.
- >> **Almost everyone will be operating in panic mode.**

Protecting Your School if You're a Teacher or Administrator

Teachers, school administrators, school board members, law enforcement officers, security personnel, and parents are responsible for securing their schools and protecting students, faculty, and staff from violent criminals. In this section, I provide practical advice on how to fulfill that responsibility.

Beefing up school security

TIP

Here's a checklist for what schools can be doing to beef up their security:

- ❑ A single entrance/exit for all common traffic — one way in, one way out — in a bulletproof vestibule with a metal detector (see Figure 14-1)
- ❑ One or more armed guards
- ❑ Steel doors on every classroom that lock during class times
- ❑ Numbers or letters on all rooms and exits so first responders can quickly locate the threat
- ❑ An alarm system that detects the opening of an outside door
- ❑ Cameras in every classroom, hallway, entrance, and exit
- ❑ A communication system for each classroom to contact *incident command* (first responders who take control of the scene when they arrive)
- ❑ Body armor for teachers and staff that can be put on and deployed at a moment's notice (like the bulletproof backpack shown in Figure 14-2)
- ❑ Arming and training teachers and staff — or at least allowing them to carry pepper spray (bear-spray size for longer and wider range)

FIGURE 14-1: A single entryway through a bulletproof vestibule with a trained armed guard is one of the best deterrents.

FIGURE 14-2: A bulletproof backpack adds another layer of protection.

Just as with personal self-defense, what works best is a layered approach in case one layer fails. Plan for the worst and hope for the best. Your active-shooter prevention plan must be able to do the following:

>> Detect a potentially violent intruder before they enter the building.

>> Alert first responders immediately about any credible threat.

>> Enable anyone in the building to shelter in place for 10 to 15 minutes of assault.

>> Empower teachers and staff to stop the assault — by providing training and allowing at least one or two staff members or administrators to carry weapons.

>> Provide teachers and staff the training, equipment, and supplies they need to triage injuries from weapon attacks.

Schools must be secure during school hours and all events like assemblies, athletic events, graduations, and concerts.

REMEMBER

Neutralizing an active shooter

Prevention didn't work. An armed intruder has gotten past all your safeguards and is shooting or threatening to shoot people. Now what? In the following sections, I explain how to neutralize the shooter in two different locations — the classroom or the hallway.

Don't assume a fire drill is a fire drill. Treat any unscheduled event as an active-shooter threat. Attackers will pull a fire alarm intentionally to get everyone in the building to move to a central location.

WARNING

In the classroom

Follow the procedure put in place by local law enforcement. Sheltering in place in a locked classroom is very safe. Bullets don't destroy locks and doors like they do in the movies. You can also barricade the doors with desks and file cabinets.

However, if for some reason they breach your doorway and you're forced to fight, use the entrance to your classroom as your place of ambush. The threshold doesn't give them full visibility of the room and they can't see you on either side of the door.

Because classroom doors open out, hide behind the door on the hinge side (see Figure 14-3). As soon as they crack that door open, smash the door into them, disrupting their balance. They have to use one hand to open the door, which keeps that hand preoccupied for a moment, and shoving the door into them will be a nasty surprise. Attack immediately and viciously, preferably with a weapon — gun, knife, pepper spray, improvised weapon, whatever you have. Keep driving into them and attacking until they're dead or wish they were.

FIGURE 14-3: Ambush from the knob side of the door.

In the hallway

If you get trapped in a hallway, you may need to fight your way out. If you're armed and you have body armor, put the kids behind you crouched in the corner between the wall and the floor and deploy your pepper spray or firearm. If you don't have pepper spray or a firearm, use a fire extinguisher to pop smoke and cover ground to escape or attack the attacker. Throw anything you have — a book, keys, a backpack, a purse — to distract the shooter as you close ground and attack!

Protecting Yourself in the Workplace

No matter where you work, you're susceptible to a disgruntled employee or customer coming into your place of business and taking lives. Your employer probably doesn't have any protocols for a violent intruder event, and even if they do, it's still up to you to defend yourself. Here are some general guidelines for protecting yourself:

>> If possible, have a bulletproof jacket or backpack nearby that you can put on quickly. Wearing body armor all day at work isn't practical or comfortable; you probably wouldn't wear it all the time even if I told you to.

>> Find out where the first aid kit is. If your workplace doesn't have a first aid kit, inform your supervisor or employer so they can get one.

>> If permitted, always carry pepper spray or a firearm.

>> Identify places of cover or ambush, so you know where to head before you need to head there.

>> Plot two exit routes, preferably to different doors. Most building fire codes require multiple exits. However, in the rare instance that your place of work only has one door, think ahead about the most effective way to get to it.

If you work in an office behind a desk or behind a counter or register, you have more places to store and conceal body armor and weapons, but you have less time to react to a threat. If you work the floor in a retail store or a restaurant, you have more time to react but fewer places to store and conceal your self-defense gear — you pretty much have to carry or wear any weapons or body armor you need for your protection.

5

The Part of Tens

IN THIS PART . . .

Make key assumptions about attackers and attacks that improve your ability to defend yourself.

Realize that you're likely to be on your own to defend yourself when an attacker strikes and for at least the first 10 to 15 minutes of the attack.

Gain insight into the potential impact of a violent attack on your emotional and psychological self.

Take practical steps to recover mentally and emotionally after a violent attack and start your journey to reclaim your power and control.

Harness the power of self-defense training to accelerate and deepen your recovery from a violent attack.

» Making assumptions that will save your ass

» Expecting the worst and making it even worse for your attacker

» Relying solely on yourself

Chapter **15**

The Ten Commandments of Self-Defense

The ten commandments of self-defense are rules and assumptions about attacks and attackers that improve your survival odds and give you an edge over your attacker.

Assume Your Attacker Is Armed

Criminals always want to have an advantage over their victims, and a weapon is the easiest way to improve their odds of success. Your advantage is surprise. Most criminals pick people they believe aren't likely to resist or are poorly equipped to put up a fight. By striking first, ruthlessly, and relentlessly, you neutralize their advantage. And if you have a weapon that you can use while preventing them from using theirs, they don't have much of a chance, if any.

WARNING

Just because an assailant doesn't brandish a weapon, doesn't mean they don't have one. If it's dark or the weapon is concealed, you may not see it. Assume they have one.

Never Underestimate an Assailant

Anyone who is forcefully trying to impose their will over you is prepared to harm you by any means possible. If they're brazen enough to walk up to you and demand your wallet, they'll do whatever is necessary to get it, which is why, throughout this book, I advise you to end the threat as quickly as possible. Don't wait to attack, and don't stop attacking until you can escape safely or the assailant no longer poses a threat.

Count on Your Attacker Having Friends Nearby

Like a weapon, accomplices give an attacker an advantage over a lone victim. Most times you won't even see them; they're hiding or mixing in with the crowd, standing ready to attack if you put up any resistance. By attacking and continuing your forward drive, you move off your X, which makes targeting you much more difficult.

WARNING

Don't just stand there waiting for the fight to come to you and assuming you can fight off a gang of hooligans. That's a good way to get whupped . . . and even killed.

Don't Make Yourself an Easy Target

If your attacker wanted a fair fight, they would've joined a gym. They pick the people they deem easy targets. They pick the time, the place, and the target, so assume you're going to be attacked on your worst day and their best day. Appearing distracted, disabled, weak, and vulnerable makes you an attractive target.

To avoid being an easy target, always be aware of your surroundings and steer clear of areas and situations in which you can be easily ambushed. Be armed and confident at all times, and master the simple self-defense tactics and techniques I present throughout this book, which don't require a tremendous amount of skill and are easy to execute when you're in a high-stress situation.

Be Prepared to Fight Anywhere

Martial arts competitions take place in open areas often covered by nice, soft mats. In contrast, assaults can happen anywhere — in your living room, in an office, outside in an icy parking lot, in the woods. . . . These places have obstructions and unforgiving surfaces and debris. To maintain your balance while delivering powerful blows to your attacker with your knees and feet, train to develop stomping, driving footwork and make it second nature whenever you're in attack mode.

Keep Fighting Until You're Safe

Don't assume that just because you "shook hands" the fight is over. The attack is over when you're safely out of the area or the threat is incapacitated.

A local kid got into a little misunderstanding in a bar with another man. They "shook hands" and the kid thought it was over. Unfortunately, it wasn't. The attacker left the bar, waited outside for the kid, and stabbed him to death in the parking lot. You have no idea what's going on in the mind of the person you're dealing with; don't assume they have the same moral code as you. This is why I stress the importance of training to stop the threat or leave the area.

Expect the Unexpected

When you're training, you always picture exactly how an attack will unfold, and when it actually happens, it's never as you imagined. In the real world, you'll be approached in ways you never imagined, you'll miss your target, you'll slip and fall. . . . People who use violence to impose their will over others are cunning. They've done this before, while you've only imagined it.

You can't possibly prepare for everything an assailant might do, so break down every situation into position and distance and respond with nonspecific defenses — tactics and techniques that are effective regardless of the situation and what your attacker does or doesn't do.

Don't Count on Getting Any Help

Studies show that the overwhelming number of assaults happen to people who are alone. An assailant doesn't want to fight your posse or commit a crime in a roomful of witnesses. When you're alone, be especially vigilant, pay close attention to your surroundings, protect your personal space, and don't let anyone get too close.

Don't Telegraph Your Intentions

Your attacker chose you because they think you're an easy target — you seem to be alone, unarmed, distracted, confused, and generally vulnerable. They're not expecting you to put up a fight, so don't give them any reason to believe that you know how to defend yourself or that you're armed and dangerous. They should realize you have pepper spray only when it's stinging their eyes. The only time they should know you've had some training is when your axe hands are pummeling their face and your thumbs are gouging their eyes. The only time they should know you have a knife is when it's sticking in them. They should realize you have a gun only when you present it and intend to use it.

Don't Trust Your Attacker

Ted Bundy was charming. He kidnapped, raped, and murdered dozens of young women and girls in the span of only a few years. Regardless of how charming or sincere an attacker is, and regardless of how frightened you are of what they're threatening to do to you if you don't comply, *never* leave the scene with your attacker, give up your weapon, or let them restrain you in any way.

REMEMBER

Your attacker wants to move you to another location because they can't do something far worse than anything you can imagine at your current location. They want you to give up any weapon you have because they know you can use it to harm them and escape. They want to restrain you so you're powerless against them. Fight to the death. There are things in this world far worse than death.

Chapter **16**

Ten Tips for Survivors

When someone imposes their will on you, they do more than take something from you or physically hurt you — they take away your power and free will. They destroy your confidence, and that can spill over into every aspect of your life. In this chapter, I give you some tools that you can use to come to grips with the event and maybe even turn it into something positive in your life.

REMEMBER

There's really no right or wrong way to respond to a traumatic event — everyone handles it differently and at their own pace. I've seen big, strong people recoil from life after an attack and small, delicate people turn a sexual assault into a springboard for a better life. Your response is unique to you. My hope is that the insights I share in this chapter hasten and enhance your recovery.

Reclaim Power and Control

An assault can steal your sense of power and self-determination. It can make you feel powerless and even ashamed. You replay the incident in your head, second-guessing your response to the attack and wondering what you could've done to improve the outcome.

One of the most effective paths to overcoming the psychological trauma of an attack is through self-defense training. After an attack, you realize how vulnerable you really are. That's a hard pill to swallow and the main cause for post-traumatic stress. Training gives you a response to the attack, an answer to the problem you couldn't solve before. It gives you a plan and restores hope. At the end of the day, you're alive. The ultimate goal of self-defense is to survive, and that's exactly what you did.

Take Some Time

Your mind needs time to process the traumatic event, but spending too much time in your own head can be counterproductive. You can end up in a never-ending cycle of negative self-talk that does more harm than good.

Physical activity can help tremendously, especially self-defense training. I realize that may seem like "my answer to everything," but I've trained many victims of assaults and witnessed the transformative power of training firsthand. If you don't start (or continue) training, do something physical — get outside and walk. Get your endorphins flowing. Time can heal all wounds, but physical activity accelerates the process.

Don't Fret What You Can't Recall

When your sympathetic nervous system (SNS) engages and puts you into fight-or-flight mode, you lose function of your cerebellum, which affects your recall. You have tunnel vision and auditory exclusion, and you may even black out. This temporary impairment affects your ability to remember details of the attack.

REMEMBER

Your mind has the ability to repress memories of traumatic events. It's a coping mechanism that enables you to continue to function as you process what happened. Try not to let yourself stress over your inability to remember. If you want to facilitate the process, start with the last thing you remember and try to recall what happened next.

Call the Police . . . and a Lawyer

Immediately after an assault, call the police. If you're the victim of a sexual assault, contacting the police immediately is crucial. Avoid washing or cleaning up. (I realize this is the exact opposite of what you want to do, but the more evidence law enforcement can collect, the more likely you'll get a conviction.) Act immediately — the longer you wait, the more difficult it will be to prove your case.

REMEMBER

Keep in mind that after you file a police report or even an incident report at your doctor's office, the case is in the prosecutor's hands from that point forward. You can't just drop the charges. Also, keep in mind that if you were attacked and you defended yourself, you could be charged with a crime, so proceed with caution.

Start by calling the police and saying you were attacked and you're having chest pains. Doctors can't test for that condition, but they'll document that you reported having chest pains. Months later, when you're being tried for assault and battery, your lawyer can say, "My client was so fearful for their life, they had chest pains."

As soon as the police arrive and start asking you questions, request a lawyer and remind them that you're having chest pains. Like they say on TV, "Anything you say *can* and *will* be used against you." Don't try to plead your case or defend your actions. Just say something like, "Thank you, officers. I appreciate what you do, but I would prefer to talk to an attorney."

REMEMBER

Even if you're the victim of a sexual assault, I strongly recommend going to the police with a lawyer, parent, guardian, or friend. Do *not* give your statement or be questioned alone. These investigations are tricky, and victims can quickly be turned from accuser to suspect.

Get Back into the Swing of Things

Returning to your normal routine can be very therapeutic. Fake it 'til you make it, if necessary. Your routine can put you in a better frame of mind and shift your focus away from the traumatic incident. However, if your attack was centered around a particular part of your routine (for example, you were attacked leaving a bar you frequent), and you don't want to go back there right away, alter that part of your routine.

Talk about the Incident

Everyone handles trauma differently. Some people need to talk about what happened; others don't. How you handle it is up to you. No approach is wrong as long as it's not detrimental to your physical and psychological well-being. I suggest trying to talk about it, but if it doesn't feel right, stop.

Give Yourself a Break

Take some time for yourself, away from your life and your routine. Maybe take a vacation and travel out of the area for a while so you don't see any reminders of what happened. When you're in a different place, you get a fresh slate and meet new people, and you have an opportunity to present yourself the way you want to be seen.

Seek Therapy

I recommend professional therapy to anyone who has experienced a traumatic incident because people don't always realize how traumatized they really are. Even if you have only one session, talking to someone who's not a friend or family member can be a tremendous relief. A professional can give you insights into how you're responding to the trauma that you didn't even realize.

Look for the Good in the World

Far be it from me to tell you to hold hands and sing "Kumbaya." After all, I just spent 15 chapters telling you to gouge eyes and kick groins. But the world, all in all, is generally good. If it weren't, violence would be everywhere 24/7. Yes, evil exists, and we hear about it every day, but most people want to do the right thing (or at least be left alone). Take pleasure in your relationships, friends, and family, and seek to make meaningful connections.

Become a Victims' Advocate

Some of the greatest rewards come from helping others help themselves. Surviving a violent crime equips you with unique insights that can help others cope and recover. Joining an outreach program or support group or teaching people how to defend themselves or reclaim their lives benefits you tenfold. Take it from me: Learning to defend yourself and protect others is great. Teaching others how to defend themselves, reclaim their lives, and protect others is even better.

Index

attacker (continued)

tossing, 226

track record of, 10

underestimating, 286

as untrained, 60

violence motivation of, 65

auditory exclusion, 36

awareness, 77, 81–87

awareness and avoidance level of self-defense, 39

axe hand (edge-of-hand strike), 162–168, 211

axe handle, 109–112

B

backpack, bulletproof, 267–268, 272, 279

balance, 33

ballistic body armor, 266

bars, awareness in, 82–84

base leg, 235

baton, collapsible, 108–109

bear hug, breaking free from, 203–205

biting, 41, 204, 222–223

blackjack, 108

bladed stance, 152–153

blocking, 161

body armor, 266–268, 271, 273, 276

boot knife, 115

boxing the ears strike, 183–186

brass knuckle, 112

Brazilian Jiu-Jitsu (BJJ), 26

breaking free

attacking your attacker for, 200

from bear hug, 203–205

from closed guard position, 234

from collar grab, 212–213

from double-hand grab, 201–203

from double-wrist grab, 202–203

from edged weapon attack, 251–257

from firearm attack, 257–266

from full nelson, 205–206

from hair grab, 213–214

from headlock, 208–209

from hostage situation, 263–264

from impact weapon attack, 247–251

overview of, 199–200

from rear naked choke, 206–207

by seizing testicles, 209–210

from single-arm grab, 212–213

from single-hand grab, 211–214

British Special Air Service, motto of, 12

bulletproof backpack, 267–268, 272, 279

bulletproof jacket, 93, 267–268

bullets, dodging, 257–258

bullies, 62–63, 66

Bundy, Ted, 288

bushido, 26

buttocks, attacking with, 15

C

caestus, 112

caliber, 121

calmness, cautions regarding, 45

carjacking, avoiding, 87–88

castle doctrine, 52–53

cellphone, distraction of, 75

center of gravity, of attacker, 137

centerline, 132

cerebellum, 98

cerebrum, 98

cervical spine, as target area, 145

Cestari, Carl (instructor), 1

chamber kick, 154

chest bounce, 233

chest smear, 233

chin, 14, 144, 158, 178–179

chin jab, 168–170, 177, 178–179, 212–213

Chinese kung fu, 26

chin-jab uppercut, 170–172

civil unrest, awareness in, 86–87

clavicle (collar bone), as target area, 146

clawing, 204

CLEAR, 94

clearing your home, 122

close range distance, 31, 32. See also distance

closed fist attack, 178

closed guard position, 230, 234, 238. See also position

club, 109–112, 249–250

collapsible baton, 108–109

collar bone (clavicle), as target area, 146

collar grab, breaking free from, 212–213

combat sport, 25–27, 152, 230

combative, defined, 1

commuting, protection during, 90–91

concealed weapon, 50, 120. See also weapon

confidence, exuding, 74–76

constructive force, 53

F

face. *See also* head group
chin, 14, 144, 158, 178–179
ears, 143, 222
eyes, 143, 221
forehead, 14, 188
nose, 143, 145
protection for, 158–159
as target area, 142

Fairbairn, William (inventor), 2, 168

Fairbairn-Sykes knife, 114, 115

falling, in ground fighting, 218–220

familiarity attack, 66

far range distance, 31, 32. *See also* distance

fear, 44–45, 67–69, 97

feet, attacking with, 15, 134, 149, 157. *See also* kicking

fencing grip, 116

fender bender, avoiding, 89–90

ferocity, 12–14

fight in the street, attack as compared to, 60–61

fight-hide-run response, 271

fighting stance, avoiding, 136

fight-or-flight mode
ability to fight in, 34–36
action *versus* reaction in, 37–38
defined, 97
fear in, 97
fine motor skills in, 35
gross motor skills in, 35
processes of, 23
recollection following activation of, 290

simplicity in, 37

sympathetic nervous system (SNS) in, 34–35

figure-four position, for club use, 110–111. *See also* position

fine motor skills, in fight-or-flight mode, 35

finger dart, 153–154

finger hole knife, 115, 116. *See also* knife

finger-gouging, 221

fingers, ripping, 222

"Fire!," yelling, 98, 99

fire hose, for active shooter, 273

firearm. *See also* weapon
attacking active shooter with, 272–273
exiting grip from, 265–266
for mass shooting defense, 271
overview of, 119–126
statistics regarding, 244
surviving attack with, 257–266

First Amendment, 87

fist, fortified, 112

fist pack, 112

flashlight, tactical, 93, 106–107

fleeing, 247–248

fogger pepper spray, 106

force, 33–34

force-on-force training, 123

forearm, attacking with, 15

forehead, attacking with, 14, 188

fortified fist, 112

forward driving, 159–161

forward fall, 219

forward headbutt, 188

forward roll, 220

full nelson, breaking free from, 205–206

G

getting caught, fear of, 68

gi, 206

Global Entry, 94

Good Samaritan dodge, 90

gouging, 41, 220–221

grapevine, 233–234

grappling. *See also* ground fighting
chin attack in, 14
cupped-hands strike during, 185
forward headbutt for, 188
goal in, 199
in judo, 25
knee strike during, 195
overview of, 41–42
rear elbow smash for, 193
weapon for, 105

green threat level condition, 19–20

groin group, as target area, 146–148, 194–195

grooming, as deterrent, 74

gross motor skills, in fight-or-flight mode, 35

ground and pound, 232–233

ground cover maneuver, 236

ground fighting. *See also* grappling
from bottom up, 236–239
chest bounce in, 233
chest smear in, 233
closed guard position in, 230, 234, 238
crossing edge-of-hands maneuver in, 237
escape maneuver in, 237–238
falling safely in, 218–220
fighting attacker at your side in, 228–230

voice, as weapon and alarm, 98–100

Vulcan nerve pinch, 101

W

walking, 74, 81, 132

weapon. *See also specific weapons*

for airport security, 93

ankle carry of, 122

appendix concealment of, 121–122

assumptions regarding, 285

attacking the attacker with, 245–246

basics regarding, 244–247

for bear hug, 204

benefits of, 30

body armor for, 266–268

choosing, 104–105

clearing, 246, 257, 260, 261, 262, 263

close range with, 126

concealed, 50, 120

constructive force with, 53

counterattack stopping with, 54

deadly force with, 54

deadly-force diamond and, 51

defined, 15

dodging from, 247–248

drawing, 123–124

dropped, 255

dynamic attack with, 247

everyday carry (EDC), 92, 93

fleeing from, 247–248

as force equalizer, 15, 104

as force multiplier, 15

frontal attack from, 252

hard skills with, 15–16

high (neck, throat, or face) attack from, 253–254

hip placement of, 122

hostage situation with, 263–264

importance of, 103–104

improvised, 119

laws regarding, 104

lesser, 104

lion tamer defense to, 249

low (stomach) attack from, 252–253

mechanical force using, 53

myths regarding, 49, 50

nonlethal, 41, 105–107

open carry, 50, 120

outside the waistband (OWB) placement of, 121

perspective regarding, 245

position of advantage with, 126

proactive defense with, 117–118, 125

projectile, 40, 119–126

reactive defense with, 118–119, 125

rear attack from, 254–255

retention of, 125–126

rules regarding, 117

running from, 248

safety with, 120

scanning for, 78

shoulder holster for, 122

six o'clock carry of, 122

stacking of, 105

static attack with, 247

statistics regarding, 244

in street fight, 243

testing, 105

training for, 122–126

voice as, 98–100

in the waistband (IWB) concealment of, 121

web-of-hand strike, 176–178

websites

CLEAR, 94

Global Entry, 94

My Self Defense Training, 5

Self Defense Company, 272

Travel Destination, 92

wheeling-elbow swing, 192

whip kick (direct front kick), 154–155, 196

windpipe, as target area, 142. *See also* neck; throat, attacking

women's intuition, 77

workplace, mass shooting in, 282

wrestling. *See* grappling

wushu, 26

Y

yellow threat level condition, 19–20

About the Author

Damian Ross is a husband and father of two. He's an internationally recognized expert in reality-based martial arts and has competed, taught, and coached on all levels of amateur sport since 1975. Damian created the Self Defense Training System and, along with his wife Angela, founded the Self Defense Company in 2007. Together, in 2015, Damian and Angela developed and launched Bodyguard armored backpacks and jackets, a line of concealable and undetectable bulletproof clothing that enables people to incorporate ballistic protection into their everyday lives.

Damian has a second-degree black belt in tae kwon do under his brother Phil Ross, a second-degree black belt in judo under Yoshisada Yonezuka (a ninth-degree black belt and judo legend), and a fourth-degree black belt in tekken ryu jujitsu and combatives under Carl Cestari (the "godfather" of modern combatives).

Damian was an all-state football player and wrestler at Ridgewood High School in Ridgewood, New Jersey, where he was inducted into the Hall of Fame for both sports in 2008. He was a varsity wrestling coach and football coach, a nationally ranked competitor in judo and karate, and competed in football and wrestling at Lehigh University in Bethlehem, Pennsylvania. He has also won state and national titles in judo, karate, and wrestling, winning his first national title in wrestling when he was 13 years old.

Damian has also worked security, was a bouncer and a bodyguard working details for the Grammys, the New York Yankees, and Fox News, to name a few. He has served as a firefighter and first responder in Saddle River, New Jersey.

In 1989, Damian discovered a method of combatives through a friend on the Bergen County S.W.A.T. team. It wasn't in a dojo or a seminar, but in a church basement in Paramus, New Jersey. There, he met his mentor, Carl Cestari, and discovered "the truth about self-defense." It was nothing like he had ever seen before, and he dedicated his life to learning and teaching it. Since that moment, he has focused his martial arts efforts on learning and teaching this valuable information, which he covers in this book.

You can see videos of all the techniques, instructions, drills, and applications on his website, www.myselfdefensetraining.com. You can also get all of Damian's Bodyguard armored backpacks and jackets at https://bulletproofbodyguard.com.

Dedication

I dedicate this book to my wife, Angela, my business partner, better half, and the first (and only) student I ever dated. For my kids, Damian and Olivia; my mom, Patricia; my dad and first coach, Phil; and my grandfather Cosmo.

Author's Acknowledgments

First, I would like to thank my technical editor and longtime friend, Dr. Tom Gorman, without whom this book would have been much more challenging to complete. Tom was at ground zero when I first discovered this method of self-defense, so it's only fitting that he oversee its content.

I would also like to thank instructor George Hutchings, who heads up the Self Defense Company instructor program with brutal dedication.

Thanks to Michael Archangel for being the catalyst for this journey. When I had a falling out with a former partner, Mike helped me and my wife, Angela, launch the Self Defense Company by believing in us and the mission. It was during those humble (and stressful) beginnings that we created a true vision of what personal protection should be.

I must thank my lifelong friend, and literally my first student, Pete Barry. Pete is my main training partner in the training videos and training images. Pete is the guy who never says "no" and always makes himself available for whatever projects pop in my head. Everyone should have a friend like Pete — but very few do.

I would also like to thank Roger Jones, another training partner, instructor, and friend, who not only trained with me, but also wrestled and played football with me at Ridgewood High School. Roger has been another constant in my life, and I'm lucky to have known him.

Thank you to Craig Domalewski for being more than a friend, attorney, teammate, and fraternity brother. You were and still are the voice of reason. It was your decision to stand up and fight for what's right that was critical to get us to where we are today.

I also wouldn't be the instructor, coach, father, and husband I am today if it weren't for my high school football coaches Chuck Johnson and Jim Stroker. Aside from my own father, these men helped me understand the value of and appreciation for hard work, sacrifice, teamwork, patience, and persistence. To this day, I still seek their counsel and wisdom.

Of course, this book would not have been possible without Jennifer Yee of John Wiley & Sons. Her belief in me and this project gave me the confidence and resolve to complete it. Thanks are also in order for Elizabeth Kuball and Kristie Pyles, who no doubt had to sift through my submissions and make better sense of them.

I must give big props to writer Joe Kraynak, who is truly a tenth-degree black belt master of his craft. I sent him lumps of clay, and he crafted them into something that adds to my legacy while keeping my voice and intent intact.

Special thanks to our awesome models Olivia Ross, Angela Ross, Kobie Jackson, and Pete Barry. I also would like to thank the Saddle River Fire Department and Chief Bill Salvatore for the use of the location for some critical shots.

And finally, thanks to my wife and business partner, Angela Ross, who proofread this book, served as the art director on the images, and allowed me to pursue my passion and share my time with the world while raising our two amazing kids (I don't think they'll read this part, so I'll say it).

Publisher's Acknowledgments

Acquisitions Editor: Jennifer Yee

Editor: Elizabeth Kuball

Technical Editor: Tom Gorman

Production Editor:
Tamilmani Varadharaj

Photographer: Kat Yannalfo,
Photography by SKY

Cover Image: © filmstudio/
Getty Images

Special Help: Joe Kraynak